Gables *and* Fables

a portrait of

San Francisco's Pacific Heights

Gables *and* Fables

a portrait of

San Francisco's Pacific Heights

Anne Bloomfield and Arthur Bloomfield

Illustrated by Kit Haskell

Heyday Books, Berkeley, California

The publication of *Gables and Fables* was made possible due to an exceptionally generous gift from the Victorian Alliance of San Francisco. Major contributions were also received from the following individuals:

> Anonymous
> Barbara G. Aaron
> Christopher Buckley
> Anita Jean Denz
> Douglas and Barbara Engmann
> Leanna and Robert Gaskins
> Lois Hayn
> George Fredrick Jewett, Jr. and Lucille McIntyre Jewett
> Rolf Lewis
> Robert P. Morrow III and Mary M. Morrow
> Lois and Arthur Roth
> Margaret Burnett Titus
> Steve Wille
> Mark Z. Zier and Beverly J. (Macy) McCallister

Library of Congress Cataloging-in-Publication Data

Bloomfield, Anne.
  Gables and fables : a portrait of San Francisco's Pacific Heights / Anne Bloomfield and Arthur Bloomfield ; illustrations by Kit Haskell.
    p. cm.
  ISBN 978-1-59714-055-3 (hardcover : alk. paper) -- ISBN 978-1-59714-056-0 (pbk. : alk. paper)
  1. Architecture, Domestic--California--San Francisco. 2. San Francisco (Calif.)--History. 3. Pacific Heights (San Francisco, Calif.) 4. Pacific Heights (San Francisco, Calif.)--History. I. Bloomfield, Arthur, 1931- II. Title.
  NA7238.S35B56 2007
  728'.370979461--dc22
                    2006035482

Cover Art: Kit Haskell
Cover Design: Rebecca LeGates
Interior Design/Typesetting: Lorraine Rath
Printing and Binding: McNaughton & Gunn, Saline, MI

Orders, inquiries, and correspondence should be addressed to:
  Heyday Books
  P. O. Box 9145, Berkeley, CA 94709
  (510) 549-3564, Fax (510) 549-1889
  www.heydaybooks.com

Printed in the United States of America

10 9 8 7 6 5 4 3 2 1

For Cecily, always

Contents

The Houses

On Broadway, east to west

On or near Pacific Avenue, east to west

On or near Jackson Street, east to west

On or near Washington Street, east to west

On or near Pine Street, east to west

On or near Bush Street, east to west

On Sutter Street

*W*e find satisfaction in curves and colors, and windows fascinate us, we are agitated by staircases, inspired by doors... made wanton by ceilings, entranced by passages, and exacerbated by a rug.

—*Lytton Strachey*

Introduction

Arthur Bloomfield

The seed of this book was an intention on the part of my late wife, Anne Bloomfield, to fashion a survey of historic properties in the high-profile, tourist-friendly San Francisco neighborhood within the jurisdiction of the preservation-minded Pacific Heights Residents' Association.

Anne's plan, I believe, was to give only the bare, survey-type facts about a number of the properties, sweetening the dish with some of the articles about "Great Old Houses" she wrote for the *New Fillmore*, a neighborhood monthly, over a period of about fourteen years. The circulation area of the *New Fillmore* coincides almost exactly with that of the Residents' Association: from Van Ness Avenue on the east to Presidio Avenue on the west, Union Street at the north end and Bush Street at the south.

Anne, I should say, was a consultant in architectural history, and her *New Fillmore* articles were written with affection and expertise.

Within the above-given boundaries lie the "classic" posh and near-posh blocks of Pacific Heights, the northwestern corner of which is also known as Cow Hollow, as well as the area south of California Street whose estimable housing stock was so gentrified in recent decades that the area was

promoted in Real Estate lingo from the generic "Western Addition" to "Lower Pacific Heights"—or, more amusingly, "Baja Pacific Heights."

Writing her Pacific Heights book was the one thing Anne left undone that mattered to her a lot. But I'm convinced that, even had she lived to be eighty-seven rather than sixty-seven, she wouldn't have gotten around to it. Her time was simply too taken up with consulting work, mostly guiding "good guy" developers in how to rehab their properties while keeping the historic fabric of the building or buildings in question exceedingly well in mind. Anne was extremely efficient in this work, trusted by the growing number of clients who depended on her, and that's where she spent her professional time, very happily indeed.

Shortly after Anne died I couldn't escape the feeling that "the Anne book" should be done, and that, if I may say so, it would be more attractive to residents and friends of San Francisco alike if the survey notion were scrapped and the focus put strictly on Anne's meaty Old House columns, which provide in-depth program notes for walking and armchair architectural tourists interested in people as well as pediments, historic "characters" as well as campaniles.

One hundred and ten seemed the magical number of Anne's articles to be drawn on here, enough to be comprehensive without undue repetition. It's been my highest priority to retain Anne's "voice"; inevitably, though, the housing of one hundred and ten articles all together rather than in monthly compartments required some rearranging here and there.

And it seemed only in the interests of all concerned for me to raid the labyrinthine files of this dogged researcher, my late wife, and pursue some avenues for which she had neither time nor space when turning out her monthly articles.

Furthermore, being a professional, and compulsive, writer myself I've let metaphors of my own creep in to stress or color a point. Yes, the book has become something of a blend, a phantasmal composite, if you will, of her cabernet and my merlot. "First person" statements are mostly hers—and the dazzling architectural expertise, of course. I'm responsible for the book's rhythm. I know that had Anne really done "the Anne book" we would have taken walks together to look at the houses and I might have offered a suggestion or two that would have been accepted as appropriate...To those who question my ability to bring Anne's book to light I can only say, with complete honesty, I can read her mind (we were, after all, happily married for forty-three years).

If she doesn't like what she sees, I'll hear about it!

In the draft of a preface Anne did write for her Pacific Heights book she thanks David Ish and his staff at the *New Fillmore* for giving her a free hand in subject matter and treatment over the years. For research help she thanks Gary Goss, Bill Kostura, Vincent Marsh, Michael Crowe, the Foundation for San Francisco's Architectural Heritage, the staff of the San Francisco History Center at the San Francisco Public Library, and the librarians of the California Historical Society.

To those names I would add, most warmly, Kit Haskell, the fabulous illustrator of this volume, Cathy Furniss, Michael Corbett, Alison Bloomfield, Julia Gilden, the "Hamptonians," Tom Reynolds, Dan and Juliana Duncan, George Young, Gerald Adams, Ian Berke, Sally Hanley, Max Kirkeberg, Jane Ivory, Aaron Peskin, Nancy Shanahan, Larry Campbell, Randolph Delehanty, Arland Petersen, Kevin Starr, Geegee Platt, Charlotte Maeck, Greg Scott, David Parry, Susan Pearman, John Field, Joe Beyer, John Gaul, Alice Carey, Paul Fisher, Chris Buckley and Patricia Vanderberg.

Words are scarcely adequate to describe my enchantment with the saintly and remarkable Malcolm Margolin and his extremely talented, efficient and charming staff at Heyday Books.

What Is Pacific Heights?

Anne Bloomfield

The San Francisco district known as Pacific Heights is as much a state of mind as a matter of actual geography. True, it's at the heart of the city's relatively affluent north side—not actually the Pacific side—and well above sea level, but the boundaries fluctuate according to the informant. A real estate broker will draw them much more generously than a socialite. An older member of a family prominent here for several generations will be more restrictive still.

This is a part of town where the movers and shakers of business and Society have lived for over a century. Many of them still live in the area, for Pacific Heights continues to be one of the nation's most desirable, as well as expensive, neighborhoods. Part of the attraction, for locals as well as the industrious, frequently foreign tourists crawling over its hills, is the parade of vistas from the Golden Gate Bridge and Mount Tamalpais (Vesuvius West, some call it) to Russian Hill with its high-rise apartments and on to the East Bay hills, plus, on a clear day, Mount Diablo beyond!

Even more compelling for resident movers and shakers is the presence of other movers and shakers.

To tell the history of the inhabitants is much more involved than reciting a litany of local successes. It reaches over the development of the entire western United States. In the last half of the nineteenth century and into the twentieth, the gold rushes and mines, the railroads, shipping, utilities and other businesses of this vast area were provisioned, financed and engineered from San Francisco. And the leaders of the companies that provisioned, financed and engineered tended to live, or have town houses, in Pacific Heights.

Let me give you a couple of examples. John Sabin, founder of what became Pacific Bell, built a fine house at Pierce and Pine early in his company's history. Meanwhile the silver mines of the Comstock Lode yielded its principal owners some half a million nineteenth-century dollars a month, and James Flood, the son of one of the owners, built two mansions in Pacific Heights, at 2120 and 2222 Broadway.

Often the homes of such personalities do rank as mansions, but the term "Pacific Heights" mostly conjures up an image of ample but not showy residences, freestanding amid at least a bit of landscaping, in a city where most housing is crowded onto narrow lots or into apartments.

There is an architecture typical of Pacific Heights, and found hardly anywhere else in San Francisco. It's well-bred and generally unobtrusive, characterized by large, comfortable, foursquare dwellings well suited for entertaining. The shape is a glorified box, sometimes with an entry at the side set well back from the street. Such specimens tend to rise two and a half stories, coming in a bit taller than their suburban counterparts. Expect to find a roof with four slopes or one that's hidden behind a cornice/parapet, while window placement is regular, indicating large rooms. Usually there's not much ornament in these houses. The "look" in each case was chosen from one or more of the styles popular around 1900: Colonial Revival, Classical Revival, Georgian Revival, Tudor Revival, Arts and Crafts, Château-esque.

Another Pacific Heights creature is the luxury apartment building, usually a ten-or-so-story job from the 1920s such as you'd also find on Nob or Russian Hill. Each unit occupies a whole floor—or at least half a floor, probably three thousand square feet at the least. These dowager towerettes have long appealed to wealthy persons who want to live fairly close to the business and cultural centers of the city and no longer desire a freestanding house with stairs to climb and a garden to tend. In many cases they count among their assets such a house outside the city and require a second abode of convenience.

These apartments have views and maids' rooms, and there's usually a doorman to watch over the building's entrance, a maitre-d' in blazer or braid. The exterior design of such buildings often parallels that of office "skyscrapers" of the same era: a three-part composition consisting of decorated base, plainer shaft and elaborate cornice. Ornamentation tends to be either Renaissance-Baroque or Spanish Colonial Revival.

Note meanwhile that apartment buildings with many more units often mimic the appearance of their more luxuriously furnished siblings.

And then, of course, Pacific Heights has its share of the lately beloved Victorians—Italianate, Stick and so forth, sometimes in delightful pockets of five or ten in a row and sometimes lone gingerbread wolves, so to speak, dwarfed by neighboring apartment buildings. Many, but not all, of the sometimes fussy Queen Annes that lined streets like Pacific Avenue in the early twentieth century have disappeared—not because of earthquake and fire (the huge 1906 fire was contained at Van Ness Avenue) but, in many cases, to make way for the relatively skyscraping structures that became popular in the twenties.

Arts and Crafts houses also make their cameo appearances in Pacific Heights and the area is graced by some eloquent "modern" yet historic houses by such near-contemporary architects as William Wurster and Gardner Dailey. Art Deco is not absent, and there's the occasional "Med" (for Mediterranean).

One of the things that so appealed to me as a Midwestern newcomer to San Francisco in 1954—indeed, it seemed a veritable defining factor in the city's personality—was the heady variety of styles and style-mixes I encountered in the houses and apartments arranged up and down the hills of Pacific Heights and other neighborhoods too, like so many rugged individualists joined together in some great architectural orchestra. Perhaps you as a native or a newcomer have viewed or will view San Francisco in a similar way.

Enjoy!

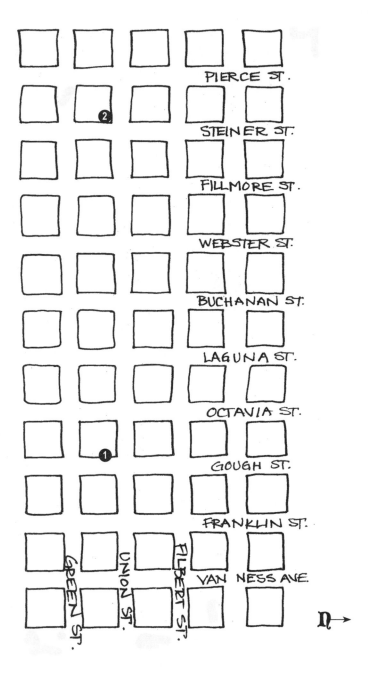

On or near

Union Street

east to west

No. 1

2645 Gough

An Octagonal Fixer-Upper

*I*n 1848 Orson Fowler, a wildly popular lecturer in the pseudo-science of phrenology, told his flock the shape of one's skull could govern personality, and the condition of a dwelling had a crucial influence on one's physical and mental health.

New Yorker Fowler sought to discover the ideal design for a healthy environment in which to live, and his answer was nothing ticky-tacky: it was that storybook curiosity, the octagon-shaped house. San Francisco in the late nineteenth century had at least five, perhaps eight, of these charming dinosaurs. Only two remain, one of them up on Russian Hill at 1067 Green, the other the subject of this chapter. Its address, 2645 Gough, puts it at the eastern end of the Union Street boutique strip, with Russian Hill just up the steep rise across Van Ness Avenue. It was built in 1861.

Fowler found that the octagon shape gave about 20 percent additional square footage per linear foot of exterior wall and was therefore more efficient in terms of heating and building costs than a more conventional footprint. He also claimed it provided more natural light and ventilation. Especially if a house of this sort had a cupola skylight, it would be virtually impossible to find an area that was not illuminated with natural light all through the day.

2645 Gough was designed with a typical octagon plan: on each floor four square rooms facing each direction of the compass, a center staircase under the benevolent cupola, and the triangular spaces on the four "extra" sides filled out with closets, bath and, on the first floor, the entry vestibule.

But Octagon House, as it is formally known, was reconfigured in 1952 when it was threatened with demolition (this was not a great period for preservation) and the Colonial Dames of California acquired it for a token single dollar. And it's no longer in its original location. The Dames had the house moved from across the street, where 2630 through 2648 Gough may presently be found. The Misses Lucy and Edith Allyne, members of the Dames, donated the space which represented the northern part of their copious property stretching along the west side of Gough from Green to Union Street.

The Allyne house on the southern half is gone but on its site at the corner of Green and Gough is the jewel-like Allyne Park. The sisters willed it to charity—valuable real estate, this, saved for the noble purpose of providing harried urbanites with a pastoral retreat.

In 1952 Octagon House amounted to a real fixer-upper. Three spinster sisters, the Misses Riley, had been living in the house in seclusion for several decades—does one encounter this sort of flight from the "real world" anymore?—and the owner since 1924, Pacific Gas and Electric, had never electrified it! *Chronicle* columnist Robert O'Brien attempted unsuccessfully to interview the sequestered sisters, and the article he wrote, probably in some desperation, only served to generate an air of mystery about this eccentrically shaped structure housing three little ladies who'd taken on some of the characteristics of myth.

There was, not surprisingly, a story about a stair-climbing ghost. This phantasmal creature took his, or her, exercise every November 24—who can say why?

Enter in 1952 Charles Warren Perry, retired dean of UC Berkeley's architecture school, to take charge of the much-needed renovation (and a shooing away, perhaps, of the autumn ghost). He took out all the partitions on the first floor to make one big space—this was tampering with the building's soul as well as that phantom, some historians indignantly complain—and replaced the rotten central staircase with one on the side. Also he added a one-story kitchen wing outside the original kitchen door, and replaced four windows, one of them with a garden door.

In the move the house was turned 135 degrees. The entry porch had been on a diagonal affording an excellent perspective to the northwest and the street life at what was originally the intersection of Gough and Presidio Road. The latter of these, now Union Street, led to "The Fort," in other words the Presidio which still may be found at the west end of Union past the boutiques—but it is of course no longer an Army post. Now the porch is on the east side of the house, facing directly onto Gough.

While not quite in one style indivisible, the exterior of Octagon House might be roped into the pigeonhole labeled "stripped Classic Revival." The cupola and interlacing blocks of wood at the house's corners are features generally associated with eighteenth-century American architecture.

The house was built, doubtless by a Fowler follower, for William C. McElroy (1819–1871) and his wife, Harriet Shober McElroy (1821–c. 1899). From Virginia and Lancaster, Pennsylvania respectively, they married in San Francisco at Gold Rush time and had one child, Emma Eliza, born in 1852. Helpfully for writers such as this one, Mr. McElroy, a miller by trade, left a time capsule under the staircase, dated July 14, 1861. He included newspaper clippings of the period, especially about the Civil War and the amazing growth of San Francisco, and added a tintype of the three McElroys and an artist nephew, whose profession was not considered quite respectable.

"We are a very good Looking old Couple

and pretty well off in this world's goods," announced the contented burgher of Gough Street; Mr. Fowler's prescription seems to have been the correct one for the McElroys.

But while they owned property on Stockton Street between Clay and Washington (now a busy, non-touristy part of Chinatown) as well as the whole east side of Gough between Presidio Road and Green, McElroy himself did not conduct a prosperous business. He worked for other people, as a boilermaker for Union Iron Works in 1854, and as a miller from 1859 on. From 1863 into 1865 he tried running a plant nursery from his property—Gough Garden it was called—but the business didn't last.

After her husband's death in 1871 Harriet McElroy continued to live in their octagon. Then in 1896 she deeded it to her daughter Emma Van Duzer who'd been a schoolteacher before her marriage. Emma's daughter Kate inherited the house, and sold it in 1917: that makes fifty-six years in one family's possession.

The house was a rental for sixty years from 1890. Tenants included the poet and journalist Daniel O'Connell, an early member of the Bohemian Club who wrote a play for the legendary Bohemian Grove summer outing (attended by tycoons and artistic types alike) while in residence on Gough. Later came wine merchant Frank Cavagnaro, and from 1910 to 1949 those three elusive Rileys.

No. 2

2325 Union Street

The Cow Hollow Church

2325 Union Street is the address of St. Mary the Virgin Episcopal Church, "the Cow Hollow church." It's been on this site at the corner of Steiner and Union, the western end of the now gentrified Union Street commercial strip, since October 4, 1891. But just how much of that original building remains is something of a puzzle. There was very extensive remodeling in 1950–51, and seismic strengthening plus other work in 1997–98. The parish, however—its name, its site, the area served, and the feeling of the place—all remain the same.

This part of San Francisco, its boundaries perennially a matter of opinion, was originally known as Spring Valley, not Cow Hollow. Thanks to the ready availability of grazing land and fresh water, more than thirty dairy farms sprung up in the region in the 1850s and 1860s, and it wasn't long before the area took on a new and picturesque name, too catchy a name to abandon later when it proved inscrutable to innocent newcomers not let in on the lore.

The St. Mary's congregation had its genesis in a Sunday school started in the summer of 1888 by Miss Florence Gay, a public school elementary teacher, a few blocks to the northwest on Greenwich near Baker.

Miss Gay began with only five young ones, but the number soon grew. By the spring of 1890 she was such a "draw" that the rector of the important St. Luke's on Van Ness Avenue appointed his new assistant, a tall, Cambridge-educated Englishman with the equally tall name of William Washington Bolton, to start a mission in her domain. Hopefully it would be built on property at Steiner and Union that just might be available.

This was a good corner. Ten years earlier the third cable car line in town, from Montgomery Street downtown to a Steiner-Union terminus, had been completed. True, there were rough shacks as well as fine homes in the area in the 1890s, but no longer those shady characters hanging around McLane's Crab House. In any event Bolton sought a diverse congregation.

The towering Mr. Bolton established the mission and led it through its formative years into 1898. He it was who tackled the formidable editor of *The Argonaut*, short, bewhiskered Frank Pixley, who owned the land on which the church still stands, and for whom a long and not uncharming alley north of nearby Filbert Street is named.

A battle of Mutt and Jeff, was it? Though a professed agnostic, and a terror to his employees and most others (editors in the old days shared with symphony conductors a tendency toward tyranny), Pixley eventually agreed to lend the land to Bolton for seven years, rent free. There was, of course, no clear indication of what would happen when time was up.

Frank Pixley died in 1895. And helpfully his widow—who, in the classic manner of spouses not perfectly matched in their religious fervor had been a devout churchgoer all along—deeded the corner property to the church. With certain stipulations, of course: the building was to be always open during daylight hours, at least one service was to be held every day, and seats were to be free. (At that time most congregations charged yearly subscription fees for the right to sit in the grander pews.) Furthermore, among other requirements, services were to be rich in ceremonial. This was as Bolton and both Pixleys preferred.

The original church building was too small to have an architect. It just got built.

One entered on Steiner Street, and the altar was where the door is now, up Union. The belfry existed, and the little cupolas along the roofline. And the interior was in the natural redwood with exposed trusswork we see today.

After the dynamic Bolton moved on, the congregation went through lean years, not made fatter by the comings and goings of a dozen different rectors in a quarter-century. Meanwhile there were a few additions and changes to the building: a choir gallery across the back, gables over the windows (so, it was said, no one would confuse this spunky little church with a barn) and the exterior seems to have been painted white.

That's how it looks in a 1906 photo of earthquake damage to adjacent Union Street—with a "20 CENT LUNCH" (to judge by a huge advertisement on its west wall) served in the building across the street where a bicycle shop may currently be found. (In the twenty-first century the co-author of this book was lunching kitty-corner from St. Mary's for an average twelve dollars, not a bad deal.)

The pace of activities quickened somewhat with the arrival of Jacob Henry Ohlhoff as priest-in-charge in 1923. The debt from settling with the Pixley heirs was paid off and this inspired plans for the future. Several architects, William Wurster, Ellsworth Johnson and the Charles Warren Perry we encountered at Octagon House, suggested improvements galore: a new foundation and roof, reversing the interior, adding space at the Steiner Street end, and construction of a courtyard and parish house.

All this improving took time, but these 1934 recommendations were carried out pretty much to the letter by 1952. A kickoff fundraising event to pay for replacing the rotten wood foundation helped energize the women of St. Mary's who scheduled countless bazaars, house tours and dances, activities usually mentioned in the Society columns, which, in San Francisco at least, continue to chronicle rather giddily the imbibings of the philanthropically inclined.

The considerable amount of work by local artists around the St. Mary's complex as it's enjoyed today should not go unmentioned: Perry himself designed, carved and gilded the sign on the Steiner-Union corner, near the bench where inspired parishioners and tired shoppers alike wait patiently for the 22 bus to perhaps turn up. Johnson designed the altar, with mosaics by Ruth Cravath, and also the sanctuary lamp, which was executed by Dirk Van Erp, and the sanctuary ceiling. The ceiling was painted by decorators Frederick and Olga Mornement, who also did the background for the Madonna at the corner sign. The fresco on a courtyard wall is by Lucienne Bloch (daughter of the composer Ernest Bloch) and Stephen Dimitroff.

Like Allyne Park next to Octagon House, this courtyard seems enchanted, removing you in a moment from all urban grit. This impression is never stronger than early on a sunny spring morning when San Francisco's famous matutinal fog is nowhere to be seen.

The longest rectorate at St. Mary's has been that of the personable Richard Fowler who came in 1966 and retired in 1999. He empowered the members of the congregation to work together and reach out. They have a solid youth program, a nursing home ministry, and much more. A recent multimillion dollar building program included seismic work, a sprinkler system, a remodeled parish hall, refurbished pews, new floors and lighting, and accessibility for the disabled.

Yes, a strong church.

Interlude

Geographically between "Great Old Houses" Nos. 2 and 3, in hilly territory a block and a half above St. Mary the Virgin, is the don't-miss 2460 Union, a mansard-roofed house with paired dormers set in the gentle slope of what suggests a scalloped ski-jump. It looks, with its mansard and tall shutters below, very French, as if Flaubert should be inside writing a novel, *Tales of the City* perhaps. This spacious gem of a house with its many-sided central gable is thought to have been built about 1872, designed by the firm of Mooser and Cuthbertson. It originally stood on a knoll in the center of a huge lot, the middle third of the square block bound by Union, Filbert, Scott and Pierce Streets, with access from both Union and Filbert to the north. In the 1890s the property was subdivided and the house torn from its knoll to appear in its present up-front location.

—Arthur Bloomfield

BRODERICK ST.

DIVISADERO ST.

③

SCOTT ST.

PIERCE ST.

STEINER ST.

FILLMORE ST.

WEBSTER ST.

BUCHANAN ST.

LAGUNA ST.

OCTAVIA ST.

GOUGH ST.

FRANKLIN ST.

VAN NESS AVE.

VALLEJO ST.

GREEN ST.

UNION ST.

N→

On

Green Street

2500

No. 3

2500 Green

Legacy of an Architect Cut Down

*T*he name of the architect of this nicely etched house on one of the pleasantest corners of Pacific Heights—stand kitty-corner from it and you can see Berkeley on a clear day—is a big surprise. William H. Lillie is known for incredibly ornate Queen Annes: the mansion, for instance, on the corner of Franklin and California diagonally across from Whole Foods, and the row of seven at 108-124 Lyon Street near Buena Vista Park. This quiet example of Colonial Revival, vintage 1898, provides quite a foil.

Lillie specialized in residences, and the index of *California Architect and Building News,* the local architecture magazine of his time, lists about fifty building contracts bearing his name. Most cost well under $10,000, but three were in the $17,000 range. Lots of houses for a man who died, like Mozart, in his mid-thirties, cut down by typhoid.

While not breaking any artistic ground, 2500 Green in its tactful style favored around the turn of the century is a satisfying piece of work. The apparent size of the house is a human-scaled two stories, but the descending hillside on Scott permits a full basement well above "dungeon" level and the four-slope roof masks a large attic. The true size of 2500 is also soft-pedalled by the somewhat different surface treatment of each story: horizontal rustic on the amply windowed basement, narrow clapboards on the first floor, and smooth wood siding on the second.

Ornamentation is restrained and harmonious. One room gently projects a bay window toward the street, another retreats lightly behind a pretty balcony. The façade sports four dignified Ionic columns and a half-moon pediment on the large central dormer above. All very orderly and proper 1898.

2500 Green must have been one of Lillie's last jobs, because he was born in 1862, in Minnesota, and died just before his thirty-sixth birthday. He grew up in Eureka, California, then moved to San Francisco at age twenty-one. For three years he called himself a civil engineer, so he knew his structural stuff. For another three years he was a draftsman for the bigshot architect Samuel Newsom (Newsom with his brother and sometime partner Joseph Cather Newsom is known for epic gingerbread of the Carson House in Eureka), then at age twenty-seven he struck out on his own.

For a young architect with only local training he did remarkably well. His houses are scattered through Pacific Heights, tony Presidio Heights just to the west, Alamo Square a mile south, and in the Haight as well. He was just making a name for himself among rather posh clients when the typhoid struck.

A word about Lillie's education in the 1880s. He did not attend architecture school, there was none west of the Mississippi. Most architects at that time simply learned by long apprenticeships under practicing architects, not perhaps such a bad way to go. Some builders *declared* themselves architects and were accepted, because the profession was not yet well organized. There were no exams, and licensing had not been heard of.

Samuel Newsom, the master under whom Lillie studied, preached a philosophy of "up-to-date" architecture with lots of ornament. With 2500 Green however, Lillie had moved beyond Newsomian trendiness into a style of pleasant understatement, a style which, with its...let's call it de-Carsonization, would have found plenty of good clients in the new century.

The client for Lillie's new direction on Green Street was a well-to-do businessman who, like his house, never made headlines. Frank Mortimer Ames didn't land in the cream of San Francisco high society, he spent his adult life selling crockery and glassware, much of it while managing the most upscale department of Nathan-Dohrmann, a wholesale and retail hotel supply business launched in the 1870s. From 1907 to 1946 it occupied the building at the southeast corner of Union Square which in its remodeled state became the home of the elegant retailer I. Magnin.

But the Ames family kept its head up in the social swim. According to *Our Society Blue Book,* Mrs. Ames and her daughter-in-law "received" (translation: "We are ready to serve tea to callers") on Fridays.

The 1900 census shows a house-load of nine souls living at 2500 Green: Frank M. and Sarah Ames, natives respectively of Maine and Massachusetts; both their children, son Frank H. Ames, a manufacturers' agent and Bohemian Clubber, and daughter Mary Gray along with her stockbroker husband and their two children; and two live-in servants as well, one Chinese (probably the cook) and the other German (probably the maid)—these were doubtless assigned, respectively, to quarters in the copious basement and attic.

Through the glass of time I see the master of the kitchen in his white jacket slicing bread (no crusts, please) for the dainty tea sandwiches surely served on Fridays. Later in the day, I imagine, the stockbroker would come home from the Financial District on that cute little "E" streetcar (door in the center) tooling its way up Union Street past dear St. Mary's. In summer give him a straw hat.

Interlude

Lording it over 2500 Green across Scott Street is the glamorous 2800 Scott, a handsomely pedimented and balconied mansion all red brick and white trim, ultrasymmetrical with a pillared entrance on its south side, which I admit to having fallen in love with. If this aristocratic palazzo looks fit for a king (or Joan Crawford, who resided here in the film *Sudden Fear*), 2500 Green with its homely finesse comes off as the house where some retainer of the monarch—his financial advisor, say, or maybe his chief steward—might have lived. Or Frank Ames.

The commanding 2800 Scott is the work of the prestigious architects Bliss and Faville and was built for capitalist William Mayo Newhall about 1905. Newhall belonged to the clan that later produced Scott Newhall, the feisty *San Francisco Chronicle* editor who famously put a story about the alleged failings of local coffee on his front page.

Because Green Street is just north of the circulation area of the *New Fillmore*, for which Anne wrote her Old House articles, she paid less attention to addresses there. I take the liberty of mentioning some of its highlights before we continue: Holy Trinity Orthodox Cathedral at 1520 (corner of Van Ness), which was built in 1909 and seems at once quite Russian as well as American in its look; the classic William Wurster "modern" at 1641, which is breathtaking in its simplicity (this pronouncedly wood-based house dates from 1940); and 1950-60, a Victorian "apartment building" of common-wall flats pressed together like pieces of toast.

Then, just below Green at 2929-31 Fillmore, is a be-eagled structure boasting bold Richardsonian arches that can only be called outrageous, considering the building's rather small scale.

And now to Vallejo Street with its fascinating parade of styles.

—*Arthur Bloomfield*

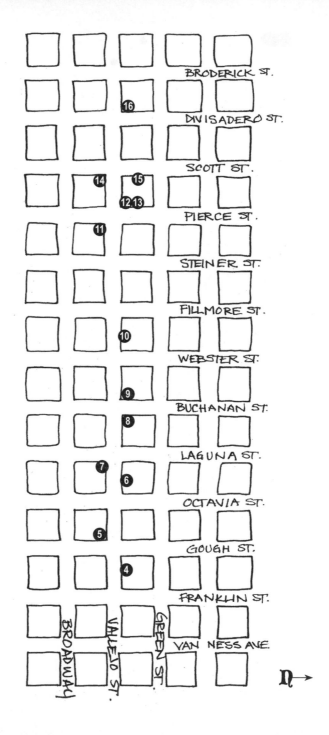

On or near

Vallejo Street

east to west

No. 4

1772 Vallejo

One Family's Landmark

The San Francisco character who caused this striking Second Empire Italianate house to be built in 1878 was a cockeyed version of the Renaissance man. Sailor, banker and mayor, Ephraim Willard Burr was a Rhode Islander who forsook the sea for California's Gold Rush and quickly jumped into the thick of business by the bay. Six years in San Francisco and he was elected mayor.

His Honor Mr. Burr reduced city spending by more than half, compromising therewith Heaven knows how many probably needed services. Whether his economy was the result of cleaning out corruption or some "small government" ideology I can't tell you. Speaking of corruption, the nimble newcomer Burr did not remain absolutely untainted: some years after founding California's first savings bank, the Savings and Loan Society, he was forced to resign because of charges he'd accepted a 5 percent commission for granting loans on Navy paymasters' certificates.

Can't you see the front page stories about that?

But Ephraim Burr, for all the colorful nature of his activities downtown, is responsible for a lovely and important house, a house that even achieved landmark status: it's officially San Francisco Landmark No. 31, designated as long ago as 1970. That was a time when San Francisco's fledgling preservation movement had developed a good head of steam in the wake of recent demolitions of fabled cinema palazzos on Market Street (the Fox, the Paramount), and in the wake too of many years of sentiment against the city's fading (but not for long!) Victorians.

Many of these had been left unpainted and even unrepaired as the Depression gave way to World War II. Then came post-war confusion as to redevelopment intentions not always honorable. And this is not to mention the "remuddling" of helpless Vics into the de-ornamented, quasi-Andalusian halfbreeds one doesn't like to think about.

The mansard roof of the grandly scaled 1772, disguising a full and bay-windowed third floor, gives the house a slightly Charles Addams look, but of a very benign sort. Notice all the felicitous detail: the richly carved balustrades at the entrance to the right, the molded corner quoins looking like so many oblong candies of impeccable provenance, the matching tiers of slanted bays, the colonnettes at the windows with their little Corinthian capitals and the reverse fluting on their lower ends suggesting packets of elegant tall cigars.

Ephraim Burr gave 1772 Vallejo to his

thirty-two-year-old son, Edmund, and his bride, Anna Barnard, as a wedding present. Can you top that? Then in due course the Edmund Burrs had four children, two boys and two girls. The daughters, Alice and Marian, lived in the house all their lives, the slightly longer-lived sister dying in 1968. They were, by the way, cousins of the Allyne sisters who racked up many years around the corner down on Gough. So pencil in ninety years for Burrs at 1772.

No wonder the house looks so intact, so true to the original design.

Alice Burr was interviewed late in life about 1772 by Junior League researchers for that pioneer chronicle of San Francisco's architectural history, *Here Today.* She told them that the actual builder of the house was her maternal grandfather, Thomas Barnard, who came from Nantucket. Miss Burr also said the house was designed by Edmund M. Wharff, and subsequent writers have repeated that name.

But in my opinion she remembered only the half of it. There was, in the nineteenth century, a carpenter/builder/contractor/architect named Wharff, but his first name was William; no Edmund Wharff of any profession was listed in the directories I've consulted. William H. Wharff, a New Englander like the Burrs and Barnards, lived nearby at Green and Laguna, he's known for some commercial buildings in Oakland and Berkeley, and

he put up quite a few houses in San Francisco's Pacific Heights.

Old Ephraim died at age eighty-five—the Burrs seem to have been especially long-lived. Edmund Burr, paterfamilias of 1772 Vallejo, had been educated at the Royal School of Mines in England and he earned a Ph.D. in chemistry in Germany. A grand tour of education! For quite a few years he listed his profession as chemist. He enjoyed staging experiments in his own lab in the backyard of Vallejo Street: should we picture a youngish Alec Guinness in Norfolk jacket, à la *Kind Hearts and Coronets?* But no fooling, he was a pro, he's supposed to have invented some reasonably crucial part of the sugar refining process and in due course he served as an executive at a succession of sugar refineries in the area.

Daughter Alice was an artist, and after Edmund's death in the 1920s she turned the lab in the yard into a painting studio. As part of the "war effort" during World War II she taught painting to recovering servicemen as occupational therapy. Meanwhile she and Marian commissioned the ubiquitous William Wurster (think 1641 Green) to design assorted residential units on other parts of their property stretching down Gough toward the Allynes. A nice gesture.

By the way, during the 1906 earthquake 1772 slipped off its foundation just as the attendant fire was halted about a block and a half to the east. Ninety-three jacks were required, but Burr House, no humpty-dumpty, was soon upright again, ready for another century or two at least.

...And as you're backing away from 1772 with your camera poised to catch all that beautiful detail you might turn around to notice, on the south side of Vallejo, a brick apartment complex of great charm and originality, an urban enclave suggesting a Norman village.

Postscript

It has subsequently come to light—thanks to the indefatigable architectural historian Bill Kostura—that the elusive architect of 1772 was actually Thomas J. Welsh, the busy Australian practitioner whose credits also include the imposing Sacred Heart Catholic Church at Fillmore and Fell Streets, near Alamo Square.

And how very interesting! In Anne's files I found copies of two sets of blueprints for the "Alice Burr studio" on Green Street. This would be on the north side of the extensive Burr property curling 'round lovely 1772 Vallejo in the western part of the block bounded by Vallejo, Green, Gough and Franklin.

The first set, from the office of architect Henry Higby Gutterson, is dated 1916 and indicates that by that time Alice already had her mind set on what must have been the successor to her seventy-year-old father's laboratory out back. The front elevation shows an apparently one-story building, a kind of super-cottage with a terrace front-and-center, capped by an arched Georgian window with fanning upper panes; the entrance is to the right. And there's an impressive hearth inside.

Then, in 1937, from the same architect's office, came plans for a remodel: raising the existing structure to second-story level, building a new first floor below and adding new entrance steps and a "hood," or near-pediment, on the north elevation. The handsome cathedral-ish window would remain, above the new hood.

And hadn't I seen it just a few hours earlier, when I was taking early morning pictures along Green Street? I rushed back in the evening and yes, there it was, the two-level super-cottage in barn-red shingle, sitting some way back from the street on a rise, between the celebrated Wurster house at 1641 and the modern flats at 1667, very much with a mind of its own: a house that looks as if it were transplanted from Carmel-by-the-Sea, or perhaps a New England town, to San Francisco's Pacific Heights.

...And a little more on Henry Higby Gutterson (1884–1954), a classmate of the aforementioned Charles Warren Perry at UC Berkeley's fledgling architecture school. In the pastorally oriented Gutterson's gracious, unpretentious designs one can find Arts and Crafts vocabulary merging with period revival modes. Although he designed about twenty houses in the Berkeley hills (in the Rose Walk area, etc.) after the disastrous 1923 fire, the largest concentration of his residential work is in St. Francis Wood, the leafy upscale subdivision west of San Francisco's Twin Peaks. He was the influential supervising architect of this area from 1914 until his death forty years later, and, as Berkeley preservationist Susan Dinkelspiel Cerny has computed, he designed approximately one hundred of its five hundred and fifty houses between 1913 and 1951.

No. 5

2461 Gough

Swanky Shingle and Friend

A case here of absolutely un-identical twins. The aesthetically macho Shingle Style house at the southwest corner of Gough and Vallejo and the relatively ethereal dwelling behind it on Vallejo were built in 1904 as a compound for two brothers, John and Joseph Maillard. (The member of this San Francisco clan with the highest profile would be the late and much-elected Republican congressman William Maillard.)

Separated by a wrought iron fence, the sibling houses shared a large garden (still impressive as seen from Gough Street) through which visitors walked to enter Joseph Maillard's now-independent house at 1815 Vallejo.

The brothers Maillard agreed to use similar building materials but the designs of the houses reflected their individual tastes. John's house at the corner, a meaty edifice suggesting the big architectural statement of some country estate, was designed by a local architect or architects (more on who in just a moment), and shows the influence of the celebrated Bernard Maybeck in its heavyweight woodwork: muscular balustrades, beefy pediments, a chest-thrusting two-story bay at the corner.

A very carpenterly house, in short: a bold affair that might have been crafted by Fafner and Fasolt, Wagner's giants in the building trade.

Brother Joseph, meanwhile, opted for a relatively delicate house inspired by the romantic Victorian cottages of the English Lake Country. Notice the tall fan-topped Georgian window at the center of the façade and the decorative diamond of an opening over the present front door. Joseph apparently designed 1815 himself and had his plans approved by the British architect John Corly.

John Maillard's corner house was sold in the 1930s to a Pacific Gas and Electric executive named Swank. The Swank family had the house for approximately fifty years, during which time they turned the original ballroom (a basement staple of many large Pacific Heights houses at the turn of the century) into a garage. A more recent kitchen remodeling dispensed with such dinosaurs as butler's pantry and servants' dining hall.

Now to unscramble the chaos relating to the name of the designer of 2461 Gough, the John Maillard house. According to a flyer put out by the real estate broker offering it for sale about ten years ago, the architect was a brother-in-law of Maybeck's known as Howard White. But just as there was no Edmund Wharff (see Old House No. 4) there was no Howard White. But Maybeck's brother-in-law John White (1870–1941) was a draftsman in the office of, and then a full partner of (from 1908) the architect George H. Howard Jr. Thus Howard and White.

Maybeck's other brother-in-law, Mark White, ten years younger than John, ultimately became Maybeck's partner. John White is even less well known than, and is often confused with, his brother Mark—not to mention the mythical brother Howard White! He was not much of a mixer or joiner, had no children, and was known to his own relatives as "the mystery man."

John White's affiliation with George Howard, whose family had pioneered the gentrification of exurban enclaves on the San Francisco Peninsula as a haven for aristos, resulted in about seventy jobs on the Peninsula alone. George Howard in an earlier and different collaboration did the landmark design for Burlingame's 1894 arcaded train station. (Howard himself was one of the founders of Hillsborough, one of the poshest addresses in the United States.)

According to a program note by Bill Sonin in a catalog for a Berkeley house tour in 1986 devoted to Maybeck and his legacy, there are at least eight houses in San Francisco designed by that amazing character "Howard and/or White." And that description of authorship would seem to be the safest in relation to 2461 Gough. With a strong tilt, I suspect, toward "John White."

Comparing the somewhat Maybeckian style of 2461 with the more colorful and, one has to say, eccentric quality of such prime Maybecks as the Roos house on Jackson Street in Presidio Heights, one would have to agree with Bill Sonin's assessment that while Howard and/or White's "distinguished houses are worthy of recognition," their architecture "lacks Maybeck's creative innovation." Their designs, he goes on to say, "run from Swiss chalet through Tudor Revival and even reach castle-like grandeur, as evidenced by some of their mansions on the Peninsula."

No. 6

1940 Vallejo

A Slice of Park Avenue West

The flower-lined walk beyond the arch at the entrance gives the visitor to 1940 Vallejo a sense of privacy before even ringing the doorbell. And the marble floors just inside this tony apartment house prepare one for high-end comforts above. The exotic tile and plaster decoration visible from the street carry on into the vestibule and lobby, putting a romantic nostalgia into uninterrupted play all the way to the apartments.

And this is an apartment building with *views,* a vertical charmer standing tall in one of the several pockets of vintage luxury "high-rises" scattered about Pacific Heights (think of the 1900 block of Broadway as well) and Russian Hill (see along Hyde Street on the cable car line just to the south of the "crookedest street"). These pockets are baby cousins, you might say, of larger concentrations of such housing stock along New York's Park Avenue or, on a somewhat more intimate scale, Chicago's Lakeshore Drive.

1940 Vallejo like most of its luxurious brethren has just one apartment per floor, with light and air to spare. Find here twelve "houses" reaching up toward the sky. Ownership in such buildings tends to be cooperative—a corporation owns the building and its stockholders have the units—and that is the case with 1940 Vallejo.

When it was new in 1928, this glamorous building avoided, or should we say sideswiped, Art Deco, the latest architectural rage. Although here and there it looks with its slender vertical panels and crisp decorative metalwork as if it might zig right into Deco, 1940 Vallejo sings a somewhat different song. Rental apartments of the late 1920s cheerfully ran with the Deco craze, but the luxury co-ops did not. At this address feast on the smooth but boldly punctuated stucco surfaces and the buttony polychrome tiles in subtle tones of tan, lavender and green—fantasy Moorish/Mexican, you might say. They stamp the building as a fascinating and ultrapersonal example of Spanish Colonial Revival, a style decidedly popular in the first half of the twentieth century.

1940 Vallejo, I think, is like a handsome woman of early middle age, bracelets quietly jangling, who loves the sun and remembers to put on sun block.

The apartment interiors here combine Quality with conservative fashion. There are broad archways between rooms, and generous moldings divide the walls into paneled spaces easy to decorate with the spare Vlaminck or Klee. The large living and dining rooms are on the north side with its enviable bay views, while the best bedrooms enjoy south light on the street side.

The architect of this good living was Carl

Werner (1875–1943) who came to the Bay Area from Philadelphia at the age of twelve. A graduate of MIT in 1898, he worked for several years in the office of Julius Krafft who designed such San Francisco mansions as the Flood house at 2120 Broadway (Old House No. 21) and the Heller place at 2020 Jackson (No. 51). Werner had plenty of opportunities chez Krafft to learn the tastes of "luxury" clients.

From 1903 to 1914 Werner was the junior partner of Mathew O'Brien and their work received considerable attention in the architectural press. Thereafter he practiced alone. He was noted especially for Masonic buildings. San Francisco's Scottish Rite Temple at Sutter and Van Ness, later the Regency Cinema, was a product of O'Brien and Werner. On his own, Carl Werner did Scottish Rite or Masonic temples in Oakland, San Jose, Petaluma, Santa Rosa, South San Francisco, Stockton, Santa Barbara, Fresno and Bakersfield. He also designed the YMCA on San Francisco's Embarcadero, a Colonial Revival City Hall for South San Francisco, and seven Christian Science churches. In the mid-1930s he worked on the Alameda County Courthouse.

Interesting to ponder the influence of Werner's "public" buildings on the elegant and should we say courtly style of his apartment house on Vallejo.

Werner invested more than his architectural talents in 1940 Vallejo.

He purchased the site from the owners of the mansion previously thereon, filing for a building permit on March 5, 1927, with "1940 Vallejo Street Inc." listed as owner. On June 29 title passed from Werner to a future resident, Mercantile Acceptance Corporation president Harold Snodgrass, and in September Snodgrass transferred title to the co-op corporation. The whole project seems to have been conceived by Werner and financed by Snodgrass' M.A.C. Snodgrass called 1940 Vallejo home for ten years. Residents were in place in '29, just before the Crash set off the Great Depression, which doesn't appear to have vastly shaken the new residents of 1940 Vallejo.

Werner may have sold units through his Masonic connections. Certainly Louis Ghirardelli of the well-known chocolate-making family was a Mason. So was Clarence Wood, a founder of the East-West football game benefiting Shriners Hospital for children—his widow lived at 1940 for more than fifty years.

Other early residents—a number of the men, by the way, belonged to the ultra-exclusive, and ultra-conservative, Pacific Union Club across from the Fairmont Hotel on Nob Hill—included Anson Herrick who'd been an accountant for the 1915 Panama-Pacific International Exposition, former Kansas City socialite Mrs. Curtice Dodge, rancher Jacob Brack, and

Honolulu Oil Corporation president Albert Mattei who was a fishing buddy of ex-president Herbert Hoover. The two almost perished in a fire one year on a fishing expedition.

"In" San Franciscans, these, who doubtless could be found dining on bourbon, petrale sole and charcoal-broiled steaks at Jack's restaurant down-town. The men, of course, generally lunched at their clubs—say, does the Bohemian still feature that signature raisin bread toast?

And Werner himself never moved from the house he'd built in laid-back Alameda, across the bay, in 1907.

No. 7

2628–32 Laguna

The Wrong Coxhead's Railroad Flats

*W*ell, what are railroad flats? One-story units with all the rooms falling into formation off the same side of a long narrow hall. Suitable for mysteries, perhaps, like Alfred Hitchcock's multi-compartmented *The Lady Vanishes,* or maybe a slapstick comedy featuring many doors plus an exposed area—the long hall—in which a comic figure, let's say Robin Williams in drag, doesn't want to be spied.

But enough of fantasy. Buildings like 2628-32 Laguna with their stacks of three elongated flats (nine-room flats, sometimes, from "engine" to "caboose") were very popular basic housing in the early part of the twentieth century, probably as a response to increases in population and land costs in tight little San Francisco. They were a way to achieve density without losing amenities like privacy and spaciousness.

And with the city's perpetual housing shortage, they continue to serve. One simply has to keep track of all those rooms in a row; one or two might be mere cubbyholes.

The San Francisco definition of a flat seems to be a unit with its own front door at the street and usually occupying a whole floor in a building. One enters the three-story "railroads" by climbing a few steps to an open vestibule set into the mass of the building. Three doors open off the vestibule, one to each flat, and two of the doors admit immediately to individual staircases (steep ones!) to the second- and third-floor units respectively. As a little boy Arthur noticed that the door handles on the three doors were often oval-shaped.

Each flat generally has full-width front and back rooms, and between them runs the long narrow hall which may jog around the staircase. The middle rooms receive sunlight from light wells—down which Hitchcockian ladies don't usually vanish!

Numerous bay windows—some here are set into tall quasi-canisters—are standard design procedure in railroad-flat structures. In general, a big cornice hides the roof: it's usually decorated with toothlike "dentils" and/or "egg and dart" alternations of oval and pointed gestures, rather like those you'd see on a Classical Revival or Queen Anne house.

There are some interesting extras at 2628-32: the ovoid porthole windows, for instance, and note the handsome curved glass in the bay windows. The puzzle here is the architects named in the building contract: Coxhead & Coxhead. Ernest Coxhead designed some of the Bay Area's most inventive architecture (see, for instance, Old Houses Nos. 15 and 58). Coxhead & Coxhead were known for manipulating scale and limiting decoration to one large element. Portholes aside, I don't see anything unusual or trendsetting about this building, and its construction date of 1902 is not especially early for this building type. Maybe Almeric Coxhead, Ernest's older, less famous, and terrible-tempered brother, designed 2628-32.

But there's no question about the client. She was Valence Bloch (there's a city on the Rhône River named Valence) and her parents, Jean and Adele, had come from France to San Francisco in the 1850s. Jean was a commission merchant for many years, a profession then identified in the census by the now-quaint job description "capitalist." Daughter Valence was the longtime secretary of the Golden Gate Park Commissioners.

Another puzzle is birthdates for the Blochs. In the thirty years between the 1880 and 1910 census reports, the parents grew thirty-five and thirty-seven years older respectively, but the children aged only nineteen or twenty. Perhaps they imbibed some magic elixir from the Rhône Valley!

No. 8

2090 Vallejo

Williamsburg Transported

A little old lady in Berkeley once told me this Georgian Revival beauty was her favorite of Clarence A. Tantau's houses. Hmmm, you might have expected her to choose among his Berkeley creations, which relate more closely to the so-called Bay Area Tradition, that stylistic orientation associated with Bernard Maybeck, Willis Polk and a number of others.* The East Bay–based Tantau (c. 1884–1943) worked under San Francisco City Architect Loring P. Rixford and Bakewell and Brown, all trained at the Ecole des Beaux-Arts in Paris, before starting his own practice in the teens. Later he was consulting architect for the developer of ultra-upscale Pebble Beach, where a "New Riviera" was being created on the Monterey peninsula, and in 1924 he collaborated with Lewis Hobart on a new central section of the partly burned-out Del Monte Hotel (later the Naval Postgraduate School). About the same time he came up with a "courtyard" house in Berkeley, 190 Alvarado Road, in a much less modern-looking revival of Spanish Colonial than we recently encountered in Carl Werner's Vallejo Street apartment house: the Berkeley house has a tri-portaled stable, historan David Gebhard opines, that is "hardly credible" in the Berkeley hills.

Then during the Depression, a terrible time for architects, Tantau supervised the work of our old acquaintance William Wurster at Pasatiempo near Santa Cruz. His star rose again with the design of the San Francisco building at the Golden Gate International Exposition held on Treasure Island in San Francisco Bay in 1939.

Here on Vallejo Street, in 1919, Tantau played with Southern Colonial ideas, especially in the thick-mortared brick walls, the restrained white trim, and the steep roofs with chimneys at the apex and return angles creating "elbows" at the base. He added two sensuous notes: the pediment over the front door curves into a pair of voluptuous wave crests, and the bay window, offering a sumptuous bay view, projects over Buchanan Street on an unnecessary but delightful series of rounded moldings.

In sum, a house that might—almost—have been transplanted from Colonial Williamsburg.

For this house which was ranked among the top one percent of all the city's buildings in a 1976 Planning Department architectural survey Tantau had, no surprise, a rich client. B. F. Schlesinger as he was known, the B definitely for Benjamin and the F probably for Franklin, was a transplant from the Midwest belonging to a clan that owned department stores all over

---

*Bang together the heads of a number of independently minded architectural historians and you'd find that sources of inspiration for this "Tradition" include the Shingle Style, the Arts and Crafts movement, Art Nouveau, Viennese Secessionism, Japanese landscaping, Spanish Mission Style, Pueblo Indian Style, Swiss chalets, miners' shacks and Queen Anne!

the United States. Arthur, a genealogist and music critic, suspects he was a distant cousin of the great conductor Bruno Walter, a Berliner whose real name was Bruno Schlesinger, and B. F. was indeed one of the early major supporters of the San Francisco Opera when it was launched in the 1920s.

B. F. arrived in San Francisco shortly after the earthquake and fire of '06, probably in his twenties, and quickly became the assistant general manager of the Emporium, the Market Street department store closed for some years now, its sterling façade to be retained in the twenty-first-century Bloomingdale's project.

Was B. F. related to an owner of the Emporium, or did he simply have department stores in his blood and stage a career coup? In any case, by 1914 he'd become the store's general manager and soon the employees were calling him the Big Chief. And he was living at 1718 Vallejo just west of Franklin.

In 1923, comfortably settled into his new Georgian digs with his wife and four sons, B. F. resigned from the Emporium and bought a number of other retail venues along the Pacific Coast including the May Department Stores, B. F. Schlesinger and Sons in an Emporium-like building in Oakland, and, as flagship, the lamented City of Paris in San Francisco on Union Square where Neiman Marcus now stands.

The City of Paris Dry Goods Company is fondly remembered by San Franciscans who bought books on its ground floor from well-informed female sales associates of a certain age, then descended to a basement called Normandy Lane where a courtly, perhaps even titled gentleman suavely presided over the wine department, and one lunched at a serpentine counter featuring baby cinnamon rolls as a signature offering. Help! Where is the time machine to take us back?

The store even had a branch, or office, in Paris itself, at 9, Boulevard de Strasbourg. The urbane Paul Verdier, often spotted prowling City of Paris aisles, was the perennial president, but B. F. chaired the board, and a son was treasurer.

Alas, the family had some personal problems. One of the sons died early; another staged a fake suicide, sending his car into the Columbia River, and had to spend the rest of his life in exile abroad. By the time B. F. sold 2090 Vallejo in 1939 he'd retired. He died in 1960.

The only other owner of 2090 until recently was Arthur Berain Dunne, a Harvard-educated attorney who was a governor of California's State Bar and head of the Republican County Central Committee. (I might note here that, while only about 15 percent of San Franciscans are registered Republicans, they tend to live in affluent areas like Pacific Heights.) In 1944 that feisty attorney Vincent Hallinan, father of San Francisco's recently defeated district attorney, charged Dunne with subordinating the interests of the State Bar to those of the mighty Southern Pacific Railroad.

But the Hallinans are another story, and even if Dunne was on the SP payroll, he did take excellent care of his Tantau house.

No. 9

2100 Vallejo

Georgian Minimal

*L*ow key, low key! The mini palazzo designed by the seriously underdocumented Houghton Sawyer across Buchanan Street from the Schlesinger house claims an exterior which is for the most part Inconspicuous. Except that it stands out for a simplicity at once stubborn and felicitous.

In past decades when the house was swathed in romantic vines this austere personality registered somewhat less; now 2100 Vallejo is as clean-shaven as the plans Sawyer drew for the house at his downtown office in 1911.

The rigorously symmetrical Vallejo Street front and the loggia-dominated Buchanan Street side emerge for the architectural sightseer in plain stucco, the simply adorned windows on the resolute face of the building relieved just a little by semicircular transoms on the main floor. The house's restrained aesthetic is pursued further in a loggia filled with lattice to avoid disturbing the plain walls. Yes, there's a cornice, but it doesn't call attention to itself. Even the surrounding garden, which covers three times as much ground as the house, is subdued behind a tall hedge.

Now, the entrance to 2100, up a little walkway on the west side of the house is Impressive, but you have to peek to see it.

It's lovely! Beneath the semicircular balcony are a pair of fluted Doric columns supporting a garland and a group of moldings—dentils, egg and dart, and a succession of rolls and curves—matching those of the cornice. Above the balcony is a large arched opening highlighted by a wide and graceful incurve. Deep recesses hollow out the arch at street and balcony levels, while inside 2100 a grand staircase does nothing to detract from the aristocratic and not unsensuous aura of the entrance.

There have been some changes over the years. When the house was vine-covered it was never painted; it had, in fact, been designed not to be painted and was a sort of sandy color with some textural relief, maybe even sparkles—subdued ones of course. In its present white paint job the effect strikes me as awfully bland. But Arthur says he's bowled over by what he calls the house's "milk of inhuman beauty." Perhaps he has a point.

Meanwhile the secret garden seems to be bucking for LeNôtrian status.

(By the way, unpainted stucco can be found on another two important San Francisco houses, both on Russian Hill: one is John K. Branner's 940 Green, dating from 1922; the other is Sawyer's baronial 1001 Vallejo at Taylor, a storybook

1905–06 mansion associated with City of Paris' Paul Verdier.)

For a 1911 house, 2100 Vallejo was a decade or two ahead of its time in offering a version of Georgian or Colonial Revival stripped to a minimum. Bare bones, you might say, but what bones! Sawyer was giving his client the very latest architectural thinking, an elegant, uncluttered design with references to the nation's colonial past.

And his client—well, technically his client—was no less than Alma de Bretteville Spreckels, the amazing character who gave San Francisco the California Palace of the Legion of Honor, the museum of European art in Lincoln Park overlooking the Golden Gate. Not long after 2100 Vallejo was built, she commissioned the high-profile Spreckels mansion at 2080 Washington Street, designed by George Applegarth (Old House No. 61). The contrast between the two houses raises some fascinating speculations: why the change in architects, why the change from super-restrained to super-ornate? And the answer lies almost certainly in the six-foot Alma's feisty, ambitious, not exactly understated personality.

Alma was not born with a silver spoon in her mouth or a Pacific Heights mansion in her name. Struggling as a young woman to pay for art lessons, she became an artist's model, attracting the attention of no less than the distinguished sculptor Edgar Walter, uncle of the Abstract Expressionist Nell Sinton, who lived in Old House No. 44 on Divisadero a number of years later.

It wasn't long before the tall and voluptuous Alma was switching gears to pose nude for suggestive oils for the walls of watering holes along the so-called Cocktail Route on Kearny Street south to Market and thence up Powell toward Union Square.

Enter now Adolph Spreckels, Charles Laughton look-alike and scion of a family with a fortune in sugar. Papa Claus lived on Van Ness Avenue until his stately pile was lost in the conflagration of '06, son John had a suitable house around the corner on Pacific, and son Adolph, who was exceptionally fond of boats, racehorses, and women (choose the order), had a place in Sausalito, across the unbridged Golden Gate.

Alma and Adolph proceeded to have a long affair, and eventually she persuaded this bon vivant to marry. A little girl was soon added to the family and a couple of years later Adolph installed, or tried to install, wife and kiddie in 2100 Vallejo.

Whether Adolph prompted Sawyer's aggressive avoidance of glitz or the architect was left to his own creative devices is not known; but the latter was very likely the case. In any event, this elegant low-key palazzetto was *not,* as her lively biographer, Bernice Scharlach, makes abundantly clear, the sort of mansion Alma had in mind.

Alma had title to the house, Adolph

paid for it, and by 1913 it was Alma's brothers Oscar and Gus, the latter always her lackey, who settled albeit rather briefly into Vallejo Street. Alma would duly proceed to the Applegarth house of her dreams—she'd been thinking about it when she was a child delivering laundry to back doors rather than Sawyeresque or Applegarthian portals.

Most of Alma's family did very well thanks to the Spreckels connection: one of her nephews, Charles de Bretteville, was even president of Spreckels Sugar forty years later. I would guess that brothers Oscar and Gus were established in stockbroking and real estate respectively through her offices. The parents were made comfortable too.

The oldest brother though, he made it on his own. Alexander de Bretteville started out as a machinist. By the time Adolph and Alma were married he was already manager of Main Iron Works, rising later to vice president.

Alma Spreckels maintained that her de Bretteville ancestors were French nobility who escaped from the Revolution to Denmark. Her father's name would seem to confirm this: Viggo le Normand de Bretteville. She didn't invent the particle "de" before the name, Viggo was using it as early as 1882, when she was only a year old. He was a farmer then, near Lake Merced. By 1894 he'd moved the family to Francisco Street between Polk and Larkin, a

Russian Hill address he had for the rest of his life. The 1900 city directory lists him as a teacher of languages, with Matilde de Bretteville, Alma's mother, a masseuse.

And what of 2100 Vallejo? After Oscar and Gus moved out, perhaps in 1915, Alma rented it to stockbroker Eyre Pinckard. Only in 1919 did Alma give title to Oscar, who in turn sold to the Pinckards in 1924. In the thirties Sawyer's quiet masterpiece was acquired by prominent businessman Louis Benoist, whose widow, Geraldine, died only recently, in Pacific Heights of course, aged more than one hundred.

A bit more about Houghton Sawyer. *He* was born with a silver spoon in his mouth, arriving into a well-off family in San Francisco in 1871. And he lived to the age of ninety. He had the finest education possible, at Berkeley, Stanford, MIT, London, Paris, and Rome. Setting up shop in his hometown, this cultured pro probably had a small office and could lavish personal attention on his well-heeled clients. Adolph doubtless chose him because he was socially acceptable: there's something, of course, about a Houghton!

There are few known works of Houghton Sawyer, but all are of high quality. Besides 2100 Vallejo and the Verdier mansion there are, for instance, a couple of Nob Hill apartment houses, 1001 California Street, kitty-corner from the Fairmont Hotel, and the especially characterful 901 Powell, behind the Fairmont. Near the Presidio Wall, north of Lake Street, he did 2 Fifth Avenue.

In Pacific Heights you should also note the lovely brick house at 2518 Buchanan two and a half blocks up the hill from 2100 Vallejo.

Some years ago its owner was William Kent Jr. of the great clan that donated Muir Woods to the public domain and developed the upscale "Seadrift" area at Stinson Beach. Arthur remembers Mrs. Kent serving tomato soup with cream floating on top before sending him and her son to the movies one Saturday afternoon: three cable car lines including the Jones Street "dinky" would land them at the Paramount! Later the house belonged to the Milton Esbergs, good friends of the great Wagner-ian soprano Kirsten Flagstad, who sang a number of seasons with the San Francisco Opera—her most traumatic appearance came after local veterans' groups tried to ban her because she'd returned to Norway during World War II to be with her husband.

What first caught my eye about 2518 Buchanan was its patterned brickwork, a rare variant of Flemish checkerboard creating subtle stripes. There's also a fairy tale colonnade—seek it out.

No. 10

2250 Vallejo

A House Dunn up Brown

*A*n architectural pastry chef seems to have gotten hold of 2250 Vallejo.

Ornament is king here, with a deeply modeled "top band" (or call it a frieze) contrasting pleasingly and not undaringly with smooth walls. Most of the band is foliage, traced in garlands and assorted Renaissance-style arrangements along with exaggerated scrolls. Pretty bold stuff—I'm reminded of the *New Yorker* cartoon in which a waiter asks a diner with a well-stacked plate of food before him, "Well sir, is it intense?"—and perhaps best not to analyze it too closely. This frieze, by the way, is as remarkable as the north wind face on 2004 Gough, near Clay.

Ornament doesn't stop at frieze height. Consider the doorway below with beveled glass plus attached and freestanding columns; big fat dentils (that toothy molding again); and an airy metal balcony rail to cap things off.

Then, above the frieze, observe more dentils and a wide-projecting cornice on modillion blocks. Crane your neck some more and you'll see that even the gutter downspouts boast column-like capitals and—this is for true downspout aficionados!—arrow-headed "attachers."

It comes as something of a relief, no pun intended, that the ornate passagework on 2250 is limited in area and the rest of the façade is plain. In fact, the basic building resembles the standard early twentieth-century house of the well-to-do in Pacific Heights. An elegant box, in short, with ample and very regular openings. The ornamentation stems from Classical architecture via Renaissance and Georgian derivations.

Houses like this were built to shelter the lives of well-off people who were accepted in Society partly because they and their possessions didn't attract undue attention. Well, the frieze James Francis Dunn thought up for 2250 Vallejo in 1901 is an attention-grabber all right, but because it's so beautiful.

Dunn was known for unusual ornament. He certainly had an exuberant, near-manic approach to icing his architectural cakes and left an exceptionally colorful legacy, including the friskily Frenchified Montellano apartments at 2411 Webster (Old House No. 34); the Alhambra apartments, with their Moorish fantasy, at 860 Geary on the edge of the Tenderloin; the almost Gaudi-like Chambord apartments, with their bulging, exotic bays, on the northeast corner of Sacramento and Jones on Nob Hill; and the curling-and-squiggling Art Nouveau flats at 1347 McAllister, near Alamo Square. Not to mention 798 Post Street downtown, with its rustication gone mad.

Somehow it doesn't come as a surprise

that Dunn, a Francophilic Irishman from San Francisco's South of Market (long before it was the SOMA of the dot-com era), was his own worst enemy, an alcoholic who died young. It must have been his delightful flights of architectural fancy that kept him going.

Dunn specialized in multi-unit dwellings, but here on Vallejo Street he and his then-partner Albert Schroepfer produced a single-family house and did it well. (And Arthur suspects they are turning in their graves after hearing about the dozen mailboxes lately visible.) Their client was one James Madison, who'd made his money in packing and shipping. He was a Dane, born in 1860, who'd come to this country as a teenager to join his father and stepfamily.

The father was a ship owner as well as master mariner, so James moved naturally into the financial side of shipping. By the time he moved into 2250 Vallejo, he was secretary of the Alaska Salmon Company. Later he owned businesses in dried fruits and canning, and he managed the Sun Maid Raisin Growers Association. In that capacity he joined California's wine growers in opposing Prohibition.

Madison never forgot his Danish upbringing. He promoted trade between the two countries, he managed the Danish exhibit at the 1915 Panama-Pacific Exposition down the hill from 2250 Vallejo, and he was a founder and president of the Danish Old People's Home, the Aldersley, in San Rafael. He even persuaded a group of San Franciscans to donate a park in Denmark. For these activities the king of Denmark made Madison—whose name must originally have been Madsen—a Knight of Danneborg in 1917 and Knight Commander eight years later.

Madison/Madsen also made news, in 1895, by joining other San Francisco business leaders in financing the San Joaquin Valley Railroad to compete with the Southern Pacific, which they perceived as skimming all the profits off California agriculture. But as usual, SP came out on top.

Mrs. Madison, Jennie, was the shipping and raisin magnate's junior by eight years; the couple married in 1877 and had four children. After his death in 1927 Jennie stayed on at 2250, selling it in 1949. The Madisons literally left their mark, since the initial M is charmingly perpetuated in the wild Mr. Dunn's wrought iron balconies.

No. 11

2670 Pierce

The House That Graft Built

Read here about the contractor who created the house that graft built, and the profits that accrued to the contractor who created the house that graft built, and the high-priced jobs that made the profits that accrued to the contractor who created the house that graft built. And read about the mayor who recommended the jobs that made the profits that accrued to the contractor who created the house that graft built, and the city board that held up legitimate permits while the mayor recommended the jobs that made the profits that accrued to the contractor who created the house that graft built.

Translation, please! Back in 1906 the Board of Public Works was stalling building permits until applicants agreed to use an expensive contractor, Deneen Building Company, recommended by Mayor Eugene Schmitz, for whom Deneen built a mansion at 2501 Vallejo, across the street from 2670 Pierce; and 2670 Pierce was the new home of, and probably designed by, none other than Jeremiah Deneen, proprietor of said building firm.

One stalled permit was for a Chinese theater that Deneen jacked up to $16,000 after architects estimated only $4,000. Another was for a house of prostitution he built for three partners who'd gotten the previous building on the site condemned and demolished free by the City of San Francisco. Mayor Schmitz and political boss Abe Ruef supposedly shared in the brothel's profits, and it received police protection. Well, Police Commissioner W. H. Leahy owned a piece of Deneen's firm.

These people all figured in San Francisco's infamous graft prosecutions of 1906–09. Boss Ruef had engineered the election of his puppet mayor (who was, by the way, president of the Musicians Union Local 6) and Board of Supervisors. The whistle was blown on Ruef and friends by a dynamic quartet consisting of editor Fremont Older, former mayor James Phelan, sharp businessman Rudolph Spreckels, and prosecuting attorney Francis Heney. The graft trials were front-page news all over the country, with shady streetcar and telephone franchises far overshadowing Deneen's relatively minor peculations.

Jeremiah Deneen completed 2670 Pierce peacefully enough, moving in with his wife and four children. But by spring of '07 the trials had put an end to the Deneen Building Company, and its master sold his new manse in November of that year. He continued as a relatively small-time contractor until his death in 1911, aged not much more than fifty.

Hailing from St. Louis, Deneen had arrived in San Francisco about 1891, a young man already calling himself "builder." His twenty-year career in San Francisco included several more houses in the square block containing 2670 Pierce, and several in the 2200 block of Green, not to mention the Schmitz house, which comes on as an architectural (and maybe political?) soulmate of 2670.

The half-timbering of 2670 allies it with one of the high styles of the early twentieth century, the Arts and Crafts movement. The terms Tudor Revival and Elizabethan also come to mind in the zero-setback sidewalk overhang of the bays, steep-roof dormer windows and clinker brick, not to mention the half-timbering. All these derive from early-day city houses of England and northern Europe.

Of course the designer of 2670 Pierce—Deneen, while something of a scoundrel, was obviously no mere dog-paddler in architectural waters—was building a "modern" house, very 1906 in every respect, including as it does visual symbols of the handwork ethic of William Morris and Gustav Stickley's famous A & C movement.

Was the next owner Packard and Cadillac dealer Cuyler Lee, the man who sold cars to Deneen's pals, such diverse folk as a redlight liquor dealer and the superintendent of schools? Possibly so. In any event, the handsome 2670 couldn't shield Lee from trouble any more than the hapless Deneen; he was involved in automobile accidents, he was arrested for speeding, his marriage failed, and he lost both car agencies.

Read all about it in a top-of-the-page story in the *San Francisco Call* of June 9, 1910. "As foretold in *The Call*," the reporter cried, "Cuyler Lee has lost the Cadillac agency, although at the time of the announcement he professed not to know that any change was contemplated."

Meanwhile, in the next two columns, entitled in delicate floral type "The Smart Set," one's eye might have fallen on the following..."Through an unfortunate coincidence it is suspected that a young man in our local smart set knows the secrets of the boudoir in the home of one of our prominent girls, and all on account of an accidental exchange of suitcases. Both were invited down the peninsula..."

Gilbert and Sullivan, where are you? Or should it be Oscar Wilde?

But back in 1907 Cuyler Lee was riding high, running the auto endurance race from San Francisco to Monterey in a tall new Packard. The Lees were a Social Register family from Michigan, car country. The 1910 census shows six of them at 2670 Pierce, along with three live-in servants, immigrants respectively from Scotland, Denmark and Japan. Arthur voted for the Dane as head of the kitchen (and her name, as if from central casting, was Miss Jorgensen), but apparently it was the Scotswoman who did the cooking.

It must have been after the Lees separated that the master of 2670 was fined for being late to jury duty. He'd overslept in his digs at the Bohemian Club.

No. 12

2701 Pierce

Arts and Crafts Grandeur

One Saturday morning in 1960 a courtly eighty-four-year-old gentleman received a young biographer in his office on the twenty-sixth floor of the Russ Building on Montgomery Street, the same office he'd been driving downtown to for thirty years (lately he was piloted by a chauffeur). With the utmost patience and cordiality, he recalled his role—a crucial role—in bringing San Francisco's much-loved Opera House into being.

The elderly gentleman was Charles Kendrick, one of San Francisco's great movers and shakers, no longer on the battle lines but ultra-alert. It was the same Kendrick, just back from the war in 1919, and known as Major Kendrick, who bought 2701 Pierce and lived in it for thirty-five years. And more about him in a moment...

The house dates from 1904 and is the work of William Curlett, whose architecture is all over San Francisco's downtown: the Shreve Building at the northwest corner of Post and Grant, the Phelan Building at Market, Grant and O'Farrell, the tall narrow bank building on Market facing Third, and so on. He was also the author of Senator Phelan's Villa Montalvo, that Saratoga Shangri-La for musical events on the edge of what is now Silicon Valley.

The elegant Richardsonian portal of 2701 Pierce leads to one of the grandest Arts and Crafts mansions in San Francisco. But grand? Isn't that a contradiction in terms when connected with the label Arts and Crafts? Doesn't Arts and Crafts imply a small house, usually one story—even when it's one of those "ultimate bungalows" of Greene and Greene in Pasadena?

Well, 2701, even if it looks with its awesome superstructure rather like a great liner slowly steaming up Pierce Street (or perhaps a tilted Lake Michigan lapping at a North Shore Chicago estate), is in fact a veritable catalog of Arts and Craftsiana. Hallmarks of the style are a low-pitched roof with gabled dormers, multiple roof planes, textured exterior walls, horizontal rows of windows, boxy porch columns, wide eaves on braces and exposed rafter tails, and sometimes decorative half-timbering as well. 2701 claims all of the above except the porch columns and rafter tails.

The Arts and Crafts philosophy emphasized handcrafting and the dignity of labor, rejecting factory-made objects, and followers of this Word designed houses to *look* handmade. Certainly 2701

Pierce is all about workmanship and fine detail executed with affection. You can almost see the carpenters at work in their overalls.

In 1904, when the house was built, the Greenes had barely begun their architectural journey and Gustav Stickley's *Craftsman* magazine was in its infancy. So Curlett probably derived his ideas for 2701 from the English originators of Arts and Crafts, William Morris and C. F. A. Voysey.

Curlett was born in Belfast, Ireland in 1846 and trained and began his career in that country and England. He came to California in 1871 and by the 1880s was designing mansions ranging in cost from $23,000 to $90,000, this at a time when ordinary houses cost $4,000 or so. (Curlett would feel at home today in Pacific Heights, where the sky-scraping prices for its grander houses make the neighborhood average out as the second most expensive place to live in the U.S.) Meanwhile he became a fellow of the American Institute of Architects. If you have that 1987 reprint of *Victorian Classics of San Francisco* from Windgate Press, the index can guide you to photos of seven mansions designed by the firm of Curlett & Cuthbertson. Alas, only one is standing: 1409 Sutter Street just west of Franklin, with its charming tower.

Curlett, now at the top of his profession, designed 2701 for his family. Living

with him were his wife, Celia, to whom he gave title to the house, and their children, Aleck and Ethel. The 1910 census indicates their live-in servants were a Japanese couple named Akomoto. There was also a country house at Menlo Park where this highly successful architect died in 1914. Celia Curlett held onto the town house a few years longer.

Major Kendrick, who was a real estate broker, born south of Market and later known as the president of Schlage Lock and a member of the planning commission, moved in with a houseful. The 1920 census reported a mom and dad with two sons and two daughters aged twelve to one, plus a set of grandparents and a live-in housekeeper and nursemaid.

...And back to that Saturday morning in 1960...Charles Kendrick quietly told the young writer who was working on a history of the San Francisco Opera that a chance meeting with John Drum, a member of the campaign to build a much-needed opera/symphony hall (we're talking 1919) was a turning point in the protracted tale of how San Francisco finally achieved its War Memorial Opera House in 1932.

By the end of 1919 the committee trying to raise $2 million for the project had, said Drum, less than half what they needed. This troubled the live-wire Kendrick, who loved good music and was also as it happened influential in the war veterans' organization known as the American Legion. So, a few days later, when he saw Drum again, Kendrick suggested, "You know, I think if you can turn the whole project into a War Memorial I can get the veterans' support." The idea was to somehow combine, in a new complex of at least one large building, a music hall, art museum and facilities for veterans' organizations.

And that is what emerged a dozen years later, but in the form of two similarly faced buildings (on Van Ness Avenue between McAllister and Grove), and only after much bitter wrangling, especially because leaders of some of the veterans' organization were no more friendly to "culture" than latter-day congressmen out to kill the National Endowment for the Arts. Major Kendrick and his colleagues were patient and persistent, and they saw their goal achieved.

No. 13

2727 Pierce

Destination House

The big-chested, all-white Casebolt house sitting higher than a judge on its large lot, way upstage so to speak, and guarded by a pair of great palm trees, is the house in this book closest to fiction. Well, it's not exactly the Tara of Cow Hollow, but...

In 1866 Pierce Street at this location was a country road leading down to Washerwoman's Lagoon, and the presently numbered 2727 was the newly built manor house of the hollow, standing alone in sloping fields. It overlooked vegetable gardens and cow pastures, a barn, a windmill, and a rustic lake complete with waterfall and island. Idyllic!

The man who chose to build the romantic 2727 (one can't help waxing lyrical about this charmingly formidable structure) was one Henry Casebolt, a wealthy carriage builder, inventor, and transit operator. Originally from Virginia, he came to San Francisco in 1851, traveling 'round the Horn with his wife and eleven children—a man, you might say, who needed a small hotel for his brood. He quickly opened a blacksmith and horseshoeing shop which expanded without delay into a wagon and carriage factory: surely he was hitching his wagon to prosperity.

In 1865 the lively Mr. Casebolt was commissioned to build a horse-car line on Sutter Street from Sansome to Larkin as part of a project to develop the inaccessible and sparsely populated sandhills out Sutter—just where now you'd find numerous boutique hotels, the elegant Fleur de Lys restaurant, and the Plush Room cabaret. The contract for this pioneering transportation work was worth approximately $165,000.

But the operation entailed huge financial risks. Casebolt had to invest his own money, take control of the company, manage the property, etc., all the while thinking about thirteen mouths to feed. Within a year, thanks be, the horse-car line was operating successfully and destined to become the important Sutter Street line. A series of franchises granted over a period of twenty years extended the operation all the way out to the cemetery at Presidio Avenue in one direction and the ferries in the other, with connections up and down Polk Street. Casebolt's success brought him national fame and he received contracts to build cable lines in Chicago, Kansas City, Philadelphia, Cleveland and St. Louis.

Also among Casebolt's accomplishments were the swiveling "balloon car," which mimicked a turntable at the end of a line and saved the driver the effort of unhitching and hitching the horses; the "bobtail car," designed for ladies, with velvet carpets and sofas; and the lever-operated cable grip, which is substantially the same as that used on the cable cars of today.

After this transportation wizard's death in 1893, 2727 Pierce was sold to close friends of the Casebolt family, the Gruenhagens. Theodore Gruenhagen was owner and manager of the eponymous and long-established candy and ice cream store on Kearny Street near Market, approximately where Maskey's later flourished.

The Casebolt house is a masterpiece of the Italianate style. And a local one-of-a-kind. Far from standard architectural equipment in Cow Hollow or any other San Francisco neighborhood is the Corinthian column-supported central porch flanked on each side by a staircase, with capped wooden urns at the base and top of each, and spooled balustrades accompanying the visitor ascending from right or left. With balcony and double-hung windows above, it all seems the perfect study in three dimensions for a grand and tasteful wedding cake.

And still so redolent in its pristine handsomeness of another era that the presence of an SUV parked up the drive seems an anachronism awaiting prompt correction.

Postscript

Once again we have historian Bill Kostura to thank for new information: it has come to light that the architects for this City Landmark (#51) were William C. Hoagland and John J. Newsom. John Newsom was the eldest brother of Samuel B. and Joseph Cather Newsom of Carson House fame.

No. 14

2660 Scott

A Farr Mansion for
Teddy Roosevelt's Cousin

One rich and influential client of the architect Albert Farr said to a reporter: "There is no information I can give you on my house that will be of interest to anyone; it is just a plain house for plain people to live in and it answers the purpose beautifully."

Well, a less ascetic-sounding capitalist might have put it a little differently, but there's truth in that quote. Farr, who in his forty-four-year practice designed houses in a great variety of styles, from Shingle through Tudor and French Château Revival and on to Jack London's Wolf House at Glen Ellen, preferred to submerge his architectural identity behind a functional house that served unflamboyant clients' wishes and personalities.

"A plain house for plain people," that is pretty much what Albert Farr designed in 1901 for Harry and Catherine Babcock at the corner of Scott and Vallejo. Money was not a question with them: she was a cousin of President Theodore Roosevelt and he was a son of William F. Babcock, one of San Francisco's earliest rich men. But the money didn't have to show.

Founding president of Spring Valley Water Company, the ancestor of the San Francisco Water Department, Babcock Sr. developed reservoirs to stretch the city's water supplies over the dry months and occasional dry years. His basic business was import-export, while he dabbled in a variety of investments ranging from a PG&E predecessor to a diamond mine that turned out to be a hoax.

Harry Babcock was born in 1857 in his father's elegant Italianate house overlooking the tree-studded slopes of then-fashionable Rincon Hill, where the Bay Bridge rises now, with the new South Beach condos nearby. By the 1880s the family moved to still more palatial quarters in Marin County, reached by an early version of the still-running Sausalito ferry.

Harry spent his entire working life in papa's firm, Parrott and Company, which later became the Babcock Estate, controller of much downtown real estate. City directories, and even his obituaries in 1930, when the term was not tossed about so much as previously, called him a "capitalist." Perhaps a relaxed baptismal name like "Harry" doesn't quite match such a solid business type, or go with the formally elegant house at 2660 Scott. But then, of course, the house is "plain."

With details, of course, that subtly point up affluence—the best taste.

The handsome gateposts in rusticated brick and the Corinthian-columned entrance to 2660, curve-pedimented and half-hidden on the south side of the house, hint at the elegance within. Meanwhile most of the house looks the very model of masculine simplicity, smooth wooden walls relieved only by dignified moldings above the windows. The sensuous curves of the gateposts and door hood are repeated on the dormer windows that peek out above the cornice, which has dentil molding rather larger in scale than strictly necessary just to hide a gutter.

In short, Georgian Colonial with a vengeance and a slight manipulation of scale.

No. 15

2710 Scott

A Coxhead Breaks the Rules

*I*t's tiny. It's plain. It's asymmetrical. It's even altered. So what, says the architectural devil's advocate, is so special about 2710 Scott Street?

Well, it's one of the truly original creations that helped spark the so-called Bay Area Tradition in architecture, an innovative path concerned with closeness to nature, natural materials, the "essence" of California (a tad vague, that, but no matter) and also involving the selective borrowing of imagery from earlier architectural styles.

The great Ernest Coxhead is the author of this 1893 house, heaped with praise in the works of two noted architectural historians, John Beach in Sally Woodbridge's *Bay Area Houses* and Richard Longstreth in *On the Edge of the World.* Coxhead, in partnership with his relatively silent, or perhaps one should say design-wise-invisible brother Almeric (such a Wagnerian name), began with only a small lot on a downhill site. And even for 1893 the budget—$4,200—was very little. But the client, fifty-year-old Charles Murdock, a boutique printer and sage from Boston, was a very interesting and challenging man to build a house for. He valued new ideas, he didn't care about show and fashion.

So Ernest Coxhead went to town and created a house that broke a lot of rules. It turned out a kind of visual Surprise Symphony, almost as jolly as Haydn at his jokyest. And now for a tour...

The dwarf-friendly entrance with its "mantelpiece" crown admits asymmetrically to a long hall almost oppressively low of ceiling: paneled in natural redwood, it's a miniature gallery from some English manor house (Coxhead was, in fact, born in England and didn't hide a certain nostalgia for a homeland look). At the end of the tunnel, so to speak, is—flash!—a skylit staircase with many turns, accented by a graceful bannister also in redwood.

The staircase space is the spiral spine of what John Beach calls "a series of staggered-level platforms stacked around it," the first landing opening into the dining room, with windows overlooking the view to the east out back, and another giving onto the living room, which occupies the entire front of the house above the whimsically squashed entrance.

This interesting living room enjoys a carved fireplace in redwood and windows facing north and south. Up two more landings are two bedrooms to the rear, and still further up is the attic room with handsome dormer window which performs its solo turn on the Scott Street façade: a façade which, in its studied asymmetry, reminds Richard Longstreth of the artists' houses E. W. Godwin put up in London's Chelsea in the 1880s.

Longstreth calls the façade "a sea of shingles," a happy turn of phrase considering Coxhead's high-pitched roof with its upturned ends. A different kind of "high" can be found around the corner and down Green Street where the Coxheads' own house, at 2421, went up some months after Charles Murdock's. With a towerlike façade sans slope it weighs in, perhaps, with a touch of German Expressionism of the dark, fairy tale sort, intended or not.

Fascinating calling cards for a new San Franciscan, these Coxhead houses. Reverse a few years and we find the talented Englishman moving rather precipitously to Los Angeles, ten or more days' journey from home, to meet a building boom head on. The promise of work for an Episcopal diocese seems to have been Coxhead's motivation, for during the period 1887–89 this "boy wonder" from Eastbourne designed the great majority of southern California's new Episcopal churches, including Pasadena's All Saints, which was demolished in 1923, and the presently altered Church of the Angels, also in Pasadena.

Word of new American architectural activity had reached England through the pages of *British Architect* and other avenues. Setting up shop in L.A., the twenty-three-year-old Coxhead didn't

forget his proper ecclesiastical Gothic, but he warmed meanwhile to Richardsonian Romanesque and the Shingle Style. A new colleague named Willis Polk who'd worked in the East and Midwest helped show Coxhead the way. By the time both men came to San Francisco in 1889, their different office temperaments had made for a stormy working relationship, but they remained close friends and influenced each other's work.

And back to 2710 Scott...

The original owner was no less interesting than the architect and his design. Charles Murdock had moved to San Francisco as a child and in due course became widely respected in the city's intellectual community. He counted among his friends, and clients, Bret Harte, Robert Louis Stevenson, John Muir, and the painter William Keith. He ran a small business devoted to "fine" printing, but with characteristic modesty he never used that term, simply identifying his firm as "book and job printers." They did handbills, tickets, theater programs, lawbooks, catalogues, magazines: regular commercial printing.

But Murdock, with no formal technical training in printing, was known for the outstanding taste and simplicity of his graphic design. His work, in short, had style. He printed the first stories of children's author Kate Douglas Wiggin and the first issues of the *Sierra Club Bulletin*.

His most famous "product" was *The Lark,* San Francisco's precious and impertinent little literary magazine of the 1890s, the first issue including Gelett Burgess's unforgettable

I never saw a purple cow
I never hope to see one.
But I can tell you anyhow,
I'd rather see than be one.

The Lark also showed off the talents of writers and artists Bruce Porter, Ernest Peixotto, Florence Lundborg and Newton Tharp. Murdock cheerfully indulged their outrageous demands, which included rough Chinese bamboo paper that kept breaking the metal type.

Murdock was active in the Unitarian Church and frequently attended the services led by the inspirational Joseph Worcester. Scarcely confining himself to matters artistic, Murdock was a state assemblyman in the 1880s, served on San Francisco's Board of Education in the 1890s and was a member of the reform (!) Board of Supervisors 1907–16.

Renaissance man? Looks that way.

No. 16

2700 Vallejo

A Wedding Cake to Hollywood's Taste

2700 Vallejo is pretty enough to be a movie set—and it was. Debbie Reynolds and Tab Hunter made *The Pleasure of His Company* here, with a fabulous wedding scene as star of the show.

There were real weddings here too, for 2700 was the home of a prosperous second-generation San Francisco businessman, Clarence Enrico Musto, who with his wife, Marie, had five children. After Musto died in 1927 his widow moved to Atherton but daughter Kathleen inherited this startlingly white house, and with her surgeon husband (who frequently left for his operating room before daybreak) lived in it for many years.

It's not the sort of house easily surrendered...although one might add that in more modern times children of wealthy families sometimes became hippies and preferred not to live in relatively staid Pacific Heights.

As a piece of architectural wedding cake this cinema veteran almost rivals the celebrated Spreckels mansion at Washington and Octavia Streets, Old House No. 61 in this collection. It has similar balustrades and tall, round-headed windows with fan-shaped transoms, and in proper Beaux Arts fashion the doorway sports pairs of fine Corinthian columns. Perhaps 2700 is a bit too pretty, somewhat lacking in soul. But that impression might be fed by

the fact the Mustos' peroxide blockbuster follows our account of 2710 Scott, such an amusing little Coxheadian devil.

The architect in this case was Henry C. Smith, a seasoned confectioner at the drawing board who knew how to strut his Beaux Arts stuff. He received a lot of attention in the top San Francisco architecture magazine of his day; pictures of 2700 took up four pages of the January 1916 issue. Born in San Jose in 1873, Smith practiced in San Francisco for the first forty years of the twentieth century. Around 1905 he and his then-partner Louis S. Stone invented "stepping stone" apartments—but that's another story.

Clarence Musto, proud owner of 2700 Vallejo, was president of the company that supplied marble for the City Halls of San Francisco, Oakland and Los Angeles, San Francisco's Temple Emanu-El, St. Ignatius Church and Sts. Peter and Paul, the Monadnock, Home Telephone and PG&E Sutter Street buildings downtown, and lots of banks. Their stone, of many different colors, came from all over the world, especially Italy, the western United States, and Mexico.

And was the house's overwhelming *white* some metaphor for marble?

In Clarence's day the Musto company was known as "Joseph Musto Sons—Keenan Company," but it had started out in

1866 as the very small "Musto Brothers, marble importers." Founder Joseph was born near Chiavari, an Italian Riviera town about twenty miles from Genoa, and not, of course, far from Carrara of marble fame. Unhappy participant in a defeat of the Italian war of independence, the twenty-two-year-old Musto arrived in San Francisco as early as 1851. After various experiments in the gold country he settled into an industry where most of the workers were Italian.

The Mustos' young business duly became a marble sawmill, powered by steam and with a payroll that, as late as 1899, averaged little more than $100 a week. Clarence and his younger brother Guido (who later built a house in Presidio Heights on the southwest corner of Washington and Walnut) inherited the business in 1904 and were joined two years later by their brother-in-law Joseph Keenan. Under Clarence's presidency the company expanded mightily, taking advantage of the building boom after the 1906 earthquake and fire.

Joseph and Maria had seven children, the first five of whom were girls, not considered suited to running a business dealing in marble, dry goods or spaghetti. Joseph appears to have kept a tight rein on his household, perhaps like Elizabeth Barrett Browning's cinema father played by Charles Laughton with unctuous nose well up in the air. During his time only the oldest child married—to an artist named Eduardo Tojetti—and she soon returned to the family

roost. A musician, by the way, she founded the Public Library's music department.

Then the dam broke: within a year of Joseph's passing in 1904, sons Guido and Clarence and daughter Carlotta—the last-named already thirty-six—all married. Joseph's death also created the Joseph Musto Estate Company, which still controls a lot of downtown San Francisco real estate for the benefit of Joseph's heirs.

After their marriage Clarence and Marie Musto lived in a not particularly posh part of Nob Hill, building 2700 Vallejo only in 1915. It's as if they were waiting until they could afford the house of their—and a film location manager's—dreams.

Interlude

Riding up Divisadero Street in the family car as a child—perhaps we'd been walking down on Marina Green, watching steamers come in the Golden Gate—one couldn't help noticing a dynamic, wood-based house that looked distinctly "modern" amidst a cliff of traditional mansions more on the order of the Musto and Babcock residences just discussed. Still a striking wedge in Pacific Heights' architectural pie sixty years later—and not too rich, one might add—2660 Divisadero, just kitty-corner from the Musto place, is a lasting credit to its architect, John E. Dinwiddie, a name to be mentioned in the same breath as William Wurster and Gardner Dailey. Dating from 1938, it's an excellent example of International style, with Moderne overtones in the angled shadow-box picture window.

—*Arthur Bloomfield*

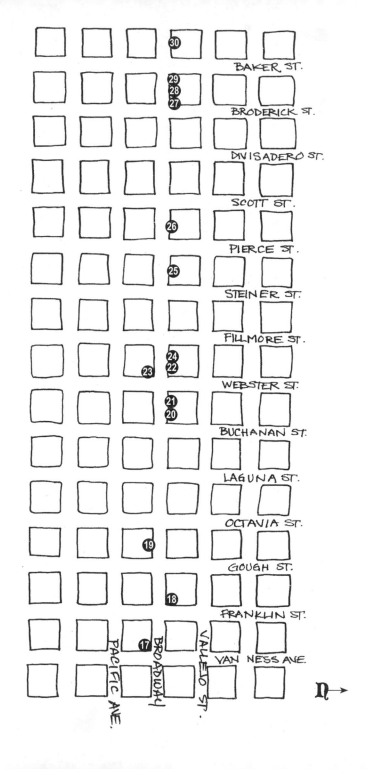

On
Broadway

east to west

No. 17

Van Ness and Broadway (SW corner)

The Church with a Brogue

t. Brigid's has stood at the corner of Van Ness and Broadway since the Civil War. Not this building, to be sure, but the parish has worshiped on this site—the church, alas, is presently closed—for more than one hundred and thirty years.

The city's eighth Catholic parish after the pioneering Mission Dolores, St. Brigid's has always been an Irish congregation. Most window donors had Irish names: McGinnis, Kiernan, O'Brien, Doherty, Sullivan, Ryan, O'Connor, Murphy, Casey. The 1902 fund-raising committee chaired by John Burnett included Messrs. Frank Kilduff, Charles McCarthy, Frank Sullivan and John C. Welch. And pastors for St. Brigid's first century were Aerden, O'Neill, Doogan, Callahan, Birmingham, Cottle, Cantwell, and O'Connor. Just to list these names is to hear a brogue roaring down or issuing sinuously from the pulpit à la Barry Fitzgerald.

And then, of course, St. Brigid herself was an Irishwoman, friend of St. Patrick, the man with a Day.

And so is the architecture Irish. The gray granite of St. Brigid's reminds of Ireland's coasts. Decorative borders have interlace designs from the edges of ancient Irish illuminated manuscripts, and the many sculpted or glass figures of angels, saints and mythical creatures evoke a people rooted—literally and literarily—in the Irish soil. The omnipresent tablets of the ten commandments recall the harshness of Irish life.

The windows themselves are Irish, designed and built by a stained glass firm in Dublin, the Harry Clarke studio. Notice wonderfully intense blues, reds and greens. And the colorful sanctuary carpets came from Donegal, handwoven by the Dun Emir Guild.

The overall architectural design is a composite: call it Richardsonian Romanesque Revival. "Romanesque" for the round arches and simple volumes from early medieval architecture; "Richardsonian" after the nineteenth-century designer of Boston's Trinity Church and thanks to the rough rock texture of the stone facing; "Revival" because of the detailing on the Broadway façade that copies the kind used on European Romanesque churches.

And note: the stones are San Francisco curbstones, recycled. That may explain the differences in color. Façade details—door surrounds, arcades and such—are made of terra-cotta, manufactured to the architect's designs by Gladding, McBean, of Lincoln, California, the only remaining West Coast manufacturer of architectural terra-cotta. The firm probably has the original molds and could remake pieces if needed.

The composite nature of the design comes from its prolonged construction history. What we see today is an end result in the wake of perhaps six different building periods, with nothing remaining from the little wooden original of 1864.

The present structure's foundations were laid in 1896 and the basement opened for services in 1897. No architect is listed in the announcement of construction—probably Father John Cottle, who arranged for the recycling of the granite curbstones, chose the size and shape of the building. Perhaps an unnamed parishioner with building or engineering experience contributed significantly to the project.

The next phase of work, in 1902–04, resulted in a steel-reinforced superstructure, but with a Van Ness Avenue façade different from today's: it was set well back from two short corner towers. Shea and Shea were the architects—well, you wouldn't have expected Jorgensen and Slimowitz.

Now the style was set: the rough stones, the rounded arches, the wheel window on the east elevation with stepped arcade above. Next, in 1930, the Van Ness end was largely reworked to increase seating capacity. Architect this time out was Henry A. Minton, who did a great deal of work for the Catholic Church, including the Chinese-roofed tower one sees driving north on Highway 280 from San Jose, part of a school for missionaries off to Asia. Minton revised the great wheel window and put previously used curbstones at the edges of the current tower's newly added height, filling inner surfaces with smoother, newer stones.

Another major remodeling took place during Father Cantwell's pastorate, in 1947. It included an entirely new set of brilliant stained glass, two sacristies alongside the curved apse, and new interior decorating. Probably from somewhat later are the diagonally striped cream and tan marble columns and the lincrusta wainscoting.

Then, in 1965, the tower's roof and top story were added, St. Brigid's reaching a little further than ever into the sky.

No. 18

1700 Broadway

Mayan Tragic

Curves, spirals, zigzags, plates, buttons hanging about the entrance—well, all that stuff is typical of numerous one-step-below-luxury apartment houses along Broadway, Vallejo Street, Pacific Avenue. It's the language of the 1920s. But you will not find peering down from every Spanish Colonial Revival doorway in Pacific Heights the tragic Mayan face with the exotic shell headdress that graces, if that's the word, the entrance of 1700 Broadway.

What, one might wonder, is the message?

Like the exterior, the vestibule and lobby of the thirty-six-unit 1700 are pseudo-Spanish, part of the near-kitschy wave of more or less Andalusian design washing over the neighborhood after the last word had been said in Victoriana and Queen Anne-ism. There are polychrome tile accents, wrought iron fixtures, double-slope painted ceilings, and a facing wall like that behind some Spanish altar. You're almost in church.

The architect of 1700 Broadway was just striking out on his own—the time is 1928—when he landed the contract for this building. He was a recent graduate of UC Berkeley's architecture school, his name was Douglas Dacre Stone and in time he'd be the first name on a well-known shingle

trumpeting the firm Stone, Marraccini and Patterson. In the late 1950s he was part of the team of architects for the Mies van der Rohe–inspired but not very inspiring Federal Office Building that infuriates so many of us as we try not to see it hovering gracelessly over the north end of Civic Center. But we stray from the topic...

In 1928 Stone did another "Spanish" apartment building, at Pacific and Laguna. The following year he was into Zigzag Moderne for the Mary Bowles Building at 1721 Broadway in Oakland. Then in 1939 he remodeled 216 Pine in San Francisco's Financial District, removing its Beaux Arts exterior and lowering the lobby to give it that stripped-to-essentials International style look. And there were lots of hospital jobs as his career progressed, a thing of workmanlike stuff with flashes of briliance here and there.

Rather as the ever "hip" composer Stravinsky switched from Toonerville neoclassic to grumpy serial music, Stone ran through all the approved styles of his time, even seeming to embrace Brutalism in his later years. After his retirement his firm turned out the high-rise Sequoias retirement complex on Geary Boulevard in that style—and that's where many Pacific Heightsers go to die after they give up their big houses.

Stone won his commission for 1700 Broadway from Marian Realty, which was the real estate arm of the Rousseau Brothers, an architectural clan that put up millions of unremarkable but pretty residential square feet in mid-twentieth -century San Francisco. Not always wanting to do the designing of what you could call their "comfort architecture" themselves, they tended to hire inexpensive young architects, as recent UC graduate Stone must have been in 1928.

Now, Stone may not emerge as the most inspiring of the architects described in these pages, but he did come up with that conversation piece of a Mayan.

No. 19

1815 Broadway

Atlas and Associate Were Here

The Indian Atlas figures holding up, uh, nothing in particular by the doorway of 1815 Broadway aroused my curiosity. Was this slightly Asian-looking building with the wide bank of windows perhaps a school? A conference center? Some other sort of institution serving chicken and peas for lunch? Certainly there's not another residential building in Pacific Heights like it. Well, despite appearances to the contrary, it's presently a ten-unit apartment house. But what was it originally?

Depends on your definition of original!

Original in this case could refer to a pre-1920 configuration involving two separate houses, or to the somewhat radical surgery which produced what we see today. City records show that the "alterations" of 1920 clearly shaped the 1815 Broadway of the twenty-first century. A go-ahead was given for the contractor to "join houses as shown," as well as change internal partitions, add bathrooms, etc. So what we see today is a sort of "new original," a self-contained building born of previously separate elements. Call it the Case of the Siamese Twins in Reverse.

Further research reveals that the six-window section sitting forward of the rest was formed out of the "original" house on the right plus a gap-bridging section in the middle. The house on the right had in its first form a lot of open space to the rear, and that space remains. The pre-1920 house on the left, and its altered self, were and are set modestly back in relation to the right-side element, like Jeeves to Wooster.

And a very interesting point: you can still see a Victorian bracketed cornice at the roofline, giving a taste of what the earlier "left" and "right" elements probably looked like before a sort of Shanghai fenestration was introduced.

One of the pre-1920 parcels was owned by the Bateman family, building contractors, and the other by Edwin and Harriet Shoemaker—he was with the North Pacific Coast Railroad that ran merrily from Sausalito to the Russian River resorts in west Sonoma County via Tomales Bay. Both families were absentee landlords. It was around 1917 that the two lots were assembled by a real estate broker who probably envisioned demolition and a tall apartment building. But the new owner, as of 1920, had a less costly idea.

Enter here Miss Louise Mahoney, a local artist specializing in pastels, who chose as the architect of her remodel none less than the elegant Houghton Sawyer, author of our Georgian Minimal at 2100 Vallejo (Old House No. 9). Known for gracious ornamentation derived from Classical architecture, Sawyer in this case explored Hispanic influences (but in a vastly different style from Douglas Stone's, down the street at 1700) with simply stuccoed walls, arches, a balconied rear patio, casement windows—and the Indians.

Louise Mahoney painted likenesses of private gardens and images from the Panama-Pacific International Exposition of 1915. Her work was exhibited several times by the San Francisco Art Association and elicited, to judge by one example, kind but not glowing reviews, and she's recognized in Edan Milton Hughes' biographical tome, *Artists in California, 1786–1940.*

Her vision for the new 1815 Broadway, which she christened "The Studio Building," was a group of studios for artists—live-work units, to use contemporary parlance. The windows all across the front were not strictly architecture for architecture's sake, they were designed to let in plenty of the north light artists prefer.

Miss Mahoney, who sounds an appealing and formidable character (should we be thinking Margaret Rutherford, or perhaps Judi Dench?) died in 1925, aged only fifty-six—she didn't have much time as mother hen of her studio-rich Shangri-La. She willed the building to her younger sister Emma. The two of them had lived together, like so many Pacific Heights spinsters of the day, and run an Asian Art store on Grant Avenue. I suppose they lunched on chocolate cake at Townsend's, shopped at the City of Paris, attended the Friday afternoon concerts of the Symphony under "Papa" Alfred Hertz at the Curran Theater, and belonged to or were luncheon guests at or maybe even swam at the Western Women's Club.

Now all these spinsters...Are we allowed to ask: were they unlucky in love, too choosy, victims of repressive fathers or chaperones out of E. M. Forster, asexual, lesbian, just plain scared off by starchy family values? Obviously there were scant opportunities for romantic experiment seventy or eighty years ago in Pacific Heights, and more stiff upper lips, amorous or not, to maintain.

In any event, Emma died about 1933 and left the property to one Jerome Landfield, ordering him to give lifelong care to her wire-haired terrier, Patsy. Landfield had quite a history of his own: he'd taught Slavonic languages at UC Berkeley, was a sometime painter and had married a Russian princess, Louba Lobanoff-Rostovsky. His views on her troublesome country were solicited by San Francisco newspapers not well versed, apparently, in pre–Iron Curtain Moscow-watching.

Alas, with Louise Mahoney's passing the artist tenants at 1815 Broadway vanished and were replaced by ordinary folk like secretaries, middle management types and so on. But the romance of Houghton Sawyer's stalwart Indians remained.

No. 20

2104 Broadway

The House That Sugar Built

The daughter of one of Frank Van Trees' clients remembered her mother complaining of the architect's drunkenness and her having to fall back on decorators for much of the design work on her new house. Well, tipsy or not, Van Trees was responsible for a dozen or so of the many restrainedly elegant, vaguely Classical Revival houses that characterize Pacific Heights and have provided very comfortable living for the people who settled therein.

Yes, he was a Society architect—his clients included A. P. Giannini of Bank of America fame and Charles Crocker of the Nob Hill Crockers—but a good one. Van Trees' 2104 Broadway is the house that sugar built. Beet sugar.

Its first owner, Robert Oxnard, was vice president of the American Beet Sugar Company and secretary of Western Sugar Refining, Spreckels Sugar and the Pajaro Valley Consolidated Railroad, which served the Spreckels plant near Salinas. And yes, there is a connection to the southern California city of Oxnard: it was named for the younger brother and business associate of the sugar executive who called this Broadway house Home from 1899 until his death in 1930.

Conservatively Classical, with a superstructure reminiscent of an old Cunard Line leviathan, 2104 doesn't yoo-hoo for attention. Call it a box, but what a box! The dignified "masculine" façade is simply stuccoed, three evenly spaced windows per floor decorated with scroll and shell motifs on beds of foliage. They're like great crests, these design salads in military formation. The entrance is a study in graceful formality, composed with Ionic columns, marble steps and fine woodcarving and ironwork. A whiskey lover, perhaps, this Van Trees, but he certainly had a clear eye for felicitous detail.

Too bad 2104 is wedged into a rather narrow city space not permitting it to state the full case for its estimable east elevation. Matter of fact, the Oxnard house when viewed from Broadway and Buchanan is upstaged by its shorter neighbor 2100, a corner palazzetto with a lovely loggia dominating its Buchanan Street side. A touch of Venice here: this Bliss and Faville charmer from 1917 suggests a house for Henry James, after he received a really good advance for a new novel.

Idle thought: would Robert Oxnard have been at home in the more delicate, less emblazoned house on the corner? I doubt it, he was all business, like Mr. Wilcox in *Howard's End*.

At all events, Oxnard was born in Louisiana about 1854 into a family involved in the sugar industry—doubtless propelled by slave labor—and at eighteen he began working as a correspondence clerk with a sugar exporter in Havana. Sounds as if he didn't mind seeing a bit of the world. By 1876 he was refining sugar up in Brooklyn and he stayed with that enterprise for a dozen years, building it up considerably. It was only in the late 1880s that he came to California. He came on the offensive and bought a refinery in San Francisco, to bang heads with the established Spreckels sugar interests.

But two sugar companies did not make a "sweet," if you will, and Oxnard and Spreckels soon formed an alliance.

Meanwhile Robert Oxnard and his younger brother Henry acquired immense beet sugar acreage in San Joaquin Valley. Then, in 1898, like some Biblical character waving a wand in a large tapestry, Henry created the town of Oxnard to accommodate workers at the $2 million sugar refinery he was building there. The next year saw a possibly tiring Robert Oxnard holing

up in his new Van Trees house, where he would live quietly for three decades.

But not too quietly. While gradually reducing his involvement with Spreckels he did retain interests in American Beet Sugar and Savannah Sugar Refinery of Georgia, and he continued to own sugar-producing land in California, Louisiana and the Cuba of his youth. He died without issue but left a $1 million estate, and a wife, Nellie, who stayed on at 2104 for several years.

Census facts from 1910: there were four, count 'em, four live-in servants at 2104 Broadway to minister to Robert and Nellie: an English maid, Miss Cassidy, and a Swedish maid, Miss Peterson, a Chinese cook, Jew Suey Fong—yes, it was often the Chinese retainer who took charge of the kitchen—and another Chinese, Jew Pook, who was master of the laundry. From a mountain of sugar came their presumably not very generous wages.

No. 21

2120 Broadway

Palazzo Fakery

ornelia McKinne Stanwood, headmistress of the Sarah Dix Hamlin girls' school from 1927 to 1946—Hamlin's was and still is housed in the palazzo at 2120 Broadway—used a ruler at in-house dances to measure the distance (the exact number of inches has not come down to us) between adolescent partners: nervous, pimply boys, one supposes, and young ladies in their frilly ballroom dresses being dragged desultorily through the mysteries of foxtrot, waltz, and, if we're talking the wartime years of the Good Neighbor Policy, the rumba as well.

All very pre-Britney Spears! Nowadays middle-aged folk walking along Broadway are confronted with young ladies from school exhibiting enough flesh—and in uniforms, yet!—to send Mrs. Stanwood into a veritable tizzy. She was, though, according to all reports, a wonderful woman.

All the preceding is just part of our story…

The Renaissance palazzo at 2120 Broadway is really a fake, having been built of mere wood. Fake or imitation architecture has, however, a long and honorable history. The word "renaissance" means rebirth, and the capital R variety refers to Italians of several centuries ago discovering and imitating the civilization of ancient Rome. Palazzo architects like Alberti and Brunelleschi imitated and adapted for their contemporaries the buildings of the old Romans who had

imitated and adapted for their purposes the architecture of the ancient Greeks. Then in eighteenth-century England talented architects like William Kent and James Gibbs imitated and adapted the Renaissance buildings that had imitated, well, you know…and we call that Georgian.

After that, Georgian homages to the past were imitated in colonial America and the whole visual ideology had yet another creative rerun in the decades bracketing 1900.

2120 Broadway, built in 1900–01 by Julius Krafft, architect of the lamented St. Paulus Lutheran Church at Gough and Eddy Streets (it burned a few years ago), borrows Ionic columns from the Greeks, serene proportions from Palladio, pediments and balustrades from the Georgians, a four-slope roof from the Colonials, and so on. It even borrows the idea of a magnificent bronze fence from an earlier San Francisco "house" put up for the same family, the Floods, at 1000 California Street on Nob Hill—that one is now the fortress of the Pacific Union Club.

Yes, 2120 Broadway is just another Flood mansion, part of an architectural deluge if you will.

The clan's founder was James Clair Flood, an ex-saloon keeper who struck it big with the Comstock Lode. His starter house, in 1878, was an oversized wedding cake called Linden Towers in exurban Menlo Park, east but not too far east of the train tracks. Then in 1885 he had 1000 California built by Augustus Laver. His neighbors were named Stanford, Hopkins and Huntington, as in hostelries to be.

Next, J. C.'s children James Leary Flood (1867–1926) and Cora Jane, known as "Miss Jennie" (1862–1929), cooperated on the house at 2120 Broadway: she owned the land and he, in what one assumes was some courtly division of labor appropriate to the day, signed the building contracts. James Leary, while really living at leafy Linden Towers, used 2120 as his town pad for ten years, his sister residing in another part of this uptown Ritz. Then he built the fourth Flood mansion, up Broadway at 2222 (more on Old House No. 24 later), while Cora remained at 2120.

Now we must back up to tell you that Papa Flood was one of the four Irishmen, Flood, Fair, Mackay and O'Brien, who manipulated the stock of Nevada silver mines into an unbelievable pile. *Rheingold* stuff. Flood and O'Brien then founded the Nevada Bank, later a major component of Wells Fargo, where some of you doubtless bank today.

The elder Flood died in 1889 but son James Leary let no mold gather on the family's business interests. Conspicuous was the arrival of the Flood Building, which continues to hover imperially over tourists and locals alike as they wait for the cable cars at the Powell and Market Streets turnaround.

Miss Jennie sold or donated 2120 to the University of California Regents in 1924 and moved to the Fairmont Hotel, across the street from 1000 California, then returned to Broadway to live in her late brother's digs at 2222. In 1928 her old house was bought by Mrs. Stanwood of measuring fame, who promptly ushered the Hamlin school, named for its first headmistress, into the generous new quarters. At this time Hamlin's was a boarding and day school and Mrs. Stanwood had her suite upstairs. A graduate of Berkeley and the progressive Mills College, she had been a suffragette and is remembered as a dynamic, compassionate person who served on the State Board of Charities.

The Hamlin School (the dated moniker "Sarah Dix Hamlin" has been dropped) continues to respect the mansion's beauty, keeping intact ornate interior details right down to the ancient spiky shower heads. The benign lions standing (sitting?) guard over the entrance are in fine shape. Only one thing is missing: Arthur remembers in earlier days a life-sized toy cable car that sat on the school grounds, ready for budding transportation aficionados to enjoy.

And a little more about 2120 Broadway's architect, Julius Krafft. He grew up and studied for his calling in Stuttgart, Germany, came to San Francisco in 1874 and worked for the prolific vernacular architect Thomas J. Welsh for a dozen years, then set up his own office. His practice extended from 1888 into the 1940s, alone at first—with Bernard Maybeck a draftsman in 1894—then with his sons from 1906.

No. 22

2200 Broadway

Fifth Avenue Hunk

*I*f you want to make a fortune, hire swanky New York architects, and build a rosy-cheeked mansion confident as a *Titanic* on a hill overlooking San Francisco Bay, it helps to start with a rich father.

Capitalist/clubman Joseph Donohoe Grant, longtime squire of 2200 Broadway, born in San Francisco in 1858, was the only son of the Scotsman Adam Grant, partner in Murphy, Grant and Co., San Francisco's premier dry goods store for half a century. When the young J. D. was seventeen years old City Hall assessed the personal property of his father's company at $325,000, the thirteenth largest assessment in town. So much for a silver spoon in the mouth.

Adam's store, built in 1867, was four stories of iron-clad brick at 100 Sansome Street, heart of the Financial District. It burned in the conflagration of '06, but J. D. replaced it in short order with the Adam Grant Building which is still part of the downtown scene.

Nine years prior to the unhappy events of 1906—a major earthquake attended by a terrible fire contained just six posh blocks to the east of 2200 Broadway—J. D. was newly acquiring his handsome neoclassic mansion at this address, a gorgeous pile of brick and stone "dignified and stately"

as a Gilbertian peer but demonstrating a certain verve, an aristocratic touch of cool theatricality. 'Twas just a pied-à-terre: J. D. and his beautiful young wife, Emily Macleay—she, by the way, was fifteen years the capitalist's junior—spent much of their time at their exurban Burlingame house or on one or another of their western ranches. But the house on Broadway was constructed *con amore*, no doubt about that.

The actual building of 2200 was the work of Mahoney Brothers, contractors for the characterful Hearst Memorial Mining Building on the UC Berkeley campus, the perfect-postured St. Francis Hotel, dowager of San Francisco's Union Square, and the handsome Flood and Phelan buildings which continue to lord it genially enough over less urbane structures along the middle blocks (well, not quite the blighted mid-Market blocks) of Market Street. The Mahoneys knew how to "build strong," a challenge indeed on the new mansion's cliffside site next to an alpine Webster Street heading scarily down from Broadway to Vallejo Street far below.

The architects, scarcely staples in San Francisco, were New Yorkers H. Hobart Weekes (c. 1867–1950) and Philip Hiss (1857–1940), the latter probably a forebear of the controversial witch-hunt figure of the 1950s Alger Hiss. This pair designed a number of Long Island mansions for the rich and famous, a building at Yale University, and the old Gotham Hotel in Manhattan.

The urbane Weekes, bearing the same name as a recent-day *New Yorker* editor (and, by the way, Alger Hiss' son Tony "discovered" San Francisco's hole-in-the-wall Hunan Restaurant in a celebrated article in that magazine) is credited with the important Belnord Apartments at Broadway and West 86th in Manhattan, a slightly racy Renaissance affair of thirteen stories, much medallioned and keystoned and noted for the unusual way in which its windows vary in size, enframement and embellishment.

What Weekes and Hiss came up with for J. D. and Emily Grant was a balustrade-wrapped creation of marble floors and paneled walls, heaven-reaching ceilings, four very grand rooms on the main floor—and the upper levels not skimped either. Well, all it takes is money, servants, and taste.

The pillared front entrance looks over a near crescent of a driveway that surely beckoned the latest brougham of Cadillac or Pierce-Arrow. It's framed by a pair of sculpted urns, the more easterly of the two peopled by a strange flock of sorrow-weighted types shouldering cares different from those of the typical extremely wealthy householder, be he J. D. Grant or Bill Gates.

J. D. went to local public schools. Today he doubtless would have attended Stuart Hall in a mansion just down the block, part of the complex containing the Sacred Heart private schools for young gentlemen dressed in white shirt, khaki pants and good cheer, and young ladies identifiable by their plaid skirts, little red sweaters and fog-chilled knees. Then after graduation from UC Berkeley it was the Grand Tour for him and a bit of ranch management before settling down to the drudgery, one supposes, of the dry goods business.

Oh dear, one yearns for more Pacific Heights houses containing avant-garde composers, seething philosophers, feisty painters, writers of good books, stars of stage and screen and concert...well, later on there'd be Francis Ford Coppola, Robin Williams, novelist Alice Adams, architect Julia Morgan, film critic David Thomson, Bishop Karl Morgan Block, columnist Herb Caen, publisher Willie Hearst, painters Nell Sinton and Jane Berlandina, sculptor Fletcher Benton, actor William Patterson, violinist Naoum Blinder, violist Germain Prévost, bookbinder Florence Walter, museum director Walter Heil, author Richard Rodriguez, marketing whiz Walter Landor, architects Albert Lansburgh and John Field, cookbook writer Joyce Goldstein, novelist Robert Mailer Anderson, opera directors Gaetano Merola and Kurt Herbert

Adler, conductors Michael Tilson Thomas, Josef Krips and Edo de Waart, tenor James Schwabacher, logician Francis Rigney, "private eye" Hal Lipset, mystery writer Erle Stanley Gardner, and should we mention Danielle Steel? This doesn't count writers Frank Norris, Gertrude Atherton and John Steinbeck—three locations for him, one above Pacific Heights Cleaners on Fillmore!

But dry goods was not the line J. D. would stay in. By 1912 he'd converted Murphy, Grant and Co. into a real estate holding company. Meanwhile he presided over Columbia Steel, was first vice president of General Petroleum and became a director of countless corporations. And he was of course what the society pages of the day termed a "sportsman," and belonged, naturally, to the exclusive Bohemian Club—from the age of twenty-four!

Emily for her part was director of the Women's Board of the 1915 Panama-Pacific International Exposition, which gave us the Palace of Fine Arts, well in sight of upper Broadway looking toward the Golden Gate.

In his spare time J. D. was active in nurturing the Academy of Sciences in Golden Gate Park and a lifetime trustee of his friend Leland Stanford's university down the Peninsula. In 1920 he helped found the Save the Redwoods League and enthusiastically chaired it for twenty-one years, earning the naming of a J. D. Grant Redwoods Grove in Del Norte State Park. Big business, in short, seems not to have inhibited Grant's environmental concern and one suspects he was what would now be called a *moderate* Republican.

Unfortunately the Grants lost part of their panoramic view from Broadway and Webster when the last of the Flood mansions, a door to the west, was built on a lot extending further than the Grants' toward subterranean Vallejo Street. But the two families remained friends and the Grants stayed on—while they were in town—until J. D.'s death in 1942 and Emily's six years later.

Then the Sacred Heart Schools bought the property, converting palazzo to academy while scrupulously maintaining its regal exterior for passersby to enjoy—a walking tour troops past at about 12:30 p.m. daily.

No. 23

2201 Broadway

Six Styles in Search of a House

*I*f this house were anywhere but across from the Grant and (final!) Flood mansions its unconventional beauty would have attracted a lot of attention. That beauty stems in large part from a complex, and elegant, stylistic mix. Ask half a dozen architecturally knowledgeable people to find the proper textbook pigeonhole for 2201 and you'd probably get half a dozen answers, all of them correct.

One would say Beaux Arts for its symmetry and grandeur, another Mission Revival for the tile roof and flat walls with bricks laid in basket-weave patterns. (Incidentally, if you figure in the Grant mansion as well as the Italian Consulate at the corner of Broadway and Webster, and the Bourn mansion a few steps to the south, you have a mini-city of patrician brick in this little bit of Pacific Heights.) Yet another classifier would opt for Classical Revival because of the dentil moldings and arched doorway, also the symmetry. And Georgian, of course, is the name for the projecting center pavilion, the balcony, and the contrast of red brick and white. Meanwhile the block-and-ball corners might recall the "chains-for-drainpipe" effect (it's a little like threading a belt through pants loops) in Japanese architecture. And why not say

Venetian for the loggia and zero setback? Secessionist could be the word to catch the abstract blocky forms and limited geometric ornament.

But enough! To me 2201 Broadway is simply an original creation that uses familiar elements in a highly individual way that doesn't add up to a "style" for architectural historians to place in a neat box.

I especially like the way the center pavilion's extra height balances the length of the wings; and the smooth brick of the house with its intermittent diagonal to-and-fro design makes for a delightfully playful, almost impish effect. For his mastery of proportions and textures the architect of this highly satisfying and not unsensuous house, a veritable work of art, goes well to the head of the class.

The creator of 2201, which dates from 1914, was G. Albert Lansburgh, a feisty little man with impeccable credentials who was especially known as a theater architect. He it is who's responsible for the interior of San Francisco's War Memorial Opera House, finished in '32, with its star-shaped chandelier suspended from an exquisite turquoise "sky"—although a plaque inside the Opera House has led the uninformed to believe the building was solely the work of Arthur Brown Jr., a slight that

Lansburgh felt until his dying day, in 1969, at the age of ninety-three.

Speaking of opera, that balcony fronting 2201's central pavilion can't help suggesting some upwardly aimed serenade sung by an ardent tenor eyeing his Juliet or Rosina perched an inconvenient distance above the stage. Bring a ladder, the lady wants to say.

Panama-born in 1876, then orphaned, Lansburgh was educated in San Francisco schools, worked a summer in Bernard Maybeck's office while attending UC Berkeley, did a term as well in the office of Julius Krafft, author of the Hamlin School mansion, then set off to Paris with Maybeck's blessing to attend the prestigious Ecole des Beaux-Arts on the Left Bank. Ten San Francisco architects, Lansburgh included, earned the coveted "diplome" of that institution. The Beaux-Arts was the western world's best training ground at the turn of the century, and Beaux-Arts thinking shaped post-earthquake San Francisco rebuilding after 1906.

Lansburgh's concentration on theater work had to do with his enjoying the patronage of Morris Meyerfield Jr., president of the Orpheum Theater and Realty Company. Albert's attorney brother Simon was counsel for the firm and succeeded Meyerfield in 1920. Albert designed Orpheums in Los Angeles, Salt Lake City, Kansas City and St. Louis, but not the theater currently named Orpheum in San Francisco. On San Francisco's Market Street he was responsible, in 1921–22, for the Golden Gate and Warfield, which evolved through the years from cinema palaces (in the case of the Golden Gate, cinema and vaudeville) to legitimate theater and pop music venues respectively.

Back in the 1920s the neighboring Golden Gate and Warfield construction teams actually raced each other—sounds like something out of a movie—to see who would open first. The Great Theater Race!

Lansburgh also repaired the twin-onion-domed Temple Emanu-El downtown after the 1906 fire (Rabbi Vorsanger had been Albert's childhood guardian), and in the mid-twenties he was a consultant, along with Maybeck, for the new Emanu-El being built at Arguello and Lake at the west end of Presidio Heights. He also designed a synagogue in Oakland, and credit him too with the charming retail buildings in downtown San Francisco at the southwest corners of Sutter and Grant (a real jewel box, this one) and Geary and Powell, kitty-corner from Union Square.

Another consulting job was on Los Angeles' Shrine Auditorium, a giant but acoustically friendly venue to which the San Francisco Opera used to tour. In New York, if the philanthropist Otto Kahn had had his way, before dying in 1934, there would have been a new Metropolitan Opera a bit west of Carnegie Hall, its backstage equipment much more up-to-date than that of the Old Met, and one of its architects none other than G. Albert Lansburgh.

At 2201 Broadway in 1914 San Francisco, Lansburgh's clients were Florence and Samuel Lowenstein, whom he might have met at Emanu-El. Lowenstein was a partner in Pauson and Company, a long-gone men's store at Sutter and Kearny. The couple had been living nearby, but when they built this house they must have wanted greater formality as well as a Broadway address. The Lowensteins lived in 2201 for about fifteen years, then moved to the Palace Hotel. In those days there were a number of "carriage trade" residential clients at the Fairmont, St. Francis, Clift and other posh downtown hostelries—well, there was no Sequoias retirement facility to go to.

The next owner of 2201 was John M. Grant, not apparently related to the J. D. Grant of 2200 Broadway across the street. This Grant was a Scotsman and a banker who came to Chicago as a young man in 1895, specializing in foreign exchange. Then he worked for American Express establishing branches all over Europe: would that include the famous one near the Opéra in Paris where so many Americans have picked up their mail while abroad?

This south-side-of-Broadway Grant moved to San Francisco's Peninsula in 1922 and joined Bank of America, then Bank of Italy, in '26. Grant became one of the fabled, and aging, A. P. Giannini's chief lieutenants, achieving high rank as president of the related Transamerica Corporation. To keep the bank afloat in the Depression, A. P. ordered great economies and Grant became his hatchet man, reducing Transamerica's costs more than nine million pre-inflation dollars.

Lansburgh, meanwhile, built himself a lovely, Pebble Beachy Spanish-type mansion at 3052 Pacific Avenue, but ill health, and, I think, money problems caused him and his wife to retreat to suburban San Mateo in 1937 after only thirteen years' residence in what must have been his dream house. In 1960 Arthur, who was writing a history of the San Francisco Opera, went down to San Mateo and found a genial but somewhat bitter eighty-four-year-old Lansburgh puttering about his blueprints in a cramped Mediterranean-style apartment just a few steps from busy El Camino Real. He can still see the tiny white-haired man proudly shuffling through interim and final plans for *his* Opera House interior.

No. 24

2222 Broadway

Portal to Learning

A few pages back we left James Leary Flood packing his bags, trunks, whatever—well, actually it must have been his valet and other members of an in-house staff of a dozen or so who were doing the heavy lifting—and leaving 2120 Broadway, by chauffered auto one presumes, to take up residence one block west from his old San Francisco pied-à-terre in a new and even more impressive city venue, the "final" Flood mansion, at 2222 Broadway.

Why bother? Well, if 2120, the present Hamlin School site, must have been for Flood a virtual 10 on an Impressiveness scale of 10, the new house rated perhaps 13 or 14 out of the same two-digit figure. Which reminds me, a shade irreverently, of the waiter in Chinatown back in the 1930s who, when Arthur's father asked him what was the difference between the 50-cent and 75-cent dinner, replied with a simplicity nothing less than beautiful: "75-cent more—and better!" As is 2222 Broadway indeed.

When the new owner of 2222 strode into his "more and better" mansion one (presumably) fine day in 1914—with the trenches of western Europe about to fill up, the *Titanic* well settled in its Atlantic bed, the *Lusitania* approaching its final voyage, and the Panama-Pacific Exposition a-building down by San Francisco Bay—he entered what might be called a Roman palace of the High Renaissance, complete with interior court. That, in fact, was the architects' intent.

And why not, when your client's father was already making $500,000 a week in 1872? With money on that scale, why not purchase perfection of proportions and an uncluttered graciousness hardly equalled anywhere else in the city? City Hall, under construction at the time, suffers from ornamental overload in comparison.

Now, 2222 Broadway, which presently serves as part of the Sacred Heart school complex, is a subtle composition, ostentatious only in its tremendous scale, bucking as it were for entry into some Civic Center of a dreamer's architectural imagination. The roof overhang creates exactly the right shadow, with a perfect gentle slope above. The string course that continues third-floor window sills perfectly divides the building into unequal upper and lower sections. And the rhythm of window openings combines a textbook vertical lineup with just enough variety to spell interest.

The limitation of ornament to just one magnificent burst correctly focuses attention on the visitor's necessity, the front door—which in Flood's time, of course, would have been opened by a butler straight out of old Hollywood's Park Avenue, a posh whiskey ad or a *New Yorker* cartoon. This entrance defines High Renaissance: that's where in history Flood's architects found the notion of multiple designs on flat relief panels. It's also the source of curly-leaved Corinthian capitals on columns supporting a classically correct entablature.

Credit, too, the lofty Renaissance for the spiral fluting on these columns, and notice that one spirals clockwise, the other counterclockwise, to invite you inside—if, that is, you have an invitation.

Then there's the delicate bronzework of the door itself. Go look and marvel.

For all this felicity thank the architects, and Flood's good taste in engaging them: Walter D. Bliss (1873–1946) and William B. Faville (1866–1946), native Californians who worked for several years in the New York office of McKim, Mead and White, America's premier source of first-class Classical Revival buildings. Bliss and Faville came home in 1897 and formed an incredibly productive partnership, without the fruits of which San Francisco would be seriously incomplete. Bliss and Faville buildings include the St. Francis Hotel on Union Square, the original State Building on McAllister Street at Civic Center, the Matson and Southern Pacific buildings on lower Market Street, the Bank of California at Sansome and California, several clubs, and a flock of patrician mansions

including the gorgeous 2800 Scott (the *Sudden Fear* house) and the jewel box 2100 Broadway.

James Leary Flood died in 1926, having spent only a dozen years in part-time residence at 2222. By 1939 his widow, Maud, had moved to that faithful retirement home known as the Fairmont Hotel. Fearing her already hard-to-maintain mansion would be torn down and replaced by an apartment building, she gave it to the Society of the Sacred Heart, which now operates schools in its elegant rooms as well as in the J. D. Grant mansion and the Lansburgh-designed beauty in the same 2200 block of Broadway, and maintains all these architectural treasures well.

Interlude

Continue west on Broadway, cross Fillmore (where the view of the Italianate hill town Sausalito across the bay is especially good) and soon on the left you find 2307 Broadway, onetime home of moviemaker Francis Ford Coppola. It's an elegant and creative blend of Queen Anne and Classical Revival graced by a fan-windowed portal, an incipient octagon of a bay composed with five oblong windows, and, in a not-always-noticed comic climax, chess pieces to crown turret and gable. The date of this house, which originally belonged to George Volkmann of the Schilling spice clan, is 1892, and the architects the scantly known Kenitzer and Kollofrath. Julia Morgan of Hearst Castle and other fame made some interior alterations in the 1930s.

Down the hill at the southeast corner of Broadway and Steiner is perhaps the most sought-after house in millennial Paciific Heights, the house in which that remarkable cinema character Mrs. Doubtfire earned her keep. Scarcely a day passes that locals walking in the area are not asked by guidebook-toting tourists from Europe and other parts of the U.S. where might the house of Mrs. D be. Its date is 1893, the architect J. B. Mathisen, and this house at 2640 Steiner is not, in fact, a very distinguished piece of architecture.

But down Steiner a few steps at 2715 is a lovely, more or less turn-of-the-century house that's become a favorite of mine, especially for the graceful portico sunnily centered on the south elevation, reached through a delightful oblong of a formal garden. Notice the fanlight with curving triangular panes, and the house's nice pilasters too. Alas, the best minds can't seem to find the name of 2715's architect…but wait a moment, I have a feeling those pilasters and certain lovely traceries at 2715 might have led Anne, if presented with this problem, to bring up the name of Otto Collischonn, who had a hand in Old House No. 73, several blocks south on Steiner at Clay.

—*Arthur Bloomfield*

No. 25

2470 Broadway

Country Tudor in Town

*A*s late as the 1890s the whole square block bound by Broadway, Steiner, Pierce and Vallejo was vacant—and not surrounded, one hopes, by fences with advertisements for chewing tobacco thereon.

And then, rather quickly, the block filled up, with the likes of 2670 Pierce (Old House No. 11) and 2715 Steiner. One of the first houses under construction was 2470 Broadway, a little slice of rustic chic you might say, in a style—Tudor Revival more than anything else—that flourished in Pacific Heights from about 1898 to 1910. The architects Edgar Mathews and Newton Tharp had seized on this vein. Exhibit "A" might be Mathews' 2360 Washington, built for William Gerstle in '98, Old House No. 64.

The house at 2470 Broadway is the work of two Newsoms. Not the combination of Samuel and Joseph Cather Newsom who built the fabulous Carson Mansion standing like a gingerbread cathedral up in the northern California market town of Eureka; no, in this case Samuel was paired with his older son Sidney who'd joined his father's firm as a fifteen-year-old apprentice in 1893, just as the office was preparing for the

Midwinter Fair scheduled for the following year. He became a partner in 1901.

And that is the year a widow named Alice Dillon bought the lot at 2470. She commissioned the new "Newsoms" to build a house and it was completed in '02. But Mrs. Dillon never lived in it, preferring to sell it at once, the buyer being one William Gage, the proprietor of a lumber business who fled with his wife, Louise Longworthy Gage, to San Diego after the '06 earthquake. He kept the house, however, complete with telephone number (and doubtless, also, their listing in the San Francisco Social Register) for another year before selling to Charles Hornick, a journalist who'd come out from St. Paul in 1905 to be managing editor of the *Chronicle,* only to jump ship and take the same position at the old *Call* the following year. Editor theft?

One hopes Mrs. Dillon before unloading her new house took the time to consider its architectural charms, crafted with such Tudor Revival traits as the steeply pitched side gable roof and the overhanging second story. Also notice the diagonally laid brick capping the garden wall on the way to the front door. Non-Tudor elements include the shed dormer at the attic and the hefty but simple consoles supporting the overhang. The large and lovely moldings at the eaves are composed of one row of toothlike dentils, another of egg and dart, and—an original Newsomian touch, this—a row composed with a stylized wave pattern.

The bottom line, so to speak, is a 1901–02 house that seems radically different from Stick Victorians of scarcely more than a decade before. And it marks a coming down to earth (as well as down the hill) after the Flood and J. D. Grant mansions a couple of blocks to the east.

2536 Broadway

Altered by a Page Brown Protégé

This is a house that was born twice, and retains a slightly split personality. Originally built in 1883, it was moved two alpine blocks to its present location fifteen years later, and its new owners had it quite drastically altered. With their blessing, architect Frank Van Trees:

- Stripped all the original trim
- Covered the house in brown shingles
- Built up the roof as a mansard affair
- Put into place a rather Coxheadian cornice based on Georgian sources
- Eliminated various doors and windows
- Incised an entry porch in the side bay

So thorough was the transformative updating of 2536 into a "Bay Area Tradition" look (call the "B.A.T." a subdivision of Arts and Crafts), I can't tell whether the original house was Italianate or Stick Victorian.

About all the remodelers retained was the exterior outline, including big windows at the front and on one side, and a set-back section on the other. Alterations resulted in large areas of plain brown shingled wall as on a Willis Polk or Ernest Coxhead house. The prominent new roof and its squat dormer windows de-emphasize the original fenestration, tall and vertical with leaded glass borders; added

windows are short, and arranged in bands à la Bernard Maybeck.

Any walking tourist in Pacific Heights who became familiar with Frank Van Trees via his elegantly chest-thumping 2104 Broadway (Old House No. 20) may be excused for not matching him with the infinitely less imperial 2536. In this case he was, of course, not working from the ground up—well, not quite.

As a matter of fact, Van Trees can claim some connection with the architects who designed the first Bay Area Tradition houses. Along with Polk, Maybeck and Albert Cicero Schweinfurth he worked in the office of A. Page Brown, which produced one of the very first examples of the genre, the old people's home at Pine and Pierce (Old House No. 98). Van Trees inherited Brown's practice and clientele, and he surely was acquainted with other practitioners and philosophers of the "Tradition." He even employed some of them.

The clients commissioning 2536 Broadway as we see it today probably signed up Van Trees because he was designing the new (and characteristically weighty) house for Charles Page, 2536's original owner, at 2518 Pacific—where 2536 originally stood. Van Trees needed to get rid of the older house on the site, but demolition was frowned on in those days, so why not sell the house and have it moved instead?

Even if there *was* a very steep hill down, and part of a steep hill up, between the two locations.

A note here on Charles Page. He was an internationally known admiralty lawyer associated with the firm of Page, McCutchen and Knight, predecessor of the modern-day McCutchen, Doyle, Brown and Enersen. In the 1890s he defended a sea captain whose ship was involved in a revolution in Chile, and after the 1894 revolution in El Salvador he represented one of the ousted generals. Such cases may have come his way because he was born in Valparaiso, Chile of a Chilean mother with Swedish connections and a physician father born in New Jersey. He came to the U.S. in 1863 aged sixteen and graduated from Yale in '69. After a time in Germany he settled in San Francisco, perhaps because his father owned Rancho Cotati in Sonoma County.

Sounds a bit like pre-jet-age jet-setting, doesn't it?

But what about the new inhabitants of the Moveable House? Contracts show that Cornelia Nokes, a widow with a sixteen-year-old daughter, arranged for the money and remodeling, the latter almost as expensive in 1898 as building a whole house from scratch, but the owners-to-be were

her parents, Augustus (who worked for the United States Coast and Geodetic Survey) and Serena Livingston Rodgers.

Soon installed at 2536 were the Rodgerses, Cornelia (an adjuster at the U.S. Mint) and her daughter as well as six of her seven brothers and sisters. The 1900 census also lists a Chinese cook and French maid in residence, the latter presumably lodged in the mansard regions.

The government agency employing Augustus Rodgers at a presumably well-paid level was actively surveying all over the West Coast in the nineteenth century. It published accurate maps of the San Francisco region as early as 1852. Rodgers seems to have been involved from the late 1860s until his death in 1908 at the age of seventy-eight. His family continued living at 2536. Cornelia, a proper Victorian lady, did not let herself be listed in a directory.

Her brother Augustus Jr. and her sisters Marian and Grace were still at this address in 1944—such sibling living was much more common in olden, stricter times—along with Virginia and John B. Murphy. Virginia was probably Cornelia Nokes' daughter who had turned eighteen in 1900. Virginia Murphy stayed on at 2536 Broadway until at least 1953, five and a half decades after moving in!

No. 27

2800–2808 Broadway

Chez Hellman and Dinkelspiel

At the hilltop corner of Broadway and Divisadero one heads west into that rarefied area known to locals as "the last three blocks of Broadway," an ultra-posh lineup of residential housing answering, especially after the intersection with Broderick Street, to the term Palatial. A number of the houses seem like giant exurban dwellings uprooted from vast landscaped parks or estates well outside the city and squeezed somehow onto one or two in-town lots.

Houses, in short, for upscale whiskey ads.

They're the next thing to châteaux, they boast fabulous views, they exude in some cases a massive serenity, and they must be very difficult to maintain. With no apartment houses in sight there's actually parking here, and with the Presidio Wall confronting cars at Lyon Street, the end of the road for Broadway, there's not much through automobile traffic. This is where Arthur's father taught him to drive—scarcely a car to bump into, then or now.

The pair of houses which are our subject here—they were, by the way, part of a single architectural plan—illustrate why a history of Pacific Heights tells the story of all San Francisco, even all the West. The one on the left, 2808, was the home of Frances Jacobi Hellman, widow of I. W.

Hellman Jr., the crown prince of banking in California, and the one on the right, 2800, was built for her daughter and son-in-law, Florence and Lloyd Dinkelspiel. He was a noted benefactor of Stanford University—think Dinkelspiel Auditorium where the Stanford Opera Theater has put on impressive productions—and a longtime partner in a law firm still very much with us, Heller, Ehrman, White and McAuliffe.

Dying at the age of forty-nine in 1920, just one month after his father, I. W. Jr. never came into his full inheritance but his career had soared nonetheless. He apprenticed at his father's Farmers and Merchants Bank of Los Angeles and with his Nevada Bank of San Francisco. Shortly after his father founded the Union Trust Company in 1893 he became its manager, in his early twenties yet. By 1916 he was president, having built up the firm significantly.

Isaias W. Hellman Sr. is the man who made Wells Fargo the name-brand bank we know today.

One of a number of young and entrepreneurial Jewish pioneers who came to California from Bavaria not long after the Gold Rush, I. W. was just eighteen when he arrived, penniless, in 1860. He went on to create and nourish a great bank in

Los Angeles, then came to San Francisco in 1890 to rescue the Nevada Bank, which had been founded in '75 by Messrs. Fair and O'Brien. They had poured into it the incredible wealth of the Comstock silver mines near Virginia City just over the state line into Nevada.

Wells Fargo likes to boast about its origins in the Gold Rush of '49: its logo and advertising emphasize the stagecoach of that era. Actually though, Wells, Fargo & Company was one of many express companies: don't forget United Parcel. There were no banks in California then, and Wells Fargo earned a reputation for reliable deliveries of gold dust sent to city and town from mining communities. Its agents also bought gold dust, and that led to the undertaking of banking functions. But the express business, delivering things and people, was their main focus.

Hellman Sr. bought the banking part of the concern in the 1890s and the express continued independently, well into the twentieth century. In 1905 he grafted his Wells Fargo banking operation onto the larger and stronger Nevada Bank, and then his other creation, American Trust, was merged with the Wells Fargo Nevada National Bank after his death.

But this story is about Frances Hellman, daughter-in-law of I. W. Sr.

A photograph of her published in 1916 shows a truly lovely woman with dark hair and gentle eyes. It's the finest portrait among those of hundreds of women hailed for their work in promoting the Panama-Pacific Exposition of the previous year. She was also keenly interested in Mills College, the progressive women's college across the bay in Oakland—a trustee, in fact, for twenty-seven years until her death in 1959, aged 82, at 2808 Broadway.

She donated a gym and a pool to Mills, and her children gave it $100,000 for music scholarships in her honor. She loved music, serving long years on the boards of the San Francisco Symphony, Opera and Community Music Center. And her granddaughter, Nancy Bechtle, is president of the Symphony as I write.

She was born Frances Jacobi, daughter of Frederick and Flora Brandenstein Jacobi—he was a prosperous liquor importer and Flora was the sister of Max J. Brandenstein, founder of MJB Coffee. Here in a Hellman/Brandenstein connection we have an example of the linkings that tie together so many of San Francisco's great merchant Jewish families.

In the early 1890s Frederick Jacobi moved his family to New York, so when Frances was married in San Francisco in '98, it was at the home of her maternal grandparents, the Joseph Brandensteins. Because of a recent death the wedding was smaller than originally planned, only one hundred guests, all relatives and very close friends.

The family to which she gave birth

included I. W. Hellman III, Frederick J. and Marco Hellman, all bankers, and the daughter Frances who married Mr. Dinkelspiel and moved into 2800 Broadway. When 2800 and 2808 were conceived, in 1927, the houses were designed under a common Tudor Revival hat—a gracious one to be sure—and with a large central open space. The architect was Willis Polk and Company, but that doesn't mean the celebrated Polk himself, because the master died in '24.

The actual designers were James H. Mitchell and Angus McSweeney, who carried on Polk's practice into the Depression. A graduate of the architecture school at UC Berkeley, Mitchell had been in Polk's office at least since 1919 and his local colleagues thought enough of him to elect him secretary-treasurer of their chapter of the American Institute of Architects.

Postscript

Could the composer Frederick Jacobi, born in California in 1891 and educated in New York and Berlin, be Frances' younger brother, or at least a close cousin? This Jacobi studied the music of Pueblo Indians in Arizona and New Mexico about 1920. From 1936 he taught at New York's famous Juilliard School, and his violin concerto was premiered by Albert Spalding with the Chicago Symphony in 1939, performances following with the New York Philharmonic. Pierre Monteux conducted a Jacobi symphony in San Francisco in the mid-1940s.

No. 28

2880 Broadway

A Polk Palazzo More or Less

2880 Broadway, which Willis Polk designed for Albert and Mina Ehrman in 1913, is and is not like an Italian Renaissance palazzo.

Yes, its arches, columns and roofline balustrade speak a Classical vocabulary, a vocabulary transmitted along that great line from Greek to Roman to Renaissance to Georgian to Beaux Arts. But at the same time it's not a truly Classical house, mansion, palace, whatever, because the canted corner at the left of the front façade confounds symmetry and the nearly equal stories reject Renaissance proportions.

Polk did achieve what his clients wanted, the then-popular serenity of Classicism. Yet he suited the house to his clients' modern needs. He played, for instance, on the direction of sunlight (a coveted thing in often foggy San Francisco), superbly lighting the grandest rooms with the canted corner windows facing southwest from two levels. Then, with an almost painterly sensibility he invited shadows onto the façade by recessing openings behind columns.

The serenity of 2880 comes from a rhythmic repetition of very few elements: Ionic columns, matching pilasters attached to the façade, paneled wall sections, half-round arches. In this felicity Polk could be considered an architectural Johannes

Brahms—think of those elegantly spaced "pillar" chords at the close of his third symphony—as well as an expert in drawing-board chiaroscuro.

To meet his clients' 1913 needs, Polk gave the Ehrmans a fifteen-foot-high main floor and a thirteen-foot floor above. A "basement" twelve feet high takes advantage of the steep hillside running north from Broadway to give the owners another floor of gracious living with views. That challenging hillside, by the way, is the main reason the last blocks of Broadway remained empty until just before 1900. Some landowners in the area, Frances Hellman of 2808 Broadway among them, waited almost twenty years before building on the precipice.

2880 has much less wall and more glass than any Renaissance predecessor. By Classical standards, in fact, its roof comes down too close to the windows, rather like a mop of hair allowed to fall perhaps too trendily over a young gentleman's expanse of forehead. And the feet of the house could be said to be too close to the street. But let's not be too critical, there's nothing amateurish about Willis Polk's 2880 Broadway.

Polk, it should be noted, took advantage of his modern materials. A reinforced concrete foundation tames the plunging hillside, and a wood and stucco super-structure gives the flexibility and strength to crowd the front of 2880 with glass.

The Ehrmans must have liked their $40,000 house, expensive for 1913. They lived at 2880 for forty-eight years and celebrated their golden wedding anniversary there in 1949. They seem to have lived rather quietly, in spite of an end-of-Broadway address, world-class views, and tall, elaborate rooms that beg for entertaining. The Ehrmans don't show up in newspaper stories or other sources that historians consult. I suspect they considered it unmannerly or *nouveau* to court publicity or pay for it.

Money wasn't in question. Albert L. Ehrman was a stockbroker of long standing and president of the San Francisco Stock Exchange in 1920–22 and 1931–33. Those were difficult years for the exchange, right after World War I and during the worst of the Great Depression. The exchange's board of governors remembered, and paid Albert Ehrman tribute on his ninetieth birthday in 1960.

Albert was born in San Francisco, the elder brother of Sidney Ehrman (see Old House No. 30), whose name is still on the door of Heller, Ehrman, White and McAuliffe. Their father was Meyer Ehrman, one of the city's many pioneer Jewish merchants. A wholesale grocer, M. Ehrman and Co. included as partners Samuel Sussman and Samuel Wormser, who later formed their own firm: surely you've bought tins of veg with the S&W logo on the label.

No.29

2898 Broadway

Bliss and Faville Brick

*T*his beautiful brick house is the first building in a most distinguished series. Begun at this address in 1899-1900, that series continued with the St. Francis Hotel in 1904, the Bank of California in 1906, the Geary Theater in 1909, Cathedral House in 1910, the last Flood mansion (Old House No. 24) in 1914, the Southern Pacific and Matson buildings on lower Market Street in 1916 and 1921, and the State Building facing Civic Center Plaza in 1926.

These are only the cream of the crop, and for other estimable buildings in this world-class series look to Oakland, Atascadero, Tahoe, Sacramento, Berkeley, Piedmont, Kentfield, and of course San Francisco, where the *Sudden Fear* mansion built for a member of the landowning Newhall clan may be found, pretty as a picture, at Scott and Green.

All right, if you figured the architectural firm responsible for the cream-etc. listed above was Bliss and Faville you get "A" in the course.

Walter Danforth Bliss and William B. Faville got together in New York, where they worked for the great architects McKim, Mead and White, Faville having previously taught architecture at MIT while still a young man. In 1897 these budding maestri of the drawing board came west to Bliss' native city and founded their elegant partnership, which endured for twenty-seven highly productive years.

Almost all their buildings are Italian Renaissance Revival in style. Bliss and Faville's interpretation usually featured tall, slender Corinthian columns and other delicate ornamentation. There was generally lots of ornament, but always in exquisite taste. Note that their version of Renaissance Revival differed from those of their best contemporaries such as Frederick H. Meyer, a more straightforward designer who favored fewer columns, and Lewis Hobart, who relied wholly on line and proportions and downplayed ornament.

2898 Broadway, which is Bliss and Faville's earliest known design, borrows, as a matter of fact, from the Dutch rather than Italian Renaissance. The stepped profile against the sky, the use of brick, the dark color and white trim, all recall Amsterdam. Meanwhile the house's columns have the slenderness that became Bliss and Faville's trademark.

The brickwork is special. It includes window arches, inset panels, corner quoins, a tapering wall at the double basement—what fun the team must have had with all this! The bricks are laid in the pattern called Flemish bond wherein every other brick of a horizontal course is turned head-on, and these headers, in dark clinker brick, line up in a pleasing, almost checkerboard pattern.

As for the house's light-colored trim—window sills, radiating lintels, front steps and vestibule—all that is in marble.

The commissioning of 2898 was an inside job: the clients were Walter Bliss' parents, Duane Leroy and Elizabeth T. Bliss. Nothing like a bit of parental help to get one's business going! Young Bliss himself lived in the house as well, until he married Edith Pillsbury about 1909.

Duane Bliss was a lumber baron whose forests in western Nevada shored the Comstock mines and supplied eastern and foreign markets. An enlightened timber manager, he practiced the new science of forest preservation pioneered in Germany—a great country for forests, by the way, when you consider its fairy tale literature. Bliss Sr. was widely praised for his protection of young trees and his systematic fire patrol.

Duane Bliss had come to California from Massachusetts as a teenager in 1851. He took up lumbering on the eastern side of Lake Tahoe but was careful not to denude the shores. In 1875 he built a logging railroad from Truckee to Tahoe City, then in 1898 his operation was incorporated as the Lake Tahoe Railway and Transportation Company. Duane Jr. was its president after the senior Bliss died in 1907.

Father Bliss also helped make Tahoe a resort. He created the still-extant east-side trail, which Mark Twain celebrated in *Roughing It,* he put a sightseeing steamer on the lake in '96, and he had a large tavern and casino built.

The visitors he brought to the area influenced politicians to preserve the lake and later the Bliss family deeded 744 acres for a state park. A mountain peak east of the lake was named for Duane Bliss.

For Bliss Sr., then in his mid-sixties, the new 2898 Broadway was a combination pied-à-terre and retirement home. The house remained in the family for forty years, the pied-à-terre aspect persisting because Duane Jr. lived mainly at the family company's headquarters in Nevada. Not the first example, this, of a handsome city pad in Pacific Heights for some industrial or financial leader with much time to be spent out, so to speak, in the bush.

No. 30

2970 Broadway

Yehudi Practiced Here

When Arthur's father, court physician to the Sidney Ehrmans, made house calls to 2970 Broadway in the late 1920s, likely on a Sunday morning, he would pass a room in which a chubby pre-adolescent boy was playing away on his violin. This was, you may have guessed, Yehudi Menuhin, whose name would become a household word at home and abroad, and sometimes Dr. Bloomfield would hear the young man exclaim, "Got it!" as he mastered a recalcitrant bit of Mendelssohn or Bach.

The Ehrmans, not without great resistance from Yehudi's proud mother, had elected to pay for a giant part of Yehudi's education, musical and otherwise. The Menuhins, who lived across town near Alamo Square, were not exactly paupers, but a year of study in Paris with the great Enesco was not an item that fit neatly into their budget. Yehudi was eternally grateful.

In one of his autobiographical volumes, *Unfinished Journey,* Yehudi recalls his first meeting with Sidney Ehrman, following his debut recital at the Scottish Rite Auditorium, later the Regency Cinema, on Van Ness Avenue. The year was 1925. "A tall, handsome gentleman wearing a dinner jacket" was ushered in and delivered himself, as Yehudi says, of a flattering brief comment. Then a Rolls-Royce drew up, and a ride to Alamo Square was offered, which mama Menuhin, not about to be pampered, politely refused.

Sidney Ehrman did not give up the chase and soon had Yehudi under his benevolent wing. He was, no surprise perhaps, something of a violinist himself—and, as the story goes, had not been altogether satisfied with the piano accompaniments of a certain Miss Hellman when he was courting her some years before!

More on Sidney Ehrman from Yehudi: "Whether making money or giving it away, he rose to adverse situations...his modesty and authority, the splendor which rejected éclat and the patronage which made no claim upon the protégé, merged into [my mother's] prototypical image of a Caucasian nobleman.

"Indeed he had qualities which drew devotion from everyone who knew him... strong yet humble, wise yet simple, humorous yet serious, benevolent yet selective, with the charm of intelligence and cultivation allied to true sympathy, he was a shining example of what a man can be."

That Rolls-Royce, piloted by Barney, a Brit imported from the UK along with the imposing vehicle, would have rolled up to an end-of-Broadway mansion designed by one of California's best architects, Lewis Parsons Hobart. Credit him with Grace Cathedral, the Academy of Sciences, the Bohemian Club, the old William Taylor Hotel at McAllister and Leavenworth where opera singers stayed during autumn seasons in the thirties, Del Monte Lodge, several mansions in Hillsborough, several residences at Pebble Beach, a house in Pasadena, a park and theater in Bakersfield, the Honolulu Memorial "temple of music and water coliseum" at Waikiki, and so on...

He was still at work three years before his death in 1954 at the age of eighty-one, making adjustments at San Francisco's Fleishhacker Zoo.

The design of 2970 Broadway is Beaux Arts perfection, with a difference. While the front and center of the house is perfectly symmetrical, the pavilions on the sides are unequal. But the tiny setback of the narrow one on the right balances with great felicity the deep recessing of the wide and bay-windowed one on the left.

The third floor is even further back; if it had been brought out to the façade its height would have overbalanced the front.

You will have gathered that Hobart's clients for this 1915 mansion had deep pockets. Well, Sidney Ehrman was the son of a rich provisions merchant and a founder of the top-drawer law firm of Heller, Ehrman, White and McAuliffe which had begun, right after the '06 quake, as Heller, Powers and Ehrman. (Frank H. Powers dropped out about 1920, then Jerome B. White and Florence M. McAuliffe were added; Emanuel S. Heller died or retired about 1930, but his name graces the letterhead to this day.)

Sidney's wife, Florence, the property's legal owner, was the daughter of the celebrated banker I. W. Hellman whose acquaintance we've made in connection with real estate down the street. Florence Ehrman, who, by the way, never carried keys to her house because there was always a servant to open the door, gave herself as well as her money to the Esther Hellman Settlement House, a Jewish school for immigrants.

As late as 1962, when Sidney Ehrman was nearly ninety, he was still listed with his law firm as "Of Counsel." He died in 1975 aged one hundred and two, resident in the house he'd built sixty years before. Not long before that he had been seen, tall as ever, helped along by a cane, at his beloved San Francisco Opera.

Sidney and Florence's only son, Sidney Jr., died in Cambridge, England, in a hunting accident while still a young man. His study at Cambridge University was imported in its entirety—books, paneling and all—to San Francisco and recreated at 2970 Broadway as a second-floor sitting room. A lovely gesture.

And perhaps in a sense Yehudi Menuhin became for the Ehrmans a son...

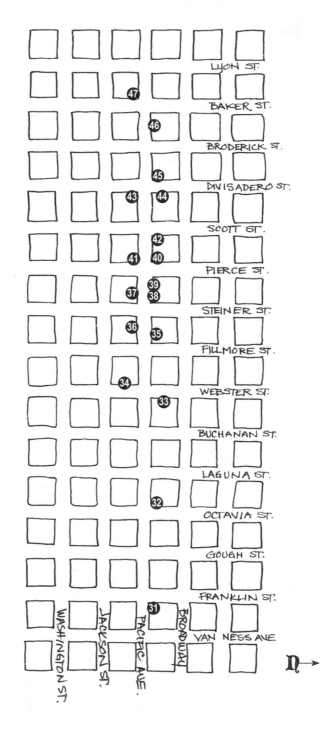

On or near

Pacific Avenue

east to west

No. 31

1782 Pacific

Goldberg–Bowen's Founder Lived Here

This Italianate jewel box, sitting pretty with its symmetrical bays, pipestem colonnettes, a whole bag of ornament that stops just short of *de trop*, can't help catching the eye, directly or peripherally, of thousands of drivers rushing down one-way Franklin Street past Pacific Avenue.

But it wasn't always so pretty. By World War II, 1782 Pacific had fallen out of caring hands and was divided into multiple units. Then, in 1957, a time when many San Franciscans, one hates to say it, were eyeing Victorians with ideas of demolition dancing through their heads, thoughtful new owners took the house under their wing and, with the help of photographs supplied by relatives of the original owners, restored it inside and out.

1782 Pacific dates from 1875 and was, as sometimes happened in those days, a wealthy man's gift to one of his children. In this case the Maine-born lumber tycoon William C. Talbot presented a lovely piece of real estate to his daughter Mary and her husband, Henry Dutton Jr.—hence 1782 being known in the architectural history community as the Talbot-Dutton house.

William Talbot had sailed to California in 1850 on the schooner *Oriental* with a cargo of much-needed lumber. Then he engaged in the lumber trade along the coast of South America and the Hawaiian Islands, in due course founding, with his brother-in-law Andrew J. Pope, the well-known firm Pope and Talbot.

The handsome 1782 Pacific was purchased in 1905 by Jacob Goldberg, a founder of Goldberg-Bowen, purveyors of fine foods. Imagine an earlier-day combination of the upscale Oakville Grocery in the Stanford Shopping Center down the Peninsula and the Whole Foods store anchoring the southeast reaches of Pacific Heights at Franklin and California Streets.

San Franciscans of a certain age remember well the tempting aisles of the Goldberg-Bowen store on Sutter Street across from the present-day Banana Republic. It was not, I should add, all luxury goods. Such stores in those mid-twentieth-century days and earlier had to have a lunch counter where working stiffs, secretaries as well as attorneys, could get their ham on rye and chocolate malt. Goldberg-Bowen rose to this basic need, but also served pies done up with a haunting galette crust I can still taste three decades on.

And now we lunch on mussels and Abruzzan stews in Belden alley.

No. 32

2000 Pacific

The House of the Three Sisters

While Victorian architecture was out of favor, the Queen Anne/Colonial Revival mansion at 2000 Pacific owed its preservation to the inaction of three aging maiden ladies, Lottie, Dottie and Maud, last name Woods, who died in their eighties and nineties, the last in 1974. Across Octavia the large and rather ugly Queen Anne at 1998 Pacific, which had been the town quarters of the Sigmund Sterns—think Stern Grove, that verdant concert venue at Nineteenth Avenue and Sloat Boulevard—was long gone by the time the last of the sisters was carried away.

Dottie, by the way, was technically Dorothy Woods, but even the Social Register accepted the somewhat informal moniker Lottie when listing her sister—come to think of it, Lotte is a good German name, not a nickname.

Maud gave up maidenhood at the age of sixty-one, but only for a few days. Her husband-in-passing was Frederick C. Hotaling of the old-time liquor wholesalers, about whom Charles K. Field wrote in 1906, in the wake of the great earthquake and fire:

> If as some say, God spanked the town
> For being over frisky,
> Why did he burn the Churches down
> And save Hotaling's Whiskey?

Evidently on the honeymoon either Hotaling was disturbed that the "chaperoning" *other* sisters were sleeping in the next cabin, or Maud was put off by her new mate's drug addiction. A suing for divorce followed forthwith and Maud returned to her sisters, the Chinese "houseboy," and her poetry. Which, one suspects, was a long way in tone from Chekhov's *Three Sisters.*

Lottie's hobby was genealogy, and Dottie gardened. They all belonged to the Century Club at Sutter and Franklin (where that estimable chamber ensemble led by pianist Margaret Tilly gave interesting concerts five or six times a season), and the Colonial Dames associated with the Octagon House on Gough Street. Sounds like they had fun, "sublimation" of the baser instincts not troubling them too much.

Oh yes, each decorated her own tree at Christmas. It's lucky there were several large rooms for the displays thereof. In fact, looking at the house from a kitty-corner position, you can see that it conveniently divides into south, central and northern sections, three evidently commodious bedrooms lined up symmetrically on the second floor for our near-Siamese siblings.

The sisters did not grow up in 2000 Pacific, they bought it in 1921 after their parents died. Their father was Frederick N. Woods, nephew and junior partner of W. Frank Whittier who built 2090 Jackson (Old House No. 52), recently the headquarters of the California Historical Society. Whittier made his money as a partner in Whittier, Fuller and Co., ancestor of Fuller O'Brien Paints. Woods had other businesses too, poultry and window glass—there's diversification, all right.

The house's original owners were Charles York, who had a big ship chandlery business, and his wife, Emma. No children, but they lived at 2000 with a pair of servants, one German, one Danish. Think of the pastry! The Yorks had 2000 built in 1894–95 by a contractor named Thomas McLachlan, who charged them $9,450. Plumbing cost an extra $1,975, and they had bought the lot separately.

The designer of what surely stands as a beautifully proportioned house, with impressive south and east elevations—it's helpful the house is on a corner—was one H. Burns. Perhaps this was the Henry Burns who did 3414 Washington in Presidio Heights, or was it Howard Burns, responsible for 1524 Bay Street in Alameda?

In 1911 the Yorks sold their pad to Curtis Holbrook Lindley, a respected mining attorney who lived across the street. He'd been eyeing 2000 with its great wheel of a rosette, toy soldier porch and paired chimneys, its not unsensuous corner bay. Lindley enjoyed several years at his new address, then his estate sold to Lottie Woods, evidently the business manager of the Sisters, or the eldest.

When the Warren Wilsons, since departed, bought 2000 in 1974 they were only the fourth owners in eighty years. By that time the house had lost hardly any visible parts, but nothing worked, grime was everywhere and the golden oak paneling had darkened terribly.

One day an aged Chinese American turned up at the door, proudly announcing, "I take care Miss Lottie, Miss Dottie fifty year." He'd been too busy cooking, serving and washing up to tend the house much. Meanwhile the Wilsons proceeded slowly, cautiously, fixing up one room at a time, encouraging the house to tell its secrets...

No. 33

2550 Webster

A Dark and Brooding Pile

*T*he dark and brooding pile at 2550 Webster—it looks as if it had been hammered together with radically enlarged children's building blocks—is often called an architectural masterpiece. It has all the Classical ideals of balance, restraint, grace, unity, repose, and we'll overlook for the moment its somewhat down and dangerous look, as if there were a little architectural Hyde in the mix along with the Jekyll.

(A postscript: the house's present state of disrepair is mystifying and heartbreaking.)

Superstar Willis Polk designed 2550 for tycoon William Bourn in 1896—and early in the twentieth century fashion caught up with its dark and daring clinker brick. Note in this magisterial house the Renaissance-inspired curving pediments, stout balustrades, profusion of lion's heads, and the massive door surround in unglazed terracotta. And ponder the low and submissive ground floor, a mere prelude to the lordly main rooms above.

Where, so the story goes, porno films were made not many years ago.

Polk's client, born in San Francisco in 1857, inherited his father's Empire Gold Mine and other inviting properties before the age of twenty: a case, you might say, of *almost* being born with a gold spoon

in one's mouth. And then, acting as the manager of these properties, young William Bourn increased their worth with tough determination and drive.

In due course this entrepreneurial steamroller became president of the Spring Valley Water Company, which maintained a monopoly over San Francisco's water supply from 1865 to 1930. And Bourn, with his fingers in more than one utility pie, was also president of San Francisco Gas and Electric, which ultimately merged with PG&E.

Meanwhile, wearing his vinicultural hat, he gave us the huge cellars later occupied by Christian Brothers in St. Helena. More than a mere business expert, Bourn also turned up as president of the San Francisco Symphony, supported local artists and promoted the 1915 Panama-Pacific International Exposition.

His architect was ten years younger and had come to San Francisco in 1889. *Enfant terrible* of the local arts scene, Willis Polk founded his own magazine, *Architectural News* (which ran for all of three issues), helped Gelett Burgess with his little literary magazine *The Lark* and loudly proclaimed the new era of beautiful architecture he and his friends had brought to fin de siècle San Francisco. His attention-craving and wildly exaggerated ways made him a lively companion around town and at Bohemian Grove outings up by the Russian River, but they also lost him potential clients.

Polk was a brilliant designer, a facile, imaginative and temperamental architect, as scholar Richard Longstreth puts it, who worked on intuition but was committed to beauty as his ultimate aim.

In addition to numerous residences (several of which make the book you are holding a little heavier) Polk is responsible for the Hallidie Building on lower Sutter Street which is called the very first glass curtain-wall structure. He did the Hobart Building, also in downtown San Francisco, he restored charming Mission Dolores, he rebuilt the mansion housing the Pacific Union Club on Nob Hill after the disasters of '06, etc., etc.

But his best client was doubtless William Bowers Bourn.

2550 Webster was Polk's first building for Bourn. He'd designed but not built Bourn houses in St. Helena about 1890 and 1894. In 1897–1898 came the "Empire Cottage" (a sort of mansion, really) and other buildings at Bourn's mine in Grass Valley. Then in 1905 Polk did the Jessie Street substation for SFG&E, setting an elegant pattern for the substation genre in San Francisco. For Spring Valley he designed the delicate Water Temple down the Peninsula and the impressive office building at 425 Mason Street in the city.

And Polk is also the author of Filoli, Bourn's elegant Peninsula mansion. Bourn sold 2550 Webster about 1924 and one can't help wondering if the house's less than totally upbeat personality didn't get to him at times, this man who seems to have loved wine and music as much as business.

No. 34

2411 Webster

One Touch of Paris

*I*t looks like some building magically transported from a Paris boulevard, only shorter and with a stucco surface over frame construction instead of stone over masonry.

Forty years ago neighborhood rumor even had it that the original owner had ordered her contractor to make an exact copy of a particular Parisian building. And yes, the exterior ornament of 2411 Webster, the Montellano Apartments, gave that rumor life. Take, for instance, the lions peering out just above your head: they have a distinctly Gallic look, something related to their troubled Grand Manner expressions and droopy manes. They seem to invite a Sarah Bernhardt to pet them.

Those lions have company. There's hardly an inch of the Montellano façade that isn't *decorated* one way or another: oak leaves, ruffled ribbons, scallop shells, two different kinds of balconies supported on giant-sized consoles or brackets, looping window divisions suggesting loosely tied scarves, egg and dart moldings, toothlike moldings, curved glass, interrupted garlands, the horizontal grooves called rustication, you name it. A pigeonholer of styles might call the whole building an amalgam of two Parisian modes, the free-flowing Art Nouveau *and* Ecole des Beaux-Arts with its taste for heavy axial symmetry.

Blinded onlookers shouldn't fail to notice the lobby, a perfect gem, a photo of which was published in an architectural magazine in 1919 with a couple of black bearskins stretched out on its marble floor. The space is oval, with arched niches, and in the photo looks very grand, maybe thirty feet across. But it can't be: it's sandwiched between a symmetrical pair of covered driveways on a lot only forty-six feet wide.

The fact is, the lobby, actually almost tiny, the ceiling barely clearing your head, *begins* to look large and grand only because of its perfect proportions. It's a good trick with scale, as if someone had run the room through a photocopy reduction process.

You might have guessed by now that that old neighborhood rumor about a copycat building out of a Paris arrondissement was wrong and there was a superbly skilled architect on site. It was in fact no one less than the colorful James Francis Dunn (see Old House No. 10) who was responsible for some of the most delightfully Frenchified and far-out apartments put up in early twentieth-century San Francisco.

He did the curls and squiggles of 1347 McAllister in 1901, the lions and wild rustication of 798 Post in 1913, the Montellano here about 1914, and the Gaudi-like bays of the Chambord at Sacramento and Jones in 1921, the year he died. That doesn't count his amusing wallowing in Moorish fantasy for the Alhambra Apartments at 860 Geary in 1913.

Dunn was something of an architectural theorist too, with two articles on apartment house design to his credit. In 1919 he declared in print that the luxury trade wanted apartment living, and "the individual house is gone." A bit of wishful thinking here—or was it self-promotion?—considering the increasing spread of suburban and in-city suburban-type tracts.

On the other hand, how many single-family houses have been built in Pacific Heights since 1919? A fun game here! Using the fingers of perhaps two dozen hands, I can think of the occasional William Wurster in a spare yet sensuous modern mode, several mansionettes on this or that newly subdivided jumbo-sized property, a few slim maidens from the elegant drawing board of John Field, the pretty anomaly in Beverly Hills kitsch that pops up here and there, a few pockets of smart, not especially modern houses on cul-de-sacs developed not so long ago. Could the grand total be about 130?

Dunn's client for the Montellano Apartments was a widow named Annie Byrne who'd moved with her husband, William, to an earlier house on the same lot about 1900. To judge by its footprint, it was probably an 1870s Italianate Victorian, a one-story affair wide and symmetrical with twin bays framing a central doorway as in 1782 Pacific Avenue. Following her husband's death, Annie lived with her two sons in this likely Victorian until 1913, and then they moved and the house was demolished, to be replaced with the fabulous Montellano Apartments.

The apartment house was the Byrnes' investment, not a speculation: one or another of the family lived in the new building for many years. Mrs. Byrne died about 1950, her sons inherited the building, and one of them, J. Charles, called 2411 home at this time. He was a real estate broker, and the family probably made a business of investing in apartment buildings: one or another Byrne lived in, and probably owned, 835 Hyde in the Tenderloin and had a connection with 1940 Vallejo, that sultry Pacific Heights damsel.

Well, here was a family that made James Dunn's predictions about apartments being the home of the future ring true.

Interlude

Around the corner from the Bourn mansion and Montellano Apartments you'll find a jazzy little apartment house I've been especially fond of since my grammar school days. As Michael Crowe puts it in his engaging *Deco by the Bay*, 2360 Pacific has a split personality, its entrance being Spanish

Colonial Revival while the upper floors are trimmed in Art Deco terra-cotta. Crowe goes on to say that the small-paned industrial sash is unusual on a domestic building. The six sculpted headdresses at the roofline look like meringue substitutes piped onto the building from a pastry tube.

Super-sleuth archivist Gary Goss tells me 2360 dates from 1927 and is the work of Bolles and Schroepfer. Edward S. Bolles was the father of John S. Bolles, the architect of the windswept baseball stadium known as Candlestick Park and the proprietor of an outstanding 1960s art gallery at Jackson Square which featured contemporary Bay Area artists.

—Arthur Bloomfield

No. 35

2418 Pacific (top) and 2420 as well

Mortimer Fleishhacker Sr. Lived Here

*O*n one of the widest residential lots on Pacific Avenue near Fillmore a wrought iron fence, head high, guards not a landscape but a cobblestoned parking lot. This is the way to a lovely house faced with dark, elegant brick laid in a formal Flemish pattern and trimmed with light-colored granite. Big shoulders, this house has—and quiet, quiet chic. Its severity finds relief at the white doorway, several crucial paces back from the house's front-and-center, a thing of graceful columns, triangular pediment and, most charming of all, a barrel-arched ceiling. All Georgian or Colonial Revival at its best.

This house, 2418 Pacific, was the home of Mortimer Fleishhacker, a cultivated heavyweight in northern California business, and his wife, Bella, who coped gracefully with an arranged marriage and achieved happiness through children, charities and her work as an Expressionist painter.

She was born a Gerstle, and her sister Alice Gerstle Levison (who, according to her obituary a bit short of her hundredth birthday, in 1973, was "totally serene, absolutely secure...and a rugged and sometimes salty individualist") lived next door at 2420 Pacific—and died there in fact, in the same room where she gave birth to the last two of four sons. More on 2420 in a bit.

...And note that brother William Gerstle lived a few blocks away in the Tudor Revival job at 2360 Washington (Old House No. 64).

Mortimer Fleishhacker Sr. of 2418 Pacific was born in San Francisco in 1868 to a modest paper box manufacturer whose partner he became in 1892. That was just the beginning: soon Mortimer and his younger brother Herbert, quite different in personality but a keen business ally, were financing and running an incredible variety of companies pyramided, it's said, on a 1,000 percent profit from the purchase and sale of an Oregon paper mill discovered by Herbert on his regular sales route.

In 1903 the brothers organized the American River Electric Company, an early hydroelectric generation venture. One thing led, as they say, to another and for a dozen years Mortimer presided over the Great Western Power Company, a serious competitor to PG&E which was bought out only in 1930.

Herbert, by the way, who lived at the St. Francis Hotel, is the one after whom Fleishhacker Zoo and the giant Fleishhacker Pool were named. He got into banking through his father-in-law, Sigmund

Greenbaum, and by 1909 was managing the Anglo and London Paris National Bank which later became Anglo-California, then Anglo-Crocker, then Crocker Bank. Soon he was enlisting Mortimer to preside over the related Anglo California Trust Company and for three decades the brothers worked together in banking.

Mortimer was the quieter and more intellectual of the two. His immense curiosity about new processes led to investments (and usually directorships or more) in irrigation, sugar-making, paper, insurance, wine and other industries. Although his own education had ended during high school, he was a regent of the University of California for thirty years. And he served as a director of the San Francisco Opera, San Francisco Symphony, the Mueseum of Modern Art, Temple Emanu-El, the Hebrew Orphanage, and so on.

Wife Bella, the painter and philanthropist, was very probably the motivating force behind the couple's patronage of photographers Edward Weston and Dorothea Lange, landscape architect Thomas Church, architect William Wurster, and especially Charles Greene of the fabled Pasadena architects Greene and Greene, who designed the Fleishhackers' artistic and amazingly unpretentious pastoral estate at exurban Woodside. Among the attractions of "Green Gables" and its grounds (yes, a pun may have been intended) is a giant reflecting pool framed at one end with a stunning Roman arcade, a gently curving Pont du Gard as it were.

The courtly longterm correspondence between Charles Greene and Bella Fleishhacker regarding plans for the estate is worth a little book of its own. By the way, in his excellent book *Greene and Greene: Masterworks,* Bruce Smith reports that after Charles Greene, the more "artistic" of the pair, brought Henry Greene, who was more the administrator of their office, to meet the Fleishhacker family, Mortimer Sr. requested that in the future he deal only with the more engaging Charles. The Fleishhacker children called Charles "Green Greene" and Henry "Pink Greene," a double-green being apparently a term of greater endearment. With great tact the Fleishhackers wooed Charles away somewhat from his fondness for Japanese-inspired design, directing him more toward an English country look.

But back to the city and 2418 Pacific, built in 1904. The architects for the Fleishhackers' more formal house in town were Henry H. Meyers and Clarence R. Ward. Meyers, a native Californian, had worked for Percy and Hamilton, architects of the First Unitarian Church, and he inherited their practice, finishing the Kohl Building on Montgomery Street and the Wilson Building on Market downtown. The Meyers and Ward partnership lasted from 1904 through 1909 and included a number of downtown buildings as well as reconstruction of Memorial Chapel on the Stanford University campus following the '06 calamity.

The seriousness, grace and absolutely understated glamor of Meyers and Ward's 2418 Pacific is a fitting symbol of Mortimer Fleishhacker Sr.'s position in the business, and artistic, community. The house matches the determined and creative Bella no less well.

And next door...

2420 Pacific is a sane, spare, serene town house. With its handsome brick, almost pre-Deco keystones and that teasingly set-back entrance, it's a tad plain-Jane compared to 2418. But the almost pastry-like columns at 2420's entrance remind us this house is no wallflower at the architectural party. 2420, dated 1901-02, is the work of solid Julius Krafft, designer of the Hamlin School mansion originating as a Flood pad (Old House No. 21), and this is where Bella Fleishhacker's sister Alice lived with her husband Jacob B. Levison, generally known as J. B. It was J. B. who bought the land for both 2418 and 2420.

A wealth of material exists about J. B. and Alice. In 1933 he had the renowned art printer John Henry Nash publish his *Memories for My Family,* and in the late 1960s Alice gave lengthy interviews which were published by the University of California's Regional Oral History Office.

J. B. was born in Virginia City, Nevada in 1862, a long way from protected Pacific Avenue, and died in 1947, in his Pacific Avenue house, as did his widow twenty-six years later. Alice, and Bella next door, were the daughters of Lewis Gerstle, who with partners had founded and run the Alaska Commercial Company, which had exclusive rights to "harvest" seal furs in the newly acquired territory of Alaska. They made immense profits.

Gerstle and his partner/brother-in-law Louis Sloss lived across from each other on San Francisco's Van Ness Avenue, a place of stately homes before '06, and they shared a summer estate in Marin County, which their children later donated to the suburban city of San Rafael as Gerstle Park.

German Jews, they considered themselves and were in fact among San Francisco's elite. And here one should note there has been through the years a much narrower gulf between affluent Jews and Gentiles in San Francisco than in some other American cities, thanks in part to the almost complete lack of an Orthodox component in the Jewish community.

But among prominent Jews coming in many cases from Bavaria the notion of Eastern European Jews' "inferiority" died hard. J. B. Levison's father, Mark, had married a woman from the frowned-on East, and add to that the fact that financial problems had forced J. B. to drop out of Lowell High, then as now a prestigious school. So it was something of an uphill swim to get the senior Gerstles' permission for their precious, luxuriously reared, next-to-last child to marry such a "poor" man as young Levison.

But Alice saw his possibilities.

At the time of the verdant San Rafael wedding of J. B. and Alice in 1896 the young man—well, he was already thirty-four—was working as marine secretary for Fireman's Fund Insurance. By March 1902, when the couple moved into the by no means unimpressive 2420 Pacific, he was second vice president.

After the '06 disaster J. B. figured out how to salvage the company and pay off claims against it and soon he persuaded the company to write auto insurance, the first company to do so nationwide. Not surprising that J. B. became president of Fireman's Fund in 1917. He retired as chairman of the board in 1937.

J. B. had a civic life as well. An amateur flute player, he served on the board of the San Francisco Symphony and the Opera and he ran the music program for the 1915 Panama-Pacific International Exposition, visiting artists to which included the pianist Paderewski, the composer Saint-Saens and nothing less than the full Boston Symphony under the demonic Karl Muck.

(Incidentally, when Arthur's great-aunt, the celebrated pianist Fannie Bloomfield Zeisler, gave her fiftieth-anniversary concert in Chicago's Orchestra Hall in 1925, among those sending congratulations was a member of the Gerstle family in San Francisco).

Alice Gerstle Levison was involved in good works as well and presided over the Mt. Zion Hospital Auxiliary and the Emanu-El Residence Club. In '06 she opened her house to suddenly homeless relatives and friends, and she even allowed Fireman's Fund to conduct business there for a while. During World War I she was with the Red Cross.

And when she was in her ninth and tenth decades—by then the Beatles had come along, and jet travel—she was taking painting lessons...

No. 36

2475 Pacific

A Utopian Farmhouse

*L*ike a proper little lady "of a certain age" the Leale house at 2475 Pacific has left a mysterious trail of clues making it difficult to pinpoint the date it first saw the light of day in this—or nearly this—location. But almost certainly it's one of the oldest houses still standing in San Francisco.

Or perhaps one should say sitting. Set well above the street, but not rising very high from its perch, it almost seems enthroned. Surrounded by open space, impeccably maintained, it remains a contrast to everything else on its urban, upscale block, including the relatively conventional houses of the Gerstle girls almost opposite. Call it a utopian farmhouse planted in the big city.

Although it looks and probably is very old, the fact is, much of what one sees from the street is later than Victorian and the house is bigger than it looks, with a full basement behind the front shrubbery and an extension deep into the lot.

The entry porch, right-side bay windows and rear extension were added between 1899 and 1913, if one goes by the less-than-annual fire insurance underwriters' maps that show the "footprints" of buildings. Historians Gary Goss and William Kostura have narrowed the date to 1904 when the additions, they say, were designed by William Curlett, architect of the Phelan, Shreve and Citizens Savings buildings downtown, not to mention our Old House No. 12 at 2701 Pierce.

Curlett carefully grafted popular Colonial Revival elements onto the existing building: the porch has Roman Doric columns supporting a proper entablature capped with a Grecian pediment, and the dentil moldings here are also a Colonial Revival trademark, and probably the urns on the roofline as well. Collectors of architectural detail will note that the porch entablature and dentil molding are extended over the front windows.

The four windows looking onto Pacific Avenue, elegantly tall and narrow with arched tops, are a shape characteristic of the 1870s or even 1860s; they do not precisely match the stubbier, straight-topped window in the right-side bay that dates from 1904.

The "original" building is shown on fire insurance maps to have been a simple 33-by-44-foot rectangle approached by a straight flight of steps a bit left of center. At the back there were a couple of lean-to additions on the right, and a porch on the left.

The main house was probably just four rooms—a rectangle, one fantasizes, that dreamt of evolving into an octagon! The forehead, so to speak, of 2475 as currently seen, with those nine scrolled brackets, the paneling and cornice as in a house of the 1870s or so, was probably present from the beginning, whenever that was.

The family who added the porch, and owned and occupied the house from 1886 to 1964(!), were the Leales, as in Captain John Leale who tells in his *Recollections of a Tule Sailor* about his thirty-four years as a ferry boat captain. But if the house is very old, as we suspect, someone must have lived in it before Captain Leale bought it on March 16, 1886.

The seller to Leale was Martha G. Charles, a widow who had bought 2475 on May 8, 1878, when her husband was still alive: he was Henry Asa Charles, a stockbroker and mining secretary born in New York about 1823. Selling to Mrs. Charles in '78 was one Richard Perry, with the price tag of $3,500 including house and lot, and that's as far back as the trail is clear...

No Perry was ever listed living or working on the 2400 block of Pacific. I've checked a list of real estate by location back through 1868 without result and this suggests that the elusive Mr. Perry was an absentee owner from, well, I'm not sure which year until 1878.

The only Richard Perry listed in directories through all these years was a drayman or teamster who lived the whole time on Austin Street, the alley between Pine and Bush, Van Ness and Octavia. He could, one supposes, have owned the house and rented it out but he doesn't seem on paper like the right Perry.

Another Richard Perry, a carpenter, is a more likely suspect, although he wasn't listed in the 1860s. Conceivably this carpenter Perry owned the property and built the house.

By looks it could have been built new for Martha Charles in '78—or it could have been built in the 1860s. A Coast Guard survey of 1867 shows no structure at all on this lot, but there was one about the same size just behind the rear property line. Was the house moved? That sort of thing happened. And if we say yes, the house was indeed moved, well, that would give "closure" to the maddening mystery of 2475 Pacific.

Thankfully there's no mystery about Captain Leale. In more than one hundred and twenty-five thousand round trips across San Francisco Bay he logged over a million miles of passages scheduled at eighteen minutes' duration. Not bad compared to present-day on-bridge commute time.

The captain's daughter Marian described him as follows: "Slight of stature, with sharp and piercing dark brown eyes, severe and well-groomed beard and black hair...(he was) punctilious, spartan, commanding, demanding the best of his fellow men at all times and bringing it forth."

Not a captain of industry like Mortimer Fleishhacker or J. B. Levison across the street, this spartan Leale, but captain of a boat! The fluctuations of nocturnal and matutinal waves were, I suspect, more soothing at times than those of the stock market downtown. In retirement at 2475 Pacific, Leale entertained friends at the back of the garden in a replica of a captain's cabin built of parts salvaged from various vessels, porthole included.

And that cabin could still be found on the property many years after the good mariner passed on.

No. 37

2505 Pacific

This Queen Anne Takes the Plunge

This is the first house in a tract—four Queen Annes in a row, 2505-07-09-11 Pacific. But, I can hear you saying after eyeing these stolid but charming gingerbread rhapsodies, how can they constitute a tract when the houses don't look exactly alike, and they're not small and ugly, like "ticky-tacky boxes."

Ah, it's a question of economics. A developer acquires, as one did here on Pacific, a piece of land big enough for several houses—and they can be rather posh, actually—and he builds them all at once, saving money with mass production and one-shot marketing. The cost-cutting quite simply enables him to undersell the contractor who builds only one house at a time.

Usually in a tract the cost cuts do result in look-alike houses with, at best, a limited number of models to choose from. Model A's floor plan might for instance be the same as Model B's but its mirror image; or Models C and D would be similar to A and B but with an extra room tacked on, or slightly different trim.

Now, since the essence of Queen Anne is variety, this means Q.A. tract houses don't look so alike as to suggest the cartoon drunk coming home late, confronting on his street a sea of copycat houses and entering, or trying to enter, the wrong one.

But you can expect, here on Pacific Avenue and elsewhere, to encounter the same height and proportions.

The tract under discussion demonstrates tract qualities in the recurrent triangular roof ends, the nearly continuous cornice line at the bottom of all four roofs, the deeply recessed front door and the painted shingles. But it's only the first and third houses that have towers—at different levels—and a fishbone pattern at roof's end. Only the second and fourth boast floral tracery in doorway pediments. And there are other rather major differences.

2505 Pacific, the titular house of this article, was top-of-the-line, the one where the developer himself lived. Notice here how the designer carries a striking diagonal from the crown of the house down two stories in an extended plunge that's not repeated on any of the sibling houses. Fascinating! In fact, the house's whole play of triangle vs. rectangle and projecting vs. receding gesture is delightful to behold. This is what Queen Anne is all about.

That clever designer of 2505 through 2511 Pacific was a William F. Smith who practiced architecture in San Francisco from about 1878 to 1910. His client was named James Stewart and seems to have been retired or simply had money—no occupation is listed in directories of the time. It was on June 22, 1889 that he bought the land for the four houses, and they were ready for occupancy in '90.

Unlike most developers, Stewart didn't sell the houses but kept them as rentals—so, in a manner of speaking, he had a horizontal apartment house. 2505 he shared with a tenant named Alonzo Hamilton, a mining expert from New York state whose household included wife, daughter, son-in-law, grandchild and three young servants from, respectively, Switzerland, Massachusetts and Ireland. Now which of these made the pastries?

A deeper question or two…How is it, one wonders, that the south side of Pacific Avenue's 2500 block is still home to so many Queen Annes—there are more than Mr. Smith's quartet here—when so many were demolished closer to Van Ness Avenue and downtown? To some extent it must be a case of families holding onto their property tenaciously.

And then, why is it the south sides of the 2400 and 2500 blocks weigh in with fewer ultra-grand houses than the north sides? Well, the grander houses are generally a little later in date.

If you're walking west on the south side of Pacific several houses beyond the Smith tract, note that the tower of 2519, designed by the distinguished firm of Percy and Hamilton, echoes that of Mr. Smith's 2509. We mention in passing the urbane 2519 with its undulating bays and eyebrows-in-the-gable not only for its architectural felicity but because its first resident, from 1892, was one of the most despised men in California.

This was John C. Stubbs, third vice president and traffic manager of the Southern Pacific Railroad. Stubbs is the man who set railroad freight charges at all the traffic would bear, so burdening farmers that some turned violent at Mussel Slough, inspiring Frank Norris' novel *The Octopus*.

No. 38

2516 Pacific

House and English Country Garden

*W*henever I pass this quiet Tudor Revival house I stop to smell the roses hanging over the little fence. The whole ensemble is like a country estate slid gently into the middle of a semicrowded city block. In contrast to its neighbors, 2516 seems a ground-hugger and rather sprawling, with a baby Sissinghurst of a garden that almost ranks as equal partner with the house itself.

The spacious lot size here is thanks to two houses having been taken down to make way for this one. The close-to-the-ground effect is rather an illusion caused by the unusual width for a house in this area, the uninterrupted sweep of roof—like but so much unlike a barn!—and a low basement as well. The English country garden effect stems from the carefully tended lawn and roses, and their openness to the observer.

(A shame that the garden was recently reduced somewhat in size to provide entry to a garage.)

The Tudor Revival style and utter English-ishness of 2516 and grounds were intentional as the couple who commissioned the house were Anglophiles as well as very conservative. Their conservatism, however, did not extend to committing to the expense of fireproof brick construction through and through; here the brick is a mere veneer on a wooden frame.

The author of 2516, Lewis Hobart, also put brick veneer on a similarly quiet downtown building of steel and concrete at Taylor and Post, the Bohemian Club. Hobart was, of course, one of San Francisco's greatest Beaux Arts architects: we met him in connection with the Sidney Ehrman mansion at the end of Broadway (Old House No. 30). Hobart's most famous work is Grace Cathedral on Nob Hill; he also designed its companions on Taylor Street, Diocesan House and the 1912 Cathedral House recently torn down.

2516 Pacific relates to the cathedral close not only through the name of Lewis Hobart but because its owner, Lydia Monteagle, donated the funds for Diocesan House as well as the cathedral's California Street portal. Doubtless she selected Hobart for her Pacific Avenue home in 1921 because of his connection to Grace.

And don't you think 2516 with its Tudor circumflexes and curvy "coat hanger" window surrounds has an ecclesiastical look, as if it were a part of some Trollopian close that floated onto a purely residential block? Could this have been a bit of an in-joke on Hobart's part?

In any event, Lydia Monteagle was born in California in 1866, daughter of New Englanders Timothy and Mary Paige who owned a lot of agricultural land in Fresno County and other real estate. She inherited a considerable fortune, and kept it separate from the money, not exactly insubstantial, of her husband, Louis Monteagle.

Lydia married Louis in 1886 when he was cashier of the Fulton Iron Works. A Scotsman some eleven years older than his bride, he'd arrived in San Francisco about 1879 and he spent his remaining fifty-four years quietly managing the respective portfolios et al. of husband and wife, as well as dealing with the attendant business, social and religious responsibilities of the pair. He was also an insurance agent, a director of the Spring Valley Water Company until it became the city's water department, a member of the San Francisco Symphony's Board of Governors, and a very active layman in the Episcopal Church.

And the Monteagles lived for more than twenty years in one of the two houses originally on the site of 2516.

Lydia was the reigning force in the family, Louis the administrator. She was intelligent, aggressive, and well able to get her own way. She has always been lauded for her good works, and she made sure she got credit for them.

Judging by her will she wanted control even from the grave, even over her sons' marriages! Her favorite charities were Grace Cathedral, of course; St. Luke's Church at Van Ness and Clay, where she contributed significantly to the construction budget and there are Monteagle stained glass windows; and St. Luke's Hospital in the Mission, where there's a Monteagle wing. Yes, she had her reward.

No. 39

2520 Pacific

From Faville to Farr

*B*elieve it or not, 2520 Pacific is two houses in one. It was originally designed by Bliss and Faville in 1905, only to undergo a radical transformation by Albert Farr a quarter-century later. It wasn't always French Eclectic.

Piecing together evidence from historical materials, one sees that the rolling entrance arch on the right side, and the exterior staircase behind it, leading to a new and recessed entry at the second level, were all part of the circa 1930 alterations. Furthermore, as a Sanborn fire insurance map indicates, this house which appears to the contemporary eye as stuccoed was originally "brick first story, brick veneer second and third."

Veneer is an outer coating for appearance only. Now, nobody would go to the expense of installing brick veneer on a house if they were going to stucco it—enough said about the original design intention here.

So...it's extremely likely, I think, that 2520 in the original Bliss and Faville concept was a brick Colonial Revival affair, rather like the Fleishhacker Sr. house a block east at 2418 Pacific. In brick it would have had its present raised quoins at the corners, and the same height, and the same window sill brackets and keystones would have been part of the package as well, in, of course, a material and color contrasting with the brick.

The currently visible mansard roof and arched dormer windows would fit either the Bliss/Faville or the Farr design, the latter commissioned by new owners who wanted a French country—read elegant country—look, but research reveals that a cornice originally projected below the roof.

A beautiful entry door was originally front and center downstairs, slightly below sidewalk level, inside a portico and columns. The house's main rooms had always been on the second floor, so putting the new entrance at that height à la Farr required little change in interior arrangement. The 1905 first floor became a basement, and scarcely an ordinary one to judge by outward appearances, these involving extension of the ground floor form to include a balustraded terrace. And don't forget the unusually high and monumental, almost operatic garage door. Where is the carriage to whisk Manon to Paris?

Meanwhile the lovely entrance arch rising at the right from teardrop side-blocks sets the tone for Farr's delightful composition, a composition that leaves Bliss and Faville somewhat if not entirely erased. Urns, stucco and shutters complete the *French* appearance.

Well, while certainly not flamboyant, this Farr house—a Farr house, one should say, when he got his hands on it—has more flourish and pizazz than his 2660 Scott (Old House No. 14), which seems to have been designed for slightly more conservative clients.

At all events, the versatile Mr. Farr has to his credit not only Jack London's Wolf House at Glen Ellen but the gracious and commanding Benbow Inn, a wonderful period piece on the way to Eureka: here at lunchtime one stirs tinkling ice cubes in tall glasses of tea to the tune of a live flutist while earnest college kids wait tables overlooking a brook.

Farr is also known for Shingle Style houses in Berkeley and Belvedere, and on San Francisco's Russian Hill at 1020 Broadway and 1629 Taylor. After 1920 he tended to produce more formal houses in one Revival style or another, houses in the East Bay enclave of Piedmont and down the Peninsula at Atherton.

Farr's clients for 2520 Pacific were James H. and Sophie Schwabacher, who bought the house in May 1929. He was a partner in the stock exchange firm Schwabacher and Company, also the president of Schwabacher-Frey, the printers and stationers who until fairly recently had a large store in their building on Market Street facing Grant.

Their son James went into music and became an outstanding recitalist specializing in intimate lieder, and a respected teacher as well.

It was Sophie Schwabacher—a brave and ebullient lady, by the way, to those who had the good fortune to know her—who opted for "French Provincial." It took Farr and the contractors Jacks and Irvine until 1932 to get their Frenchification ready for the Schwabachers to move in (think of all the endless remodeling jobs visible in Pacific Heights today, great guttings and so forth, with whole football teams of workmen), and they waited even longer for just the right decorator, but it was worth the wait because the senior Schwabachers lived at 2520 happily ever after.

And the original owners? The first client here was John D. Spreckels, oldest son of sugar king Claus and brother of the Laughtonesque Adolph with connections to Old House No. 9 (grand) and No. 61 (grander). J. D. had 2520 built for his younger daughter, Lily, who'd recently married Harry Holbrook, scion of Holbrook, Merrill and Stetson, the gas stove manufacturers and metal wholesalers.

Alas, the beautiful Lily divorced Harry in 1918—their daughter was seven—claiming cruelty and "intemperance." She said he'd threatened her with a gun, locked her in her room, been constantly drunk and would insult her in public. Sounds like a movie.

The Social Register responded by dropping the husband but keeping the wife, even after she married a San Diego doctor in the twenties. Before the divorce she'd spent a lot of time with her parents at Coronado, the posh watering place adjacent to San Diego—her father had a lot of business in that area—and that, it seems, is where her heart traveled some years before she sold 2520 Pacific.

No. 40

2600 Pacific

Mortimer Fleishhacker Jr. Lived Here

2600 Pacific Avenue hardly looks as "old" as 1936, which is when it first saw the light and may have stirred a bit of envy in the creaky innards of a Queen Anne or two in the neighborhood. But it looks very William Wilson Wurster—in its quietly modern design, its appropriateness to the site, its upscale casualness and livability.

And that white-rinsed brick exterior is, of course, a Wurster trademark.

Founder of what's often and a bit over-academically called the Second Bay Region Tradition (the first having been created by Messrs. Maybeck, Polk, and Coxhead, Julia Morgan and friends), Wurster did not as a matter of fact think primarily in terms of architectural style. Which is a paradox, we must admit, because a Wurster house is usually unmistakeably his.

At all events, what came first for him was catering to the lifestyles of the residential clients who claimed the bulk of his professional attention. He'd question them at length before even setting pencil to sketch pad.

And what pleasant living situations he'd provide! Usually a Wurster house has a lot of glass connecting the indoors to a lovely garden, a very special courtyard or a view well worth looking at. Access to the outdoors he repeatedly facilitated by putting the main floor at ground level—some fifty-five years, in the case of 2600 Pacific, before the Americans with Disabilities Act.

At 2600 Pacific the house's shoved-back L-shaped plan gives birth to a plant-friendly south/east garden which is nicely sheltered from cold westerly winds (a San Francisco summertime specialty, this) and creates behind its attractive walls a feeling of green space entirely unconnected with the paved world outside.

The client here, Mortimer Fleishhacker Jr., grew up in a much more formal house a block and a half east; that would be the 2418 Pacific (Old House No. 35) we encountered several articles back. Probably 2600 for him was more a reminder of vacations spent at Green Gables, the Fleishhackers' artistic but relaxing estate at Woodside.

A UC Berkeley graduate of 1927, M. F. Jr. founded a company that manufactured household chemicals. He was also involved in lumber, coal, taxi and billboard companies in addition to managing an increasing share of his father's many interests. And he was a U.S. Navy veteran of World War II.

Fleishhacker Jr. loved his city and served it well. At different times he was president of Congregation Emanu-El, Mt. Zion Hospital and the San Francisco Planning Commission. But of greater interest to the public at large, perhaps, would be his presidency from 1955 to 1970 of the new public broadcasting station KQED-TV, with the concept of individual memberships being put into practice during his watch, and his being instrumental in getting the American Conservatory Theater to settle in San Francisco and operate on a solid business basis.

M. F. Jr.'s creativity extended to choosing a wife not blue-blooded enough to altogether please his parents. Janet Choynski was also a native San Franciscan, her father a lawyer, her grandfather a crusading editor, and her uncle a prizefighter, yet. Her activities—which must have won her some points with her in-laws—included, among others in a diverse list, the International Hospitality Center, the Salesian Boys' Club and the San Francisco Museum of Modern Art. The Italian American community was especially close to her heart because she'd spent much time in Italy before her marriage.

The Fleishhackers of 2600 Pacific had a good marriage. And their town house was such a success that one of their children later added a Wurster house to the Woodside estate.

No. 41

2421 Pierce

Mr. Irvine's Pied-à-terre

*A*cross from the junior Fleishhackers', this corner house at Pierce and Pacific clings modestly to its hillside, encasing its ample interior in long and austere horizontals with no more windows than necessary. From the corner you don't even notice the almost inglenooky entrance, which hides from the street along the uphill (south) side of the house.

But you are quite likely to notice the gentle four-slope roof and the wide, thin, brandy-flask chimney, the squashed capital pilasters, the overscale brackets with two-tiered scrolls, the projecting upper story with intricately X-ed false balconies, the restrained Tudor detailing of subdivided window panes.

For all its escaping the walking tourist's eye, the front door is an expanse of paneled golden oak with double brackets and leaded side windows. Above is more leaded glass, lighting a two-story entrance hall with beamed ceiling, tall fireplace, balconies and more golden oak paneling, all this highly reminiscent of H. H. Richardson's residential work although the architect of this house, dated approximately 1903, is Edgar Mathews.

Each room of 2421 Pierce, including the living room that occupies the whole Pierce Street frontage, boasts individual ceiling treatment. Photos of the interior published in 1905 also show claw-footed tables, uncluttered floors, meager upholstery, broad fireplaces. Some sort of spartan machismo here, would you say? Well, Mathews' client, none less than the James Irvine after whom the southern California city Irvine is named, was said to be a stubborn, willful business man: perhaps this characterization fits the gracious but rather austere 2421.

Or was the meager upholstery dictated somehow by the new and oaky Early English look Mathews specialized in and which won for him with its brackets, scrolls and Tudor X-ings quite a number of Pacific Heights clients?

Edgar Mathews was the son of the respected Oakland architect Julius Mathews, he had an architect brother named Walter and, rather better known, a painter sibling, Arthur Mathews, whose murals adorn the State Capitol in Sacramento, San Francisco's Mechanics Institute, the Curran Theater and the Lane Medical Library at 2395 Sacramento.

The exceedingly well-heeled Mr. Irvine (1867–1947) owned the third of Orange County known as the Irvine Ranch—one hundred and five thousand acres that is—which he ruled with an iron hand. Cattle and grain were his business. His forty-niner father had bought the land in the 1860s and his descendants profit from it today, even after donating the Irvine campus of the University of California.

Born in San Francisco, James Irvine kept his Pierce Street residence for the rest of his life, either because he preferred his native city or merely as a place to hang his hat when in town for business or a social function.

His hat rack was probably a miniature work of art.

No. 42

2698 Pacific

Vesta Interest

The light-filled rotunda fronting and acting as focal point of this Classical Revival mansion doesn't actually imitate the Temple of Vesta in the Roman Forum; its sources seem at once older (in the exotic columns) and newer (the coffered Renaissance ceiling). But surely Roman are the house's rounded colonnade and low-pitched conical roof.

The round Roman temple form has a certain history in San Francisco. The noted architect Albert Pissis is responsible for two examples, the long-lost 1884 building that showed off the city's "Panorama," and the entrance to the Hibernia Bank Building at Market, Jones and McAllister—a building Arthur says he couldn't help noticing when, as a ten-year-old, he frequently took in Saturday afternoon movies at the cinema palazzos nearby.

Willis Polk weighed in too with a couple of examples, the Gibbs mansion at 2622 Jackson (Old House No. 59) and the water temple at Sunol in the lower East Bay.

2698 Pacific put its best Roman foot forward under the aegis of Newsom and Newsom, that's Samuel Newsom of the famous Newsom brothers who did the Carson House in Eureka and his son Sidney—a combination we've met before (Old House No. 25). Papa Newsom worked in several different styles current and popular during his long career, the original brothers' motto having been "up to date architecture." I find 2698 one of his (and his son's) best productions: the temple portico is beautiful, the symmetry of the house, almost a cube, satisfies, and the siting is perfect.

Note too that the smooth light-colored trim, from portico to corner quoins to window surrounds and Classical cornice, contrasts very effectively with the dark gray and heavy-textured stucco that gives 2698 its gritty (rather elegantly gritty!) complexion. Successive owners since the house was built in 1904 seem to have followed the original intent for this "pebble dash" stucco which was: *Never paint it*.

The first owner of 2698 was Julius J. Mack, another of those San Franciscans who made a fortune or two elsewhere, then built a mansion in Pacific Heights in which to enjoy the fruits of his business genius and/or luck.

Born in New York City in 1853, Mack learned financial speculation while a Wall Street errand boy. Obviously he was a quick learner: after landing in Visalia in California's Central Valley at the theoretically tender age of nineteen he quickly graduated from a bookkeeping job to organizing a local bank that prospered. At age 27 he came up to San Francisco with his profits and organized a wholesale drug firm in which his brother Adolph was a key player as well. The story goes that when J. J.'s speculations got the firm in trouble they were bailed out by Adolph's father-in-law, a founder of the Alaska Commercial Company.

Next, J. J. retreated to Bakersfield where he and Philip N. Lilienthal, also with San Francisco connections, formed the Bank of Bakersfield. Soon J. J. was speculating with a farmer named J. M. Keith in Kern County oil, and the rest you can guess: this of course was the jackpot. By 1901 Julius J. Mack was back in San Francisco, president of Imperial Oil, and ready to build his dream house. No, he was not about to settle in Bakersfield (although there are, it should be noted, attractive upscale houses in that oil-land city).

Meanwhile brother Adolph settled into the big "pebble dash" house just to the east of 2698 Pacific, a be-scrolled fortress sans portico but boasting a lovely side vestibule with etched glass and some racy rococo-ish window surrounds at basement level.

Interlude

Across Scott Street from 2698 Pacific is one of the few outright "Meds" (Mediterranean-inspired, that is) in Pacific Heights, 2700 Pacific. Scarcely a landmark, it is however a very satisfying essay in what might be termed architectural civility. All Andalusian white and terra-cotta tile, it sits on its corner comfortably, without airs, like a house imported up the coast from that residential nirvana Santa Barbara. Dated 1929, it's the work of Burlingame-based John Norberg, whose practice was mainly devoted to clients in that and neighboring suburban locales down the Peninsula.

Continue walking west on Pacific a half block and a gem of a different sort presents itself, that massive near-steamship of a vaguely Richardsonian Queen Anne/Colonial Revival mansion answering to the address 2724 Pacific Avenue. Enjoy here the elaborated symphony of fenestration dreamed up by its architect, the not very well-known E. A. Hermann. Date this one 1894. Its most distinguished resident was the French countess who helped guide the fortunes of the City of Paris department store downtown on Union Square.

—Arthur Bloomfield

No. 43

2799 Pacific

The Uninhabited House

The Ellinwood mansion at 2799 Pacific, a textbook Colonial Revival hunk complete with what was originally a barn with "eyelid" dormer and hay door, came for many years as close as any residence in this series to the category Haunted House.

Ghost-inhabited or not, this great ship of a house which stayed in the same family's hands for slightly over a hundred years remained empty for a full half-century—while a family member lived one house down Pacific—and toward the end of its slumber, in the 1970s, it resembled nothing so much as a Sleeping Almost Beauty, a house with fine detail but in serious need of a modern tricolored paint job to give it some life and charm.

Dating from 1893-94, 2799 is one of the earliest houses built on the particular Pacific Heights crest centered at and around the intersection of Pacific Avenue and Divisadero. A cable car lumbering up Pacific had paved the way.

It's a very balustradey affair, this house—note the angled or rounded balustrades on at least three levels, right up to widow's walk altitude—and that comes as no surprise to history buffs when they're told the architect of the Ellinwood mansion was J. Eugene Freeman, author of Oakland's similarly endowed Dunsmuir House, that imposing landmark standing in its meadow at the foot of the East Bay hills.

By the way, the Connecticut-born Freeman lived in Pacific Heights, not far from his Ellinwood creation, and achieved the age of ninety-five.

The Pacific Avenue elevation of 2799 boasts an elaborate central portico accessed asymmetrically from the west. Above it a pair of oval windows in pointy surrounds suggest inflated hand mirrors transferred miraculously from some giant dressing table. Meanwhile the entire west elevation running down Divisadero toward Jackson Street is supported by a stone retaining wall above which sits the "barn," which has graduated (new owners have elaborately remodeled the property) to a trendier, less rustic status.

All this summit luxe was designed for Welshman Dr. Charles Ellinwood (1834–1917), a Civil War surgeon who was an early member of the U.S. Public Health Service and founded the Marine Hospital in the Presidio. In due course he became professor of physiology and later the president of Cooper Medical College, the predecessor of Stanford Medical School in the Dickensian Gothic structure at Sacramento and Webster Streets that was only demolished about 1970.

Even in its later, jet-age days Cooper was a spooky building of twisted corridors, bereft of needless ornament: why, the office of the head of the department of medicine carried no nameplate, only a sign denoting FIRE ESCAPE

In the wake of the '06 earthquake and fire Dr. Ellinwood was burned out of the office he maintained downtown for his private practice. As a result, the basement billiard room at 2799 became the waiting room for his patients, who were forced in some cases to take that cute little cable car out Pacific Avenue for their appointments.

Billiard aficionados please note: world championships were held at least once at this address. And another interesting bit: originally the large garden to the east of the house contained three nineteenth-century specimen trees, one of them a gift from Queen Victoria.

I'm not sure what Dr. Ellinwood would think of the lap pool for urban swimming now installed in the old garden area—but, come to think of it, if he was into billiards he might have enjoyed a few laps before packing his briefcase and cabling down to Webster Street to preside over the top medical school in the West.

No. 44

2520 Divisadero

An Abstract Expressionist Lived Here

*M*rs. John Walter was a patrician hostess, a highly accomplished bookbinder, a friend of photographer Ansel Adams and the fine printer Ed Grabhorn. And she had, I think, the most beautiful female voice I ever heard, rich, dark, with a velvet buzz and a certain lilt to it. She had three daughters, and two of them when newly married and still in their early twenties were established in a pair of Tudor Revival houses nestled against each other high on Divisadero Street.

The more northerly of these houses, built in 1933, was 2520 Divisadero, and the young wife and mother-to-be living therein—Nell Sinton—would become a well-known Abstract Expressionist painter.

No, 2520 Divisadero doesn't seem like your typical house for an Abstract Expressionist, and in early middle age feisty Nell Sinton did leave this capitalists' corner of Pacific Heights for Russian Hill—not for a funky studio by any means but to a neighborhood which with its curving cornices, conspicuous Arts and Crafts presence, an art school complete with Lombardian tower and cloister-type patio, and a house, too, that belonged to Mrs. Robert Louis Stevenson, has a somewhat more Bohemian flavor than its august neighbor to the west. Upper Bohemian of course.

Nell Sinton had already studied at that Russian Hill school, the California School of Fine Arts (now the Art Institute) before settling into her posh digs on Divisadero. It was only when she sold the house in 1955 that she began the work for which she was most noted.

In 1981 Mills College held a thirty-year Nell Sinton retrospective exhibition dividing her still-active career into several periods. The earliest works, from the 1940s, were naïve and charming interiors and landscapes. From the 1960s came the Abstract Expressionist paintings, voluptuous, "loosely formal" compositions exploding in riots of color and exposing, said *Art Week*, Sinton-the-poet at her best. Next came her figurative phase, somewhat in the manner of David Park and Richard Diebenkorn. Then there were small mixed-media constructions and, in the late 1970s, a *Garden Party* series thick with social satire.

Not your generic Pacific Heights matron stuff!

And so, at age seventy, Nell Walter Sinton had refused to grow stale, working her way through new mediums and styles and telling an interviewer, "I find landscapes in human bodies and vice versa." Coming full circle, but with new power, she had recently turned to buoyant watercolor studies reminiscent, superficially at least, of her painting from the 1940s.

And what of her husband, Stanley Sinton Jr., considered "one of the quiet stalwarts" of the city. As leader of SPUR, San Francisco Planning and Urban Research, he was at the center of the campaign for Proposition H which approved two thousand units of low-cost public housing in 1968, and three years later he spearheaded SPUR's fight against the Alvin Duskin initiative to clamp a six-story height limit on new building.

The John Walter family was among the three dozen elite Jewish families who came to San Francisco in pioneer days and quickly made fortunes in clothing, dry goods, produce marketing, wood, paper, Alaskan development, etc. They all socialized together and, in a remarkable genealogical spaghetti tangle, frequently intermarried. Most of them had come from Bavaria, the town of Rechendorf for instance, which was home to the Hellman, Haas and Walter clans.

Stanley Sinton Jr. was from a similar background. Until the anti-German hatreds of the First World War, his family's name had been Sinsheimer, with various members in grain, beans, crockery and toys. Stanley's uncle Edgar also married a Walter, and his uncle Henry married a Koshland. Joining his father-in-law's business, Stanley wound up as president of D. N. and E. Walter, wholesalers of rugs, bedding and other decorators' supplies: the company still exists and long had its store in Jackson Square at the corner of Jackson and Montgomery.

Nell Sinton and her sisters, who would become Marjorie Bissinger and Carol Sinton, grew up in an ornate and rambling late Victorian that sat (if Arthur remembers correctly) behind a large palm tree at the southeast corner of Clay and Buchanan Streets, just across from the long-gone rose garden and tennis courts which were part of the nicely scaled Stanford Medical School complex now overrun by the architecturally Brutalistic—and noisy!—California Pacific Medical Center.

In late middle age the three sisters' long-widowed mother would move to a very up-to-date William Wurster house on Russian Hill where her elegant profile could regularly be spotted by passersby as she sat reading in her picture window looking down on Ghirardelli Square.

But we must backtrack to 1933 and Divisadero Street where two of the girls were settling in. While the young Bissingers' Tudor Revival at 2500 is credited to Willis Polk and Company (Polk himself having died nine years earlier), the equally youthful Sintons' 2520 was the work of Polk and Company alumnus Angus McSweeney.

Born in Pittsburgh in 1900 and trained at the University of Oregon,

McSweeney was with the California State Architect's Office for three years before coming to San Francisco in 1924. Later work includes Park Merced Apartments in 1951 and Commodore Stockton Elementary School in Chinatown, and in 1970–71 his firm was supervising architect for the new St. Mary's Cathedral designed by Pietro Belluschi and Pier Luigi Nervi.

Not surprisingly, McSweeney's 1933 house on Divisadero was more conservative in style than his buildings of a generation later. Tudor Revival as can be, 2520 has all the earmarks of the style: fake timbering with brick infill, steeply pitched roof, cross gable, groups of tall, narrow, multi-paned casement windows, overhanging second story, and a Tudor arch of course!

No. 45

2800 Pacific

Coxhead at Play

2800 Pacific Avenue, a Georgian gem designed by Ernest Coxhead in 1899, shows off this maverick architect's love of toying with scale and contrast.

At the doorway those huge curls on the broken pediment and the standout striped pillars are way too prominent by conservative architectural standards for the apparent size of the building. Same for the curved pediments over two windows and the one remaining roof dormer—there were four originally.

And note the fearless contrasts between the smoothness of the house's dark brick and the roughness of the corner quoins; between the receding roof on the house's left side and the jutting dormer; between the various planes of the front and side walls.

As if these weren't distinguishing features enough, 2800 carves a special place for itself by sitting above a grassy mound rising some altitude above the brick retaining wall at sidewalk level.

The original owner of 2800 Pacific was one Sarah Spooner, a wealthy art collector who had arrived recently from Philadelphia. Certainly no expense was spared in the design and construction of her house. Imagine the paintings that hung in this super Coxhead. Well, Ms. Spooner was not long on the scene,

because by the time of the '06 earthquake and fire Matilda and Herman Shainwald were in residence. He was head of a large real estate company, Shainwald Buckbee, which later evolved into the prominent Buckbee Thorne and Co.

Then in 1914 the property came into the hands of John A. McGregor and remained in the same family for fifty-three years. A Canadian of Scottish ancestry, McGregor had worked for U.S. Shipbuilding in the East and became in due course treasurer of Bethlehem Steel Corporation. When Bethlehem's shipbuilding division bought San Francisco's old Union Iron Works in 1905, retaining that name, McGregor soon became its president.

Union Iron Works had been launched in 1849 as the foundry of the Donahue Brothers to whom the Mechanics Monument at Bush, Battery and Market Streets was dedicated. After a profitable spell on First Street south of Market, and with new owners Henry and Irving Scott, the company moved to Twentieth and Illinois, aka Pier 70, in the 1880s, the better here to build ships. Their huge brick machine shop and administration building are at this location still, along with later buildings put up by Bethlehem.

The plant built ships for World Wars

I and II, and ship repair still goes on there.

Now, John McGregor was very civic minded and sat on the city's Park Commission (1912–18) and the Board of Supervisors (1922–26), and was also involved with the Symphony, the Boy Scouts, Calvary Presbyterian Church, etc., etc. And he loved baseball. His stage-struck son Campbell McGregor, who inhabited 2800 in the 1940s, adored opera. And he adored it so much he bankrolled a whole opera company, and appeared in one of its productions of *La Bohème* as a Café Momus waiter in the second act.

But that appearance was but the merry tip of an iceberg of unsymphonic dissension in San Francisco's operatic world, with this McGregor squarely in the middle of it.

A bit of history. The year 1948 saw the resurgence of low-budget home-financed opera in San Francisco, with "Dollar Opera" veteran Arturo Casiglia in musical charge and McGregor conspicuous among his backers. Everybody was happy. The major league San Francisco Opera saw no competition in the relatively modest efforts of the New Pacific Opera Company, which would find new friends of opera with its wallet-friendly ticket prices.

By 1953 the Pacific was still playing, not surprisingly, to good houses, but its house was not in order. Came May 1 and it was reported that Casiglia was planning a

season in November while "a Pacific Opera Company under a board of directors whose president is Campbell McGregor" was planning its own season the following March.

The McGregor-headed board had offered Casiglia a one-year renewal of his contract with several conditions, one of them being that the directors would have control of the Pacific name. Casiglia insisted the name belonged to him, he had after all been using it for thirty years, but the bill-paying McGregor countered through his lawyer Angelo Scampini that it belonged to the estate of one of Casiglia's former backers, Hugo Newhouse, and was simply lent out.

What had happened, really, was that some feeling had developed on the McGregor-led board that Casiglia was on the provincial side as an artistic director. Dario Shindell, the ambitious company manager, wanted to hire big-time singers in the East, but only the low-budget-minded Casiglia could sign the contracts. Ah, a case of stars in some people's eyes and a squeeze play in the making.

But the little guy won a round. Judge Harry Neubarth ruled in favor of Casiglia and he went ahead on his own to mount a winter of '54 season. Then, crescendo! McGregor and Shindell announced plans for their season, the first of the Cosmopolitan Opera, to take place a month after the Pacific inning.

What transpired the winter of '54 was one of the more curious spectacles in American operatic history. It was tagged by columnists the "Siamese Twin Opera Season" or the "Two Round Opera Season." Enter first the Pacific with four performances at three dollars top, then the Cosmopolitan with six more at the same price. Both seasons opened with *La Traviata*, and local fixture Colin Harvey crossed party lines to appear as Benoit and Alcindoro in both companies' *La Bohème*.

But the Pacific was really finished. Casiglia died late in '54 as if on some operatic timetable, now that his low-budget territory had been successfully invaded—by his own people. And Shindell, evidently supported by McGregor, carried his ambitions into direct confrontation with the San Francisco Opera, staging seasons with very big operatic names, Milanov, Tucker, Vinay, etc., albeit skimpy productions, backing up these stars.

By 1960 Shindell was planning a season with the Five (!) Tenors of the day, Bjoerling, Tucker, Del Monaco, di Stefano and Bergonzi all lined up in a surrealistic row. How did he engage them? By promising fees double and triple those the world-class San Francisco Opera was willing to pay.

Surrealistic? Yes, it was all too much, and then, suddenly—in all likelihood because his old Pacific Heights friends

on the San Francisco Opera got to him, although the decision was also attributed to a "seer"—McGregor, who'd been single-handedly (single-walletly?) picking up seventy-thousand-dollar Cosmopolitan deficits, blew the whistle. No more money. And the company expired in a microsecond.

Interlude

A block west of the McGregor house notice the El Drisco at 2901 Pacific, a primarily residential hotel built in 1904 by the busy firm of Cunningham and Politeo at what was then the end of the Pacific Avenue cable car line. No such convenient public transportation exists today! The hotel long served, perhaps still does, as a sort of landing pad for families from the East and Midwest intending to settle in Pacific or Presidio Heights who had not yet selected a house or apartment for their permanent home.

And the El Drisco with its tucked-away location was the local base for Josef Krips when the cigar-chomping, Mozart-loving conductor from Vienna was musical director of the San Francisco Symphony in the 1960s. His little entourage included wife Mitzi, in delicate health, and the latter's companion (later Krips' wife), the Baroness Prohazka.

Interesting where Symphony directors have chosen to live. The beloved Pierre Monteux, whose basic home was in Maine, settled for his symphonic winter into a suite at the Fairmont where friends and colleagues would join him for chamber music sessions. Outside the hotel he walked his dog Fifi and nodded appreciatively to admirers riding the cable car up Nob Hill.

Edo de Waart, the young Dutchman of many wives (not simultaneous!) who took over the orchestra some years later, lived in a succession of apartment houses on or near Pacific Heights' Lafayette Park, a convenient mile from the Opera House where the orchestra played; one of his honeymoons was in a borrowed flat on Washington Street near Buchanan.

But Seiji Ozawa, as if to underline his remoteness and inscrutability, chose to buy a house as high up Twin Peaks as you can go.

—*Arthur Bloomfield*

No. 46

2974 Pacific

Hardly Hearst Castle

*O*ne famous architect has been missing from these articles. To find what work she did in Pacific Heights (which is where she lived, on a not especially posh block) I looked in Sara Holmes Boutelle's marvelous *Julia Morgan, Architect,* and up popped 2974 Pacific Avenue.

Which is nothing more, or less, than an apartment and garage, with the whole ground-floor front devoted to garage door!

Morgan is known today for San Simeon, William Randolph Hearst's amazing castle below Big Sur—a job, by the way, that the diminutive Morgan commuted to on weekends from her Victorian on Divisadero between Clay and Washington, four blocks from 2974 Pacific: she took the Lark, the night train favored by upscale businessmen and movie stars, being met in the wee hours at San Luis Obispo by a chauffered car provided by her client.

She is heralded today as the country's best and only hugely successful woman architect, a distinction she earned when a nice woman's occupation was "homemaker." So unthinkable were women architects a hundred years ago that the prestigious Ecole des Beaux-Arts in Paris had neglected to make a rule prohibiting them, and as a consequence, and thanks perhaps to a certain chivalrous curiosity on the part of the faculty higher-ups, she was accepted in 1898 as the school's first female student. Morgan was already UC Berkeley's first female engineering graduate.

So what was the supervisor of impressive Beaux Arts structures like the Berkeley campus' Greek Theater, Hearst Gym and Mining Building doing designing a mousy, woodsy little thing like 2974 Pacific? Well, that self-effacing side of Morgan's oeuvre is well heralded in Berkeley's more desirable residential enclaves where every tucked-in, brown-shingled, garden-complementing, wood-celebrating house is rumored to be either a Morgan or a Maybeck and some of them actually are.

The apartment and garage at 2974 Pacific were commissioned in 1916. The building responds to the apartment function with big upper windows facing south that are attractively underlined by flower boxes. To house internal combustion engines safely it's a brick structure. The whole ground floor, some 25 by 40 feet, is garage: space enough for at least six modern cars, perhaps nine in 1917 when the building was completed.

2974 Pacific also satisfies Morgan's Beaux Arts—inspired love of symmetry. Detailing is unobtrusive and rustically elegant: enjoy it in the wood casement windows and the paneled and glazed garage doors that slide open (or once did: the lack of exterior hardware indicates automation). Notice as well symmetrical drainpipes held in place with Craftsman-style, star-ended metal straps.

The "common" brick is laid in Flemish bond pattern with bricks alternating long and short sides every row, a nice touch, and an extra vertical seam on each side gives the impression of pilasters holding up the floors and roof.

You're right to think a nine- or even six-car garage too much for a thousand-square-foot apartment. Actually, it was conceived in large part for the adjacent huge house at 2950 Pacific that's best seen from Broadway. 2974 is in fact part of a complex also including not only 2950 but the house at 2972 done by Newsom and Newsom in 1901. All three properties have long been associated with the Newhall family, beneficiaries of a big import-export business and the Newhall Land Company so conspicuous in California's Central Valley history.

The architectural census goes like this: the big house at 2950 was constructed about 1904 for Edwin White Newhall and his wife, Virginia; then about 1913 their son E. W. Jr. and his bride, Jane, moved into the pair of flats that then stood at 2974. Come July 1916 Jane bought the flats and immediately engaged Julia Morgan to replace them with the garage/apartment. By 1919 Virginia, now a widow, had bought 2972 and installed her son and daughter-in-law therein with their growing family. Presumably the new apartment above the giant garage was occupied by visiting friends and relations.

One can imagine a couple of excellent reasons for construction of the garage/apartment. The need to house those rich men's toys, motor cars, was surely one. Then it was appealing to get rid of the unsightly rear of the original flats, which stuck out beyond 2972 and probably interfered with light and a view of 2950's garden.

The garage/apartment design leaves two-thirds of its lot unbuilt, to accommodate landscaping. Apartment access is at the rear, where a bas-relief sculpture, a typical Morgan device, centers the wall above a full width of casement windows. And another design refinement: the brick posts in front of the garage, one with light globe, exactly match the brick gateposts and their lights at 2950's driveway.

Wonderful, subtle Miss Morgan!

No. 47

3001 Pacific

Mr. Opera's Childhood Home

*H*iding behind the trees at Pacific and Baker is a beautiful Georgian Revival house, all brick walls, white trim and fascinating roofline, the work not surprisingly of our old friends Bliss and Faville who, it seems, almost cornered the luxury market in Pacific Heights.

The mansion's trim peaks in a broad entrance with an interrupted pediment over the door and fluted columns beside it. The clinker brick, dark baked like a good French bread and slightly irregular, gives the house an aura of age. Proportions are gracious and satisfying, with an easily comprehended geometry of cubes, double squares and equilateral triangles.

The client at this address, 3001 Pacific, was C. O. G. Miller. He moved in in 1907 with his wife, Janet, and brought up four children under Bliss and Faville's elegant and multifaceted roof, with approximately five live-in servants part of the encampment.

C. O. G. (that's Christian Otto Gerberding) founded Pacific Lighting Corporation, a gas utilities holding company, in 1886 at the age of twenty-one. Three years earlier his father, banker Albert Miller, had ordered C. O. G. to enter the gas business; the senior Miller had just invested in a new gaslight manufacturing company competing with the local big one. Eventually the two merged into PG&E, but not before C. O. G. had succeeded his father as president in 1900.

When he died at eighty-seven in 1952 C. O. G. was still on the executive committees of PG&E and Pacific Lighting. He had also been a banker, president of AC Transit's forerunner the Key System, a Stanford University trustee for twenty-seven years, and a director of Fireman's Fund.

As PG&E's historian dryly remarked, "From the beginning he demonstrated a talent for finding business opportunities and a capacity to make them good."

But a much more interesting personality, I think, was C. O. G.'s son Robert Watt Miller, who lived in a jewel box on Nob Hill's California Street—with a tuxedoed butler, of course, to open the door—and served two brilliant terms as president of the San Francisco Opera, supporting during the second inning the artistic expansion of the company under Kurt Herbert Adler, who enriched the company's repertoire and hired cutting-edge stage directors such as Jean-Pierre Ponnelle.

Robert Watt Miller was born with a silver spoon in his mouth and almost choked on it. His life, in short, was not the proverbial bed of roses. To understand this troubled yet towering figure, superficially a rather forbidding character, it helps to read a perceptive and affectionate assessment in *Cadenza,* the noted conductor Erich Leinsdorf's autobiography:

"Bob Miller...looms as the strongest personality among the gallery of trustees and board members with whom I had to deal during my many years with musical organizations in America.

"In Bob's makeup was a streak of the maverick that was most attractive, setting him apart from the textbook socialite. He matured late, having lived in enforced idleness until his father died and all sorts of chairmanships became vacant for him to occupy. After he turned fifty and became active his earlier drinking problem was solved for good.

"His favorite haunt was backstage, and it was the rule rather than the exception that he got up during his wife's pre-opera dinner parties and left for the War Memorial, where he wandered among stagehands, choristers, and other participants, never taking off his Homburg [and sometimes wearing a cape!], which irritated the superstitious theater people, who frown on hats as a jinx.

"...While there was not a single trait Miller and I had in common, I count him among the very small band of my real friends. He had that rare quality of saying what he thought in words that would have been rude in a poor man but in a wealthy one were considered charming frankness."

What Robert Watt Miller thought of his father's neighbor down the street, Campbell McGregor of the Cosmopolitan Opera, one can easily guess.

So it looks from Leinsdorf's account as if Miller in his early decades had considerable growing pains thrust upon him. But how nice to grow up in a house by Bliss and Faville, so characteristic in its masculinity etched with delicacy, its ravishing textures, the sturdy Brahmsian counterpoint of its cleanly defined gestures. Not a house, it seems, in which to throw your socks on the floor!

On or near

Jackson Street

east to west

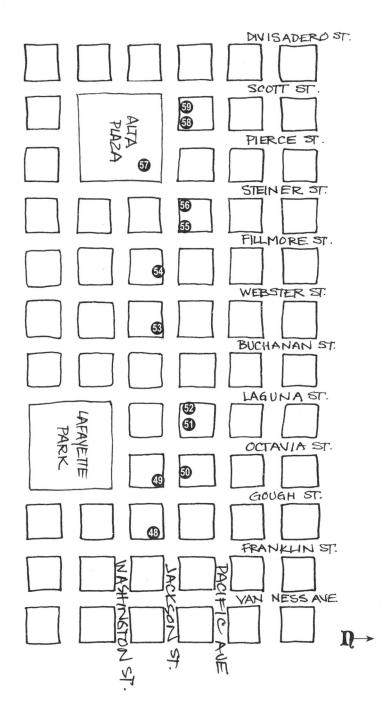

No. 48

2007 Franklin

Heritage House

2007 Franklin Street, known as the Haas-Lilienthal House, is the grand and glorious home of San Francisco Architectural Heritage, "a non-profit member-supported organization dedicated," as its newsletter puts it, "to the preservation and adaptive reuse of architecturally and historically significant buildings in San Francisco."

With these goals in mind Heritage has several kinds of activities. Volunteers serving in what could be called its educational wing conduct weekly tours of the house and occasional walking tours of various districts, and there are lecture series as well. To increase understanding of which buildings in the city should be preserved and why, Heritage's architectural historians and volunteers have surveyed Downtown, South of Market, and Richmond District areas, rating each building's architectural and historic importance. The initial survey resulted in a book, *Splendid Survivors* by Michael Corbett et al., which I strongly recommend.

Working as well in the political arena, the organization advocates the preservation of significant buildings threatened with demolition or inappropriate remodeling—what the *Old House Journal* would call "remuddling"! It testifies at public hearings, works with city agencies and, when requested, advises owners and developers. Heritage holds preservation easements too, ensuring the future architectural integrity of various buildings about town and giving easement donors a nice tax deduction.

And it takes care of—and occasionally rents out—the Haas-Lilienthal House. Which brings us to the history of 2007...

William Haas came from his native Bavaria in 1865 at the age of sixteen and three years later he joined his older cousin Kalman Haas (who was already involved in the marketing of Cyrus Noble whiskey) in the wholesale grocery business. When William was thirty-one he married the nineteen-year-old Bertha Greenebaum and in due course they had three children, Florine, Charles and Alice.

Six years later—now we're up to 1886—William Haas paid $13,000 for a commodious sixty-foot lot on Franklin Street a little south of Jackson, near the homes of several of his and Bertha's relatives at the eastern end of Pacific Heights toward downtown. In July of that year he contracted with the builders McCann and Biddell for a two-story wooden house with basement and attic, a description that doesn't quite catch the magnificence of the mansion that duly appeared on the scene. Construction was to cost, and doubtless did, $18,500—that's four or five times the average cost of a house at that time.

The architect of 2007 was Peter R. Schmidt, like Haas a German, who practiced in San Francisco from 1863 to 1894. Usually Schmidt worked with a partner—Victor Hoffman, Augustus Eisen, Charles Havens and Frank Shea in turn (the German element giving way, you see, to Irish)—but for the Haas house he was on his own. He seems to have designed several houses in the then-fashionable Van Ness Avenue/Franklin Street corridor (well, Franklin north of California Street is still rather fashionable): known survivors are 1809 Franklin and, down toward Civic Center, 819 Eddy Street.

William Haas moved his family in as soon as 2007 was completed, and the house only changed hands in 1972. Daughter Alice—whose sister Mrs. Edward Bransten lived down the street at 1735 Franklin, a handsome brick mansion built in 1902—married her second cousin Samuel Lilienthal on-site so to speak, in 1909. After father William Haas died in 1916 the young Lilienthals moved into 2007 with his widow, Bertha.

These Lilienthals inherited the house in 1927. Later the same year Alice Haas Lilienthal's brother Charles died and Alice and Samuel took in his two children, Madeleine and William, to rear along with their own three, Ernest, Elizabeth and Frances. Madeleine would grow up to live

in a monumental contemporary house in Presidio Heights designed by the pioneer modern architect Eric Mendelsohn. Like her mother, Alice stayed on in the house after her husband died. Then her heirs donated the house to Heritage, and one of them still sits on the organization's board.

So the house has had only three owners in all its [as of 1999] 113 years!

William Haas' money came from the Haas Brothers wholesale grocery business. City directory listings nailed down their trade as "imports and wholesale groceries and provisions" while another reference says they dealt in "coffees, teas, canned delicacies and cigars," trading all over the Pacific Basin. Not a firm, in short, devoted to Spam and pretzels.

When the firm incorporated in 1897 William Haas was its first president. His son-in-law Samuel Lilienthal started out in his own father's firm, Crown Distilleries, but when Prohibition loomed he joined Haas Brothers, becoming its president after Charles died.

2007 Franklin, like many houses of the late 1880s, is predominantly Queen Anne in style—witness the prominent gables, complex volumes, variety of surface materials and a tower as well—but there is Stick Eastlake ornament too. There've been a few changes over the years; in 1898, for instance, the next forty feet to the south were bought for the side garden, and a bathroom and two fireplaces with exterior chimneys were added.

Early in the twentieth century the interior was "modernized"—but the over-all effect, one should note, remains quite Victorian indeed!—and when Madeleine and William Haas joined the family group in 1927 a full apartment was added at the rear of the lot, with a garage underneath. This new bit was designed by the young Gardner Dailey, who along with William Wurster was perhaps the residential archi-tect of choice in mid-twentieth-century Pacific Heights. For clients, that is, who wanted to be tastefully up to date.

Dailey was careful not to make inap-propriate architectural waves and 2007, happy to say, looks almost exactly like its original self. The house has always been painted gray and somehow it doesn't seem to need the artistic three- and four-color jobs that have given a nice visual zest to many a Victorian in Pacific Heights and other San Francisco neighborhoods.

No. 49

1925–55 Jackson

A High End Bungalow Court

1925-55 Jackson is named, according to an old plaque on the staircase, Glenlee Terrace. And what is a terrace anyway? My dictionary defines it as "an artificial, raised, level space, as of lawn, having one or more vertical or sloping sides; also, such levels collectively." Here on Jackson Street the word is used to announce a rare type of building, one I've seen nowhere but in San Francisco.

The made-in-San Francisco terrace, usually in terms of style a combination of Arts and Crafts and Mission Revival, was developed in 1908 by Henry C. Smith, the architect who, according to the local architectural magazine of the day, designed most of the examples in the Bay Area.

This terrace-according-to-Smith is in fact a combination of several housing ideas: 1, like an apartment building it fits several dwelling units on one lot; 2, it exploits hilly terrain for maximum views, light and air; 3, like the English terrace—that means row houses—it separates units so they seem individual while still sharing party walls; and 4, as in the dictionary definition, it's a series of level spaces—on different levels—landscaped and with vertical sides.

It's also an upscale version of the so-called bungalow court, invented in southern California about the same time and usually offering low-cost housing, often for seasonal tenants, and in this case just on flat ground.

A bungalow court is one big lot with a group of tiny houses arranged in a U-plan around a central landscaped court open to the street—this of course is just a slight step up from an auto court, the early version of yes, a motel, meant for short-term guests. I've seen examples in Oakland, Santa Rosa, Sonoma, Gualala and Oakley, California; the only one I know in San Francisco is on Minna between Eleventh and Twelfth Streets, south of Market.

The literature also calls terrace apartments such as 1925-55 Jackson "stepping stone apartments" or "cliff dwellings de luxe."

The first one to come to light was, logically enough, The Terraces, at 3834-42 Sacramento Street in a relatively unposh precinct of Presidio Heights. Smith's next, containing his own residence, was La Hacienda Apartments at 3856 Sacramento. Smith also designed a terrace complex at 2255-63 Vallejo, the Heights Apartments at 2115-35 Hyde on Russian Hill, and the Hunter Apartments at 1234-54 Washington on the edge of Nob Hill. Another opus in the genre, the especially handsome and gorgeously sited Union Terrace at 1020 Union on

Russian Hill, was designed in 1921 by T. Paterson Ross.

Glenlee Terrace, although it resembles Smith's terraces, was designed by Arthur J. Laib. Building permits were approved in mid-1912, about four months after an article on Smith's terraces was published. Terrace fever?

A bit earlier Laib had built a pair (but not a complex) of houses at 1360-68 McAllister in the Alamo Square neighborhood that relate to each other like terrace apartments and sit behind an impressive retaining wall supporting a garden/courtyard. Laib practiced from 1907 to at least 1927: his known buildings, all residential, are quite handsome, many of them more or less Classical Revival.

The stucco walls, tile roofs and curvilinear parapets of Glenlee Terrace place it at least partly in the Mission Revival style. Arts and Crafts enters the picture with the clinker brick base and staircase walls, the rough texture of the stucco, the multiple panes of casement windows and the projecting beams at different level overhangs. Meanwhile there's a bit of California Bungalow in the fat, slope-sided columns of the individual entry arches.

Three styles, academically speaking, but one unified composition, with harmonious landscaping all about.

1925-55 consists of six party-wall buildings climbing the hillside. Two at the sidewalk, on different levels, frame the central courtyard/staircase; each has three stories and three units, with garages recently added. The next two buildings uphill are similar, while two in the rear enclose the courtyard/staircase and consist of two floors, two units each. Every one of the fourteen units enjoys landscaping, sun (when present) and has its own entrance, its own feeling of privacy.

The 1920 census recorded fourteen tenants at Glenlee, an average of two or three persons per unit, and four units with servants on board. Ten of the principals were young, in their twenties or thirties, so this was starter housing for some of the Glennies. The longest in residence was Charles Mount, traffic manager for the DiGiorgio Fruit Company, who called Glenlee home from 1933 to 1953.

Perhaps the most elegant was Evelyn Mendessole who owned the ultrafashionable ladies' fashion shop Maison Mendessole near Union Square. And doubtless the most interesting was cigar-chomping Prescott Sullivan, the beloved *San Francisco Examiner* sportswriter who used to stack files so high in his car you wondered how he could see to drive. If Sullivan had been a movie character he would have been played by Gene Hackman.

No. 50

1950–60 Jackson

The Swedish Connection

1950 and 1960 are really two houses although they're easily mistaken for one.

That's because they rub shoulders in matching peach-toned brick and were in fact built for the same client by the same architects, the fabled Bliss and Faville. But the house on the left dates from 1920, the one on the right from six years later. Look closely and you see that the earlier of the nestled pair has more elaborate window surrounds and a hipped roof. Both do have columned entries, with the balustraded parapet on the right balancing the third floor on the left.

Bliss and Faville designed the Matson Navigation Company's headquarters at 215 Market Street in 1921, so their first residence for the Matson family, 1960 Jackson, may have been a sort of trial run. The second residence indicates the relationship between architects and clients continued healthy.

The money to build these peach-toned gems came, of course, from the Matson Line, one of the premier passenger carriers in western waters before and after the Second World War.

There was competition for a while from the Dollar Line, later American President Lines, but most of the Dollar boats were homely affairs as devoted to freight as passengers (exceptions would be the *President Hoover* and the *President Coolidge*, the former wrecked in 1937), while the four most famous Matson liners making regular trips to Hawaii and Australia from their South Beach terminal were svelte white beauties: the *Malolo, Mariposa, Lurline* and *Monterey,* the *Malolo* in due course being renamed the *Matsonia* because "Malolo" was considered, if I remember right, a bad-luck name.

They were all two-stackers with six or seven passenger decks. The *Malolo,* according to ship historian Alan Cary, had a white and gold dining saloon and the lounge was gold and orchid with ebony columns rising out of a deep carpet of blue. The veranda café and the smoking room were oak-paneled, and she also boasted a gorgeously hued Pompeiian swimming pool. Modern-day cruise lines might want to hide their heads in envy.

William B. Matson, pater of the line, and, one suspects, not hugely interested in Pompeiian interior decoration, was born in Sweden in 1849; presumably his name was originally Madsen. He arrived in San Francisco, that magnet for wanderers, in '67 and worked his way up from seaman to captain in the coastal trade. He carried coal for the Spreckels sugar refinery, and the Spreckels family which we've met elsewhere in these articles helped him buy his first ship, a sailing schooner called *Emma Claudina.* He filled her with general merchandise and sailed to Hawaii in 1882, returning with coconuts and sugar cane.

Starting in '87 William Matson built or bought seven more sailing vessels and he called the first one *Lurline*, reputedly after a Spreckels yacht recalling an operetta whose title had been anglicized from the German "Lorelei." There were four more generations of Matson ships christened "Lurline," and perhaps it comes as no surprise that William's daughter and granddaughter were Lurlines as well.

Then in the early 1900s Captain Matson acquired steamships for the Hawaii route. Meanwhile he made investments in Hawaii—sugar, doubtless—and in oil companies. And he bought, in 1901, a mansion at 1960 Jackson for his family's residence. Fifteen years later he bought another at 1950 Jackson. In 1917 he died and his widow, Lillian, commissioned the first of the new Bliss and Favilles.

In 1914 the first daughter, Lurline, married a thirty-three-year-old from Hawaii, William P. Roth. Reaffirming the classic wisdom that it's nice to marry the boss's daughter, this William climbed the Matson Navigation Company's ladder with agility to become vice president and general manager by 1918. Soon the young Roths were moving in with their widowed mother at the new 1960 Jackson.

The second house may have been constructed so the two generations could have separate quarters. City directories and census takers in those days considered the two houses as one.

It was under William P. Roth that the Matson company created several luxury hotels in Hawaii and expanded passenger service beyond Hawaii to Australia and New Zealand. And in 1938 the Roths bought Filoli, the Willis Polk-designed Bourn estate near Woodside (this would be the same Bourn we met some pages back in San Francisco at 2550 Webster, Old House No. 33). A dozen years after Roth's death in 1963 his widow donated Filoli to the National Trust for Historic Preservation.

Also, in the early 1960s, she and her son William Matson Roth developed Ghirardelli Square, the nation's first shopping complex in an historic building.

When the elder Roth stepped down from the presidency of Matson in 1946 the two Bliss and Favilles on Jackson were granted to the Swedish government, which for some years used 1950 as the consul's residence and 1960 as consular offices. Remember, of course, that the original Matson was Swedish, so there's circularity here.

And a little footnote: in 1966 Arthur was visiting Prague, Czechoslovakia, and a waiter in a tavern asked him, a San Franciscan living five or six blocks from 1950-60 Jackson, to carry a note to his, the waiter's, supposed girlfriend, who was working—well of course!—at San Francisco's Swedish consulate.

No. 51

2020 Jackson

More Than Dull Respectability

2020 Jackson Street doesn't shout opulence, it puts a quiet and dignified face to the street—while, one might add, it looms a little imperiously over the three houses to the immediate west, which, as a matter of fact, constitute a set of exteriorly individualized tract houses, dubbed by their builders Kiernan, O'Brien and Rhine "the Italian, Spanish and French houses."

Yes, the casual observer might see in 2020's tan brick, careful symmetry and utterly rectangular windows only dull respectability. But closer inspection reveals Quality, even a little charm. All right, so it's not a house to fall in love with at first sight, but my how it grows on the walking tourist who gives it a second chance.

While noting that its walls are brick full through, not just a single thickness veneered on a frame structure—to paraphrase Gilbert and Sullivan, the house's handsome brick is no mere veneer!—go ahead and enjoy the five generous terracotta columns leading over granite and marble to the elegant side entry, the massive radiating lintels (proto-Deco, you might say) over the ground-floor windows, the coiled consoles on plain brick moldings one story above, the unusual patterns of exquisite balcony ironwork at the second level.

And that's not to mention the neat little third-floor windows which, interestingly enough, are almost square.

All this felicity combined with stone-colored brick seems to produce an American interpretation of some palazzo in Florence. Truly the house for a banker or a very conservative lawyer. Or maybe Edith Wharton, or Henry James when his royalties were good. The architect was Julius Krafft: we've met him before in these pages (Old House No. 21 and No. 35), but not as the author of a house boasting such textural richness and subtle architectural pizazz. Clearly this commission inspired him to his ultrabest.

Krafft's client was indeed a prominent lawyer, Emanuel S. Heller, founder of the patrician firm long known as Heller, Ehrman, White and McAuliffe, although no Heller was associated with it for more than a half-century. Son of a pioneer California dry goods merchant, E. S. Heller graduated from UC Berkeley and Hastings Law School, then quickly made his name in his profession. For nearly thirty years he was attorney for the San Francisco Stock and Bond Exchange.

Heller's wife, Clara, the daughter of the noted banker I. W. Hellman, a name we've also encountered in Pacific Heights, is remembered for commissioning the celebrated Darius Milhaud's cantata known as *Sacred Service*—Milhaud taught alternate years at Oakland's Mills College during the 1940s, commuting annually from his native France. She it was who signed the contracts for 2020 Jackson, over forty-five thousand dollars' worth of them, in 1902: this was ten times the average construction cost of a San Francisco house at the time.

Part of the cost went into a lavish interior with exotic woods to panel a low-beamed hall, Gothic detailing in the bayside dining room, and a Colonial Revival library on the front. Yes, very respectable indeed, and obviously not dull. Listen, the pulse of this house beats at a steady 60.

No. 52

2090 Jackson

Nazis Slept Here

Note: This article, lightly edited here and somewhat enlarged, originally appeared a dozen or so years ago when 2090 Jackson was the headquarters of the California Historical Society and open at times to the public; the house is now in private hands.

To walk through the massive front door of this Chicagoesque mansion in soft red Arizona sandstone, the door dotted with medallion-like little carved faces, is to enter some glorious time and money machine. The elaborate and fascinating interior decoration is nearly unchanged, and much of the furniture is original.

The ceilings must be fourteen feet high, and the one in the front hall is covered, like the walls, in quarter-sawn oak, with beautiful moldings, panels, beams, etc. There's not one inch of plain wall in this hall because among the acres of interestingly fashioned wood are several panels of densely patterned green wallpaper, replicating the original. The oak has beautiful clear grain with yellow highlights and it seems not to have darkened with age—the room is light!

To the right is the reception room, fairly small and octagon in plan. It still has its original rug, and a covered plaster ceiling a pastry chef might envy.

Left of the hall is the huge living room divided in unequal parts by a row of columns and arches. Mahogany is all about, in paneling, in faces and lion heads at the fireplace, in fluted and tapered columns. Here as well the woodwork has not darkened with age but looks new, satiny and beautiful. Major ceiling beams are mahogany, the rest plaster, with rosettes upon rosettes between. Some harbor bare low-wattage light bulbs which still give illumination.

Well, I could go on and on...Note as well the Turkish smoking room, a dining room lined with "mystery wood," a marvelously carved staircase, a Victorian bathroom big as a modern bedroom or maybe one of those vintage grand hotel bathrooms you might still find in Innsbruck or Brive-la-Gaillarde.

When constructed in 1894-96 the house was innovative mechanically as well as design-wise and it claims one of the first elevators in a private residence, a hydraulic Otis that ran on water and has a cab that's all metal curlicues. The original furnace, dating from a time when central heating was a new convenience, still heats the house, converted of course to gas.

2090 Jackson also came on the scene with five tiled bathrooms, and a complicated electrical system that still works.

Construction of all this luxuriance-

and-convenience cost about $150,000, an enormous sum for a century or more ago. Working with this figure was architect Edward R. Swain who designed McLaren Lodge in Golden Gate Park and was supervising architect of San Francisco's Ferry Building with its Seville-inspired tower. Swain studied locally and practiced from 1877 until his death in 1902 at the untimely age of fifty. Obviously he was a master at his craft and there must have been masterpieces up his sleeve that never came to be.

Swain's client was William Franklin Whittier, who'd come to California from Maine in 1854 and prospered in the paint business. From 1867 to 1890 he was half of Whittier, Fuller and Company, wholesale purveyors of paints, varnish, glass and mirrors, a number of which must have found their way into Pacific Heights houses.

The company came into our times as the Fuller Paint Company and is now Fuller-O'Brien. The original Fuller died in 1890 and in '94 Whittier sold out to the Fuller family. For the remainder of his long life—he died in 1917—Whittier called himself a capitalist. He had investments in real estate, was vice president of the San Francisco and San Joaquin Valley Railway and a director of San Francisco Gas and Electric.

This business whiz was a widower when he built 2090. His oldest child had already married, but the other two, in their twenties, moved in with Dad, each in a self-contained apartment. So the house was a kind of triplex behind those medallion faces. Both these children were married at the house, in 1897—what a perfect spot for a wedding!

And later the history of the Whittier mansion would go sour for a while.

Whittier's daughter Mattie Weir inherited it and kept it as her town house until early 1941. So far so good. But after she conveyed the property to the title insurance company as temporary holder, the property soon passed over to one Herman Loeper and then, a day after that, to Das Deutsches Reich. The house, in short, became the Nazi Consulate in San Francisco, a few doors or blocks from Hellers, Haases, Lilienthals, Fleishhackers. What they must have thought...

The consul, Fritz Wiedemann, was a dashing fellow, often in Herb Caen's "three dot" column, and not, to be frank, unliked by some of San Francisco's socialites. Lately he'd been living in posh suburban Hillsborough and one rather shudders to think of the warm reception he may have had from some of the isolationist locals. Perhaps more an operetta scoundrel than a raging villain, he entertained elegantly while conducting clandestine business—of a minor sort, one supposes—for his keepers in Berlin.

Then, anti-Nazi fevers running hot as well they might, he was evicted in July '41—

a false start via Japan evolved into a con-
clusive return to Germany via New York.
The house as if shuddering under a curse
remained empty throughout World War
II, producing snickers from local school-
boys who were of course connoisseurs of
all the latest good-and-bad-guys war movies, and it was held in trust for some time
by the Alien Property Custodian who later
turned it over to the U.S. Attorney General's Office.

Finally, in 1950, it was auctioned,
along with most of its contents—doubtless
no crumpled teletypes from Berlin—and
after a quick succession of several owners
was purchased by the California Historical Society, which did its best to erase the
blemish on its history.

...And here, for what it's worth, is a bit
from a retrospective Herb Caen column
in the *San Francisco Chronicle* of November 15,
1988:

> OF HUMAN INTEREST: *Whatever happened to
> Baron Manfred von Killinger, the Nazi consul
> general here before the arrival of Fritz Wiede-
> mann in 1939? Stuart Nixon recalls that he
> ended up as Hitler's gauleiter in Romania when
> the Red Army invaded that country in 1945. As
> a farewell to his loyal staff, von Killinger took a
> machine gun and killed them at their desks and
> then killed himself.*

As for Wiedemann, Nixon dismisses
him as "merely a ladykiller," a much better way to go. After the war, presenting
himself as an anti-Nazi, Fritz testified
that he had had several opportunities to
kill Hitler but couldn't bring himself to
do so because "he was my friend from the
first war."

No. 53

2209 Jackson

A Sole Survivor

This little one-story house with two bay windows comes as a surprise, almost hiding between the taller buildings on either side and set back behind a charming garden and picture-book picket fence. Freestanding there on its pygmy feet so to speak, it brings into focus another era a whole generation before the parades of two- and three-story Victorians that characterize so much of old San Francisco.

Shorn of its modern additions—silhouette in the transom, fancy railing near the front door, circle grills tacked below bay windows—the house is really very simple. The façade is symmetrically ordered, a Classical pediment tops the doorway, the roofline cornice projects only a little, the brackets under it are short and modest, the paneling vertically extending the windows is plain.

But 2209 Jackson can't help showing its charm!

This cute (but not too cute) little house is the sole survivor of Pacific Heights' first housing tract, the square block bordered by Jackson, Washington, Buchanan and Webster Streets. The block was bought in August 1870 for $45,000 by David Farquharson, one of California's best pioneer architects. Plans for the tract were actually on display a little earlier at J. W. Tucker and Company's jewelry store, and since Mr. Tucker bought several of the available lots and presumably helped finance the scheme the area was in due course dubbed "Tuckerville."

Farquharson subdivided his little townlet into forty lots twenty-five feet wide, ten on each street. Except at the corners most of the houses were horizontal duplexes with side-by-side units under a common roof. Five houses, including this one, were single units taking up twice the usual unit space.

Each owner of a unit taking up half a house got a doorway and a bay window, along with a side yard to left or right. In the duplex plan the bay windows of each unit were near each other, the separate front doors at the sides of the facades. In the case of the five single-unit houses, 2209 among them, the front door was centered between the bays.

How do I know all this? Well, the Bancroft Library at UC Berkeley has a couple of fuzzy snapshots of some of the duplexes before they were torn down. And I've seen some periodicals from 1870 and 1871 that published lists of real estate sales in the area. The five single-unit houses Farquharson sold in November and December 1870 for $6,200 to $6,370 each. The duplexes went for about $3,100 apiece between November '70 and March '71. Sales were "on the installment plan," and a few properties, no surprise perhaps, had to be repossessed.

Farquharson was born in Scotland in 1827, had come to California by 1850 and designed his first American buildings in Sacramento, nearer to the Gold Country as we call it now than San Francisco. One of these first buildings was used as the State Capitol from 1856 until the present one opened in 1870, concurrent with "Tuckerville."

Based in San Francisco from 1864, Farquharson designed prominent hotels, banks and other downtown buildings—unlike the simple Tuckerville houses these were ornate business temples.

Note that Farquharson helped pioneer construction with iron bearing columns and was involved in the beginnings of steel-frame construction. His only known works still visible are South Hall, the oldest building on the UC Berkeley campus, and the eye-stopping little 2209 on Jackson.

2209 was Farquharson's first sale on the Tuckerville block. It was bought by Frederic Clay, the proprietor of a large cracker factory who soon outgrew his little digs as he moved into finance and real estate. The next owner was Benjamin Griffith Barney, a deputy shipping commissioner. According to Bill Koolman of the Maritime Museum, shipping commissioners carried out a then-new federal law concerned with the protection of crews on foreign voyages.

The 1880 census records Mr. Barney as a native of Massachusetts with wife and grown daughters on the scene and a live-in cook and resident coachman. Quite a population tucked away at 2209. Perhaps the brick ex-stable in the rear yard was built for the coachman's charges, or even some of the two-legged creatures recorded by the census people.

No. 54

2351 Jackson

Arpeggios on Jackson

*A*nd another one-of-a-kind... With the grandeur and unusual scale of 2351 Jackson tickling my curiosity every time I passed it, I was delighted one day when my eye fell on an old photograph in the 1928 city directory that explained a lot. Because, you see, 2351 Jackson, towering over neighbors on one of Jackson Street's less imposing Pacific Heights blocks, was the Arrillaga Music College.

Further investigation revealed that 2351's grand upper portion, two stories framed by paired Beaux Arts columns—it suggests nothing so much as the superstructure of a Wilhelmine transatlantic steamer—was given over to a generous-sized recital hall, complete with organ and bathed in light coming through bold tall windows. Graduation ceremonies were held here, and monthly faculty recitals. Elsewhere in the building were studios, practice rooms, doubtless classrooms.

The school's 1922 graduation gives an idea of its scope. Five students received diplomas in piano or harmony and three went into the world with teacher's certificates in piano or voice. Four "first degree" and three "second degree" certificates were awarded in piano or voice, and there were also eight "junior certificates" and fifteen "elementary certificates" handed out.

The core of the ceremony was a student concert, sixteen numbers in all, with works by Bach, Schumann, Chopin, Debussy, Sibelius, Puccini et al. And all this a stone's throw from the big Pacific Heights (now Newcomer) School just rising across the street, the Foxhall (now Mayflower) Market down at the corner of Fillmore, and Calvary Presbyterian, of course, at the same corner.

The faculty in 1921 included several voice teachers, a dance instructor and one in "public speaking, Delsarte and stage deportment." (The Delsarte system, my dictionary reports, aimed at improving musical and dramatic expression through the mastery of various bodily attitudes and gestures). Three more professori taught counterpoint, harmony and theory, and meanwhile a flutist coached her instrument and led the college orchestra.

According to a quarter-page ad in that 1928 city directory, courses were offered in "piano, voice, pipe organ, theater organ, violin, cello, harp, flute, brass and wind instruments, dancing, opera," not to mention "theory, harmony, counterpoint and solfeggio."

The Arrillaga Music College operated at 2351 for nearly forty years, claiming to be the oldest musical college in the West, but perhaps the institution only premiered that particular wording "musical college." Its demise in 1940 may have been caused by the retirement of its director, Vincent Arrillaga, but the Depression of the 1930s, and the calls to arms as World War II heated up in 1940, may have been factors as well.

It's a puzzle how the building came by its appearance. Evidently it started life as an ordinary two-story dwelling with a little side yard and a ten-foot setback from the street. Vincent's father, Santiago Arrillaga, owned it and lived in it as a music teacher from 1882. To create the somewhat unlikely bit of architecture we see today hovering over Jackson Street's south sidewalk, the original Victorian house, probably not very unlike its immediate neighbor to the west, was not torn down (not totally, that is) and replaced, it simply grew through a series of alterations, not all of them precisely legal.

Only three building permits survive, from 1910, 1911 and 1924 for $700, $150 and $3,800 respectively. The first covered doubling a tiny house in the back yard, the last added second- and third-floor studios. The 1911 permit poses a mystery—it was for enlarging a "music room" space with "an extension to be ten feet from line of house," and if that refers to the grand hall whose front windows we see today, $150, even in 1911 dollars, would not have begun to cover such a transformation.

Here's my interpretation. Either the 1911 permit was deliberately misleading, or else Arrillaga changed his plans and didn't bother with a permit. In any event, for proper acoustics and proportions the recital hall had to be two stories high, so the entire existing second floor was demolished and alterations proceeded from there.

No architects are named in the 1911 permit, only a builder named John or Jens Hartland. I suspect that Arrillaga gave him a picture of the Paris Opera (the Salle Garnier, of course, not the late-twentieth-century Bastille Opera) and instructed him to copy one bay of it. Choice of the Paris Opera recalled Santiago Arrillaga's studies at the Paris Conservatory before coming to San Francisco in 1875.

Born in the Spanish Basque province of Guipuzcoa in 1847, he'd graduated from Madrid's Royal Conservatory. He knew the great diva Luisa Tetrazzini—after whom a now-"retro" chicken dish was named—and he'd toured as piano accompanist for the famous soprano Adelina Patti. Well connected, in short. Aristocratic looking in pince-nez and wing collar, he was the authoritative organist at San Francisco's Our Lady of Guadalupe and Notre Dame des Victoires, and then, at the time of his death in 1915, at Most Holy Redeemer.

Vincent Arrillaga studied with his father, later in the East and in Europe.

Building on his father's reputation he incorporated the Musical College in 1908 and devoted most of his life to it. By the way, he liked to call himself Vicente de Arrillaga, claiming relationship to José Joaquín Arrillaga, a native of Guipuzcoa and governor of Upper California from 1804 to 1814.

It was during or after World War II that Vicente converted his college building into ten apartments. The house had fallen silent.

No. 55

Fillmore and Jackson (NW corner)

Almost a Staatsoper

*C*alvary Presbyterian Church has been adorning the corner of Fillmore and Jackson since 1902, watching times change from its regularly altered perch.

A generation ago it looked out on a sedate old-time drugstore of the Shumate chain and a soda fountain/restaurant no gourmet would think twice about entering. Now its neighbors are a trendy coffeehouse and an exuberant trattoria with stylish comfort food and a wall-to-wall clientele of gorgeous yuppies. Clanking streetcars and antique cable cars have given way to rumbling buses snorting beneath stained glass windows.

The move to Jackson and Fillmore in 1902 marked the third of six building projects in the congregation's history [not counting the seismic work done in 2002] as well as providing the church's third location.

The first Calvary was constructed in 1854 on Bush Street near Montgomery, part of the present Mills Building site. Fifteen years later, when that area smack in the middle of the Financial District had become too commercial, and the building perhaps too small, the congregation moved to the northwest corner of Powell and Geary at Union Square. But three decades later that space was wanted for the new St. Francis Hotel, so Calvary picked up again and moved out to the present location, a new building again on a northwest corner.

The fourth building project was occasioned by the donation of a bigger and better organ in 1928. The structure at Jackson and Fillmore was duly enlarged to the west along Jackson, this construction adding the five-window portion of the building behind the second tower. Frederick H. Meyer was the designer in this case, following the general lines of the 1902 original but with subtle differences, straight window tops for instance, and simpler moldings.

The fifth building project in Calvary's history was the intimately scaled chapel which opened on Jackson behind the basic church in 1963. Suggesting a modern take on your old-time village chapel (or "the little church around the corner"), it's become a popular place for weddings. Be sure to feast on the lovely stained glass ensemble facing the street. Inside are important frescoes of the reformers Luther, Calvin, Knox and Zwingli by Lucienne Bloch, who also has work, you'll recall, at St. Mary the Virgin (Old House No. 2).

Then in 1979 came the sixth project, a modern-styled education building on the site of the earlier church-matching education building which, like the church itself, fronted on Fillmore. Robinson and Mills were the architects in '79.

In terms of real estate the present Calvary complex covers lots where ten Italianate and Stick-style houses stood in 1899; one remained until the 1928 addition and two more were taken down for the 1963 chapel. Their old neighbors remain on Fillmore toward Pacific and Jackson toward Steiner, so it isn't as if the church of 1902 totally erased the architectural feel of the area.

The original land purchased for the complex in 1900 for $70,000 included all the present and extensive Fillmore Street frontage, but along Jackson at that time it extended only 125 feet, a little less than the depth of the congregation's previous lot on Union Square.

It's been said that the Calvary buildings of 1854, 1869 and 1902 were all alike, but period pictures show differences. Their similarity lies in sticking to basic Classic Revival styles, which were popular in the early nineteenth century, lost favor in the Victorian era and were "in" again around 1900. All three claim two-story-high Corinthian columns with triangular Greek temple pediment above, but the columns of the 1854 church were not evenly spaced as in the later buildings.

The 1869 church had little cupolas on top, three at each corner: the only concession, this, to the Gothic Revival style

of four other churches at the not-yet Macyfied Union Square. This Calvary stood back a little from the street, and the column bases rested on the rusticated arcade of a fifteen-foot-high lower floor. An interior staircase (no help, one suspects, for the disabled) led to the sanctuary.

The 1902 church didn't need a tall lower-floor subsanctuary because Sunday school and meetings took place in the attached and matching education building next door to the north. The tracery from its stained glass has, by the way, been reused on the far side of its 1979 replacement.

The 1902 design of the basic church added balconies and rose windows to harmonize with the usual central columns, and the entablature above where CALVARY is spelled out, while admittedly borrowing many ideas from the 1869 building—the Colonial Revival interior for instance being very much in the spirit of '69. The 1902 architects, McDougal Brothers, were active in the Calvary congregation and must have known that similarities would help members adjust to change, always difficult and especially so for affluent conservatives when contemplating their place of worship.

At the opening service on Thanksgiving Day 1902, Calvary's beloved Irish pastor Dr. John Hemphill, who served the congregation in 1870 to 1882 and 1892 to 1907, offered this comfort:

The new church will be all the more dear to us because of the close association with the old church, for we have in the construction a million bricks from the old church; and we have the seats and the pews that were dear to us...We have placed the old pews as nearly as possible to correspond with their position in the old church, so that you shall feel at home.

The definition of "home" was graciously expanded after the earthquake and fire of '06 when the congregations of Temple Emanu-el and Trinity Episcopal found temporary housing at Calvary, with Superior Court meeting in the basement!

Hemphill also said of the imposing Calvary, which on the outside looks not unlike some nineteenth-century German opera house where a Wagner premiere might have taken place—except that the view often includes numerous cute little children being ushered in or out of nursery school—"this edifice is a workshop for Christian workers." It has remained an active one to this day.

No. 56

2500 Steiner

The Meussdorffer Arms

*B*ehold here the tallest building in western Pacific Heights, a handsome pseudo-Gothic beacon of, well, comfort and affluence. President Clinton has dined in the penthouse, and cars exiting the garage under the direction of a blazered doorman run to Jaguars and a Rolls.

Yes, 2500 Steiner is a standout among perhaps a couple of dozen grand-luxe apartment buildings scattered over the ritziest northern precincts of San Francisco in the 1910s and 1920s. Here, in what amounts to a stack of single-floor "houses," residents have all the comforts of a large single-family dwelling without stairs or garden duty. And there's that doorman.

During the 1980s there was even what struck me as excessively zealous security. The well-heeled inhabitants of 2500 must have had a good scare because for some time innocent strollers past the building had to suffer the suspicious looks of gun-toting doormen, and at night the lighting over the garage door was as blindingly bright as at the Russian Consulate during Communist days. Recently, I'm happy to report, paranoia has been replaced by a more gracious interplay with the neighborhood.

The architect of 2500, which dates from 1926-27, almost dangerously close to the great Wall Street crash of '29, went all Gothic with pointed arches, stained glass and gargoyles at the building's base, continuing in similar vein in the lobby, where rib vaulting defines the ceiling: it's supported on thin columns with bound foliage shafts and overhanging capitals.

Note as well in the lobby an imitation unicorn tapestry, more stained glass, a miniature medieval fireplace and an elevator door embossed with family crests.

The windows of 2500 line up vertically in neat upward echoes that emphasize the building's height, and the two-story "capital" at the top is crowned with a chateau-like roof visible from Marin County and Twin Peaks alike as the westernmost *high-rise* on the city skyline. Meanwhile, back inside, the visitor to one of the dozen full-floor apartments rides in an elevator cab that disdains Gothic overload. One's lifted to the privileged upper realms surrounded by nothing other than dense paneling and a grapevine cornice.

And then, in a representative apartment, the walls are plain, with only enough generalized moldings to set off the owner's individual style. Ceilings are ten feet high, mildly barrel-vaulted in the living room and with Grecian anthemion moldings in the dining room. No medieval fireplace in sight, but a vaguely Colonial Revival one, lined with black marble matching the baseboards. There are hardwood floors of course, three or four bedrooms, a library, paneled doors, you name it. All very Park Avenue!

But all this luxury plays only a second fiddle to the gorgeous bay view imbibed through huge north windows. Perhaps no one knew this better than C. A. Meussdorffer, architect of 2500 Steiner and many more of those spiffy apartment houses from an earlier day.

In Pacific Heights Meussdorffer is also responsible for three upscale "apts." at Lafayette Park, another at Jackson and Laguna, and so on. Obviously he understood the desires of people with money, and 2500, known as the Alta Plaza Apartments, was perhaps the apex of his career.

Not from an architectural or even an artistic background, Meussdorffer was born in San Francisco in 1871 into a family of hatters. From an early age he studied privately with Goswin Widder, a civil engineer turned teacher of mathematics and drawing. Later he worked in the office of Salfield and Kohlberg, prolific, and good, architects of Victorians.

Building on this foundation he set up his own office in 1897 and business was good from the start. He's said to have been a hard taskmaster with his staff, but the firm produced beautiful and well-engineered buildings. Yes, it may be a tad staid and a tad pretentious, but 2500 is one handsome devil of an apartment house.

No. 57

Alta Plaza Park

Outdoor Room Extraordinaire

*N*o, Alta Plaza Park is hardly a "house," but you could call it a great outdoor room. Or, more accurately, a number of rooms, because the park is different things to different people.

One room, or set of rooms, is the tennis courts, windswept at times but commanding great views. Another is the children's playground with slides and sand. Then there's the dog walkers' park near Steiner and Jackson in the early morning and up at Pierce and Jackson later—San Francisco Symphony maestro Michael Tilson Thomas has been sighted there with his partner, Joshua, and their standard poodle.

The joggers' park at Alta Plaza is around it, in it, up it—meaning, in the last case, those alpine steps at Pierce and Clay. Other sports, especially touch football, sometimes co-ed, are generally played near the Town School corner at Jackson and Scott. The bench-sitters' park is at street level at Washington and Steiner, the lovers' park on the hillside just above. And there's a "room" for connoisseurs of that sometimes hard-to-find San Francisco condition, windlessness, next to the row of cypresses along the crest of the park.

Then one must say that the park not only has rooms but architecture. People at drawing boards designed the staircases, terraces, paths and landscaping, then men and women installed them—and faithful retainers water the thirsty elements, perhaps as you read these words.

Even the shape of the land is a human artifact because more than a century ago it was barren and had been used as a quarry for filling other sites. There were dangerous holes, the biggest and deepest some 150 by 250 feet in size or a third of a block in the park's center.

The land had been set aside for a park early enough to prevent such treatment— "Alta Square" was one of six public squares or plazas west of Larkin Street that the Van Ness Ordinances of 1855 reserved for park use, the others being Lafayette Park, Alamo Square, Hamilton Playground, Jefferson Square and the present Funston/Moscone Recreation Center—but for a long time City Hall did nothing to develop the site (or the others for that matter). Incidentally, the eight-block-square formula for these parks was inspired in part by the notion that if a park is spacious but not *too* large, its visitors will be safe. Nineteenth-century security!

One Milo Hoadley claimed prior ownership at Alta Square and sued repeatedly to obtain it; it was only in 1888, at the Supreme Court level, that the not very civic minded Hoadley was rebuffed without recourse and finally gave up.

Houses had been going up in the neighborhood—on Clay and Steiner in the 1870s, and Scott was built up by 1885—and naturally there was growing agitation for development of the sad and barren area so unpleasantly visible from pretty bay windows in the area. But with Hoadley on the warpath City Hall had remained frozen.

With 1890 came the thaw. Property owners in the area hired a designer named R. Ulrich to prepare a plan for Alta Plaza Park and he duly came up with walks, terraces, the still-treasured "cozy nooks for rest and meditation," and plantings in the defunct quarry area that had for good reason been giving the neighbors fits.

Meanwhile a newly energized City Hall appropriated $10,000 to develop the park and in 1890–92 it was graded at last, holes filled, the still-present perimeter walls built, the Clay Street side terraced, the walks and staircases constructed, trees and grass planted.

It's been said that the great John McLaren created the plan, but I doubt it. In the 1890s McLaren was ruling over Golden Gate Park for the Parks Commissioners, and an entirely different department, the Superintendent of Streets, was charged with the work at Alta Plaza.

Whoever thought it up, the design with its handsome stairs, formally capped walls and Beaux Arts symmetry is excellent. The excavations were duly refilled and the four terraces create usable space out of the steepest natural slope, the Clay Street side at Pierce. Come to think of it, it was a bold idea in the first place to plan a park here, but then, this is ever-hilly San Francisco...

Over the years some Alta Plaza incidents have made news. After the '06 earthquake people took refuge in it. In 1938 a city supervisor thought selling it could ease a budget crunch—well, supervisors, you know—but thankfully the city attorney uttered a polite *no*. Then in 1971 a car chase for a movie was filmed on, yes on, the Pierce Street staircase, and the damage is still visible!

Mostly, though, the park has been a neighborhood joy, good to look at, or from, and a place where people meet people of like interests. In recent years the entrances have been enhanced and protected with seasonal flower beds. And lines of Japanese plum trees have been planted on the Steiner Street side. Long may they flourish.

No. 58

2600 Jackson

The Frame's the Thing

The street address is 2600 Jackson, but that's sort of a fib; the front door of this Ernest Coxhead gem is actually on Pierce Street. And what a front door—or rather, door frame. The actual door here is concealed at the side of an empty vestibule masquerading as the missing picture in an astonishing frame. Here, in short, the mundane fact of "access" gives way to Art.

Thanks to a giant puff of Coxheadian architectural steam, find at the Pierce Street "entry" columns and pilasters rising in proper Corinthian order from pedestal to a level door cornice on top, and above this a fanciful half-moon pediment repeating the cornice moldings and enclosing a huge bracket holding up, well, nothing; and then, next step above, a shield with three running rabbits in the Spanish style.

The whole marvelous ensemble is much too big for the size and placement of the house's windows, but it's needed to balance the severity (sensuous severity!) of brick walls relieved only by simple window sash. Coxhead, as we've seen before, liked to play tricks with scale and obviously he had a marvelous sense of humor, witness for instance that frame-without-a-picture at the entrance, perhaps a sly comment, this, on his client's noted art collection.

That client would be I. M. Scott, the engineer who turned Union Iron Works from the West's earliest iron foundry into its premier shipbuilders and, along the way, bought up a number of presumably estimable European paintings of the seventeenth and nineteenth centuries and works of such great Californians as William Keith and Jules Tavernier.

A bit more on the house itself. A single-story room at the Jackson/Pierce corner extends curbside walls in both directions, concealing a garden on the warm south side carved out of space originally intended as a staircase hall. On this, the Jackson Street side, the house is cut back in a variety of corners and the chimney seems to rise out of an elaborately stepped base that might have been crafted by a very bright child with building blocks; then there are characterful moldings shaped of brick, and an arched garden gate pretends to be the front door.

As for the inside, according to historian Richard Longstreth, it's full of witticisms, contrasts and magnificence.

The well-heeled Mr. Scott, who in his spare time was a UC Berkeley regent, a Stanford University trustee, Mechanics Institute president, Art Association president, etc., etc., had plenty of money to buy his daughter Alice a wedding-present house with views, garden, lots of space and even more personality.

With enviable tact Scott let the young Coxhead have his way; the architect insisted on strong brick construction, small rooms (sounds like a certain Frank Lloyd you-know) and no lavish stair hall. But the shipbuilding tycoon's order that undue extravagance be avoided went somewhat awry, construction costs rising between May and December of 1895 from a projected $4,709 to an astronomical $20,000.

Scott paid.

In June of '95 Alice Scott marred James Nash Brown, an insurance broker, but the couple had barely moved into 2600 Jackson when the unfortunate Brown died, in April '96. Alice remained single for three years, then married an Alabama-born naval surgeon with the equally triple-barreled and WASP-type name of Reginald Knight Smith.

Smith resigned from the Navy in 1905 and settled here as an obstetrician. When he died in 1937 his honorary pallbearers included twenty-seven (!) eminent physicians, among them key representatives from both of the arch-rival medical schools, Stanford and UCSF.

The Smiths lived only part-time in their Coxhead manor. But while city directories seldom listed them, social registers did. Names with a ring like Reginald Knight Smith don't, I suspect, grow on trees. At all events, after Dr. Smith died his widow did live on at 2600, among the Keiths and Taverniers, until her death in 1963 at an advanced age. Part- or full-time, she lived with those views of Alta Plaza Park and San Francisco Bay for sixty-seven years!

And then the couple's daughter Betty Knight Smith continued on at 2600 until her own death in the 1970s. Only in 1984 did the family sell. New owners repaired cracks in the brickwork and had the deteriorated sandstone entry frame replicated in a modern material. Preservationists can only say Bravo.

No. 59

2622 Jackson

Palladio West

622 Jackson looks like some lovely Palladian villa wafted from the Venetian countryside to a lawn facing Alta Plaza Park. What it is in fact is the realization of the dream of a seventy-year-old steel importer, name of Gibbs, who commissioned a brash and brilliant young architect to build him his perfect house, dignified, elaborate, but not ostentatious, a house in a class with those of his fellow moguls on the East Coast.

Willis Polk obliged with this quietly elegant essay in Renaissance symmetry which, according to Polk scholar Richard Longstreth, found its design sources in Tuscan villas, Raphael's Palazzo Pandolfini in Florence and the Temple of Vesta outside Rome. But it's not mere copy-work, it's a new whole, heralded at its birth in 1895 as "the first Classical residence in San Francisco."

Quite a payoff to George William Gibbs, this 2622, for gambling on a high-talking, publicity-seeking, twenty-nine-year-old architect who hadn't built anything on this scale.

Especially impressive is the house's round entrance portico, its beautiful proportions and serene setting—at night, by the way, when this portico is mysteriously lit, the effect is incredibly romantic. 2622 Jackson is also notable for its stone exterior, unusual for San Francisco, and the pioneering collaboration of artists who worked on it: the portico's Medusa heads were designed by Douglas Tilden, sculptor of the Mechanics Monument at Market, Bush and Battery Streets downtown, and man-of-all-arts Bruce Porter did the big stained glass stair-landing window.

G. W. Gibbs, alas, lived only two months after moving into his beautiful new residence, spending his last day, heartbreakingly one would think, but perhaps with a great calm, "directing the preparation of his grounds." Ironically the illness that forced Gibbs' essential retirement ten months earlier had permitted him to concentrate on the mansion's progress.

Born in 1824 in Albany, New York, Gibbs was the son of a Rhode Island governor who left a fortune to each of his five sons. After a proper formal education George Gibbs learned the shipping business for five years with East Coast merchants and spent four years as an independent tea importer in New York. The Gold Rush brought him to San Francisco in April 1849, but as his obituary says, "it took just two days to cure Mr. Gibbs of the gold fever, and then he began looking around for a suitable business enterprise."

With a partner he ran a general merchandise business for a while, then focused on importing iron, steel and heavy hardware—quite a change from tea! Buying out his ultimate partner he presided over G. W. Gibbs and Co. from 1876 until his death in November 1895. Meanwhile he found the time to be YMCA president, a director of Napa State Hospital and chief lay officer of Grace Cathedral, not to mention Turkish—honorary, of course—consul. Gibbs' widow, Augusta, stayed in the house until her death about 1918.

Thankfully the exquisite Gibbs House has never been seriously abused by alterations. Unintended alteration was avoided the day after the Pearl Harbor attack in 1941 when a fire alarm went off as the Japanese consul resident at 2622 was burning documents.

In 1950 the house began a long chapter as a small music school, the Music and Arts Institute. About this time the eminent and elderly Hungarian composer Ernst von Dohnanyi gave a Sunday afternoon concert in the garden, not free of wrong notes but with much charm. Coincidentally, when Dohnanyi's grandson, the noted conductor Christoph, along with his partner, the soprano Anja Silja, were here twenty years later for a production of a Janacek opera, they rented a flat in the towering house just to the east of 2622 Jackson.

Interlude

Continuing west on Jackson Street, the walking tourist passes the rather metallic 1950s modern building of Town School for Boys at the corner of Scott. Previously on this site was a large Queen Anne mansion, not very pretty as I remember, which became the home of a much younger and smaller Town School in 1942—the school had been operating in another Queen Anne over by Alamo Square, perceived by most parents at that time as "the wrong side of town."

At all events, the eighth-graders, me among them, helped move furniture into 2700 Jackson, which had been the Convent of the Sacred Heart, the summer of '42. We brats were particularly fascinated to find a barber chair up in the attic: this is where the nuns' tonsorial needs were taken care of. In due course the old chapel tacked onto the back of 2700 was reconstituted as a gym, and young Townies flew about its de-consecrated space on ropes.

Another school building of historic interest, this one still extant, is the Katherine Delmar Burke School (now University High) at 3065 Jackson, a Beaux Arts/Mediterranean affair with a lovely courtyard complete with fountain and designed by no less than Julia Morgan. As Sara Boutelle observes in her Morgan biography, the Burke School setting boasts "a pleasingly rhythmic relationship of inside to outside that is characteristic of Morgan at her best."

Then, between Town School and University High at 2944 Jackson one fairly gapes at one of San Francisco's few and best examples of streamlined Moderne. All in white, with sexily curving balconies, this compact house reaches the heights, you might say, of an earlier day's "cutting edge." It was designed in 1939 by Henry Howard, one of the several artistic sons—sculptor Robert, painter Charles also come to mind—of the noted Berkeley architect John Galen Howard who was so associated with the University of California.

Henry Howard's wife was a very petite Nicoise, Jane Berlandina, who taught art appreciation at Town School: slides of Monet, Manet and so on in a darkened Victorian parlor of a classroom on McAllister Street. I remember vividly her marionette-like appearance in a flaring skirt. There was generally a cigarette in her mouth, perhaps even while she was lecturing to us scruffy folk just in from the playfield. Ms. Berlandina was the designer of a well-remembered San Francisco Opera production of *Der Rosenkavalier* in 1940. As one critic put it, her light, witty sets "danced to the music."

Also not to be missed on Jackson, two doors west of the Coxhead house at Pierce: Ollie Lundberg's transformation of two formerly separate residences into a dazzling Moderne statement with Asian overtones. This house gleams at night like a giant FM radio receiver—dial your station! And it may be the most important example of contemporary residential architecture in San Francisco.

—Arthur Bloomfield

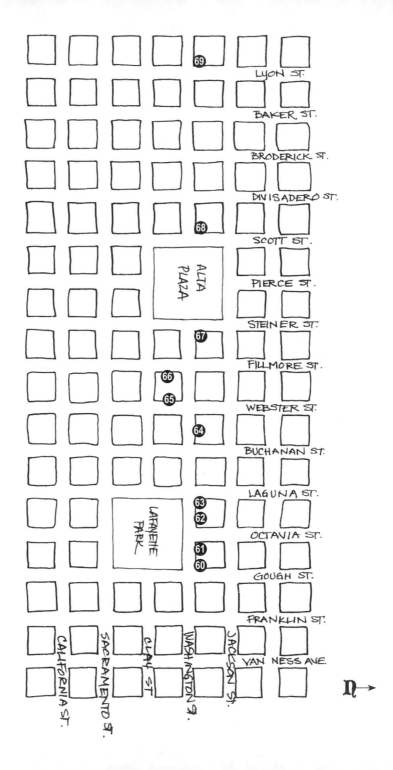

On or near

Washington Street

east to west

No. 60

2006 Washington

Monte Carlo West

The ever-pink 2006 Washington may be the most luxurious apartment building in Pacific Heights. Its full-floor apartments each claim an ultra-spacious six thousand square feet, and then there's the bonus: a heap of air space just to the west.

While the building itself occupies sixty-seven feet on its Washington Street frontage, the circular driveway and side garden take up another hundred feet, with only the porte cochère intruding. This uncapped space guarantees great light and fine views from all the west windows along a hundred feet of 2006's side wall. Not to be outdone, all the rear windows have bay views to the north, while the front ones overlook Lafayette Park to the south.

At street level the great space to the west is no perfunctory thing of mere blank pavements, it's graced by a subtly glamorous Mediterranean garden reminiscent of some five-star Monte Carlo hostelry or perhaps Julia Morgan's Hearst Castle. Lush greenery contrasts with handsome brick paving, and pine trees have been trained to enhance the views. Retaining walls pick up shapes and color from the apartment house itself.

Fantasy almost takes over here as cars enter the porte cochère then seem to vanish into an invisible garage, not far from a wall fountain flanked by Classical statuary.

2006 Washington is a large-looming but quiet companion to the property's remarkable open space, a building more dignified than decorated. First- and top-floor windows are round-headed but all the rest are modest rectangles and the ornamental metal balconies are strictly rationed. In sum there's just enough variety to keep the building from looking like a box.

The full-floor living units here have always been "community apartments." Translation: a corporation holds title to the building and pays the taxes while the individual apartment owners are shareholders of the corporation which maintains the building. This type of arrangement made its debut in San Francisco in 1914 with T. P. Ross' Greenwich Terrace on Russian Hill.

The corporation titled 2006 Washington acquired title to the land under the present building in June 1923 and construction was finished in 1925. The probable organizer of the scheme was an Agnes Mangels who lived next door in the apartment house at 2000 Washington and had connections to the Tillman family that had lived in the Victorian mansion preceding 2000 and 2006 on

Washington Street west of Gough. The new corporation bought the sixty-five feet of garden/driveway area nearer to the apartment house in the summer of '23, and the more westerly thirty-five feet (there must have been a house thereon eyed for demolition) in May '25.

And the architect of 2006? Well, no big surprise, it was C. A. Meussdorffer, author of the scarcely less impressive 2500 Steiner (Old House No. 56) which commands less acreage but does have a city park of its own to look out on.

The original shareholders in 2006 Washington were an interesting group. Count among them Roscoe and Margaret Oakes who donated much of the cream of the Fine Arts Museums' European collection—that means some Rembrandt and Hals, etc.; Dean Witter, founder of the well-known brokerage firm; financial manager Alan Lowrey and his father-in-law, railroader Charles Black; and several members of the Schilling Spice family: founder August Schilling, his son the physician and steam train aficionado Walter Schilling, and his daughter Else who was a Symphony buff and friend of Julia Morgan. Morgan it was who designed the interiors of the various Schilling apartments at 2006 in town and a house for Else at Lake Tahoe.

All carriage trade here, you see.

No. 61

2080 Washington

Sugar Cube ism by the Park

The "sugar palace," the nickname of this great old house at 2080 Washinton Street, does not as a matter of fact come from its admitted resemblance to a sugar cube; it refers, rather, to the name of the original owners, Adolph and Alma Spreckels. Everybody used to know SPRECKELS from the bags and boxes of sugar on supermarket shelves bearing that inescapable brand name.

Adolph Bernard Spreckels was prominent in the second California generation of a clan of robber barons. But even a serious historian like James Hart found their adventures superlative:

"By shrewd business methods, Claus [the father] Spreckels came to control all of San Francisco's sugar refineries and established the state's sugarbeet industry. He then financed the Hawaiian Kingdom and controlled much of its cane production and shipping. He also founded a railroad for shipping his produce by a means other than the monopolistic Southern Pacific; organized independent gas, light and power companies to combat the established public utility firms of San Francisco; and created a street railway line in opposition to the established firm.

"He and his two older sons feuded with the two younger ones over control of the family businesses and continued their fight by financing rival gas and electric companies, among other things...The second son Adolph was in the family sugar business, and his fury at the *Chronicle's* allegation that it defrauded stockholders led him to shoot publisher M. H. de Young."

And, on a gentler note:

"At age 50 he married Alma de Bretteville, with whom he donated the California Palace of the Legion of Honor art museum to San Francisco."

San Francisco is littered with sites of Spreckels mansions, but the only ones still standing are Adolph's confection at 2080 Washington and his distant relative Richard's on Buena Vista Avenue (lately a bed-and-breakfast), not to mention 2100 Vallejo, the Houghton Sawyer beauty that figured relatively briefly in the big Spreckels story (see Old House No. 9).

Papa Claus' first mansion, lost in the fire of '06, was at the northeast corner of Seventeenth Street and South Van Ness, the latter then called Howard Street in that part of town and a fashionable street it was, too—today the area could not be said to be gentrified. Oldest son John's house, also a big one, stood four blocks further south until quite recently.

Then the Spreckels household moved north.

Near the turn of the century Claus built a Pacific Heights mansion at the southwest corner of Van Ness and Clay, now the site of three large 1920s apartment buildings a degree or two below posh. John followed with his own distinguished pad at the northeast corner of Pacific and Laguna where newer construction may now be found. Baby Rudolph meanwhile put up a pillared affair at Pacific and Gough that was replaced about 1970 by the Mormon church currently on the site. Adolph was the last to build, but his mansion stands on the highest hill.

It was designed by George Adrian Applegarth working in an association with Kenneth MacDonald Jr. that also resulted in the Clift and King George hotels in the theater district downtown. On his own, Applegarth designed the Eastern Outfitting Building at 1019 Market with its delightful five-story Corinthian columns, also the Dante Hospital, now a seniors' residence, at Van Ness and Broadway, and, surely most significant, the Legion of Honor museum in Lincoln Park.

A 1906 graduate of the Ecole des Beaux-Arts, Applegarth designed with a French delicacy and sense of spatial organization. Here on Washington Street his French Baroque manner shows in the two-story Corinthian columns, intricately wrought metal balconies, round arches, etc. Since a grand symmetrical approach in the French manner was not possible on such a sloping site, Applegarth made the "next best thing" look perfect: a stone fence which steps grandly downhill in two directions from the corner of Washington and Octavia.

The house was ready just in time for Adolph and Alma to entertain lavishly when the 1915 Panama-Pacific International Exposition opened its doors down by the bay.

No. 62

2150 Washington

A Near-Wright Mansion

he lovely horizontal lines of 2150 Washington, the Phelan mansion, hint at the influence of Frank Lloyd Wright's Prairie style, but the design vocabulary—the house dates from 1914—is Renaissance Revival, especially in the expanses of buff-colored brick, the bas-relief terra-cotta arches, the broad eaves, the tile roof and driveway piers with their spiky metal lamps. The second-floor loggia seems part of the same Renaissance Revival package, but its columns, roof and glass were actually added later.

The house wraps around a courtyard, giving all the rooms windows on two sides. The front part, behind a procession of French doors capped with breathtakingly decorated arches, is actually a single long gallery, having with these prominent doors nothing to do with the main entrance which was placed, almost secretly, on the mansion's downtown side where there used to be a glass-fringed marquee.

This gorgeous 2150 Washington was designed by Charles Peter Weeks, one of San Francisco's leading architects a century ago. Like a number of his colleagues he studied at the Ecole des Beaux-Arts in Paris, and that influence can be felt in the house's impeccable symmetry.

When Weeks designed 2150 he was practicing architecture alone, between his 1903–1910 partnership with Albert Sutton and his 1916–1928 work with William P. Day—yes, their office was Weeks and Day. Weeks during his distinguished career was wholly or partly responsible for a number of outstanding buildings in San Francisco and other northern California cities, among them three grand buildings on Nob Hill, the Mark Hopkins and Huntington hotels and, across from the Fairmont, the Brocklebank Apartments which figured in Alfred Hitchcock's cult classic *Vertigo*.

1000 Van Ness, the present site of a cinema multiplex and formerly a Cadillac showroom, complete with columns topped by smiling bears, is a Weeks and Day opus from 1921; other credits include the Fox Theater and I. Magnin store in Oakland and the State Library in Sacramento.

Weeks' client on Washington Street, with a view over Lafayette Park, was another star San Francisco personality, James Duval Phelan. Native son, millionaire, son of a Gold Rush merchant and real estate tycoon, reform mayor at the turn of the century and member of the triumvirate masterminding the graft prosecutions of 1907, Phelan ordered up this house the same year he was successfully campaigning to become the first U.S. senator elected directly by the people rather than appointed by the legislature.

Actually the name of the owner on construction papers was the senator-to-be's sister Mary Louise Phelan. Neither ever married, and each had a separate apartment at 2150. It was their town residence until his death in 1930 and hers three years later.

Meanwhile the 1920 census reported a live-in staff of five maids, a "general man" and a cook, this support staff overwhelmingly outnumbering the unattached master and mistress of the house. Ida Hill had come from Finland, Rose Curran from England, Elsie Hags from Denmark, and the rest were, like Phelan's father, from Ireland.

The Phelans entertained together, timing construction of 2150 so they were ready to give grand parties for dignitaries visiting the 1915 Panama-Pacific International Exposition. Newspaper editor Fremont Older remembered Phelan as the city's greatest host since Billy Ralston, that colorful local figure who'd died in 1875.

Some of the entertaining, it should be noted, took place down the Peninsula

at Villa Montalvo near Saratoga, a Phelan property which the good senator eventually endowed as a refuge for artists, writers and musicians.

Phelan was California's leading Progressive, that being the party of Theodore Roosevelt in his later years. His integrity was rewarded with appointments to UC Berkeley's board of regents and, on a grander scale, as custodian of the worldwide relief funds attendant on the '06 earthquake and fire. As San Francisco's mayor from 1897 to 1901 he stopped boss rule, beautified parks, got a new city charter passed that initiated civil service and made the first filing for Hetch Hetchy water.

When boss rule returned with a vengeance he joined Rudolph Spreckels and Fremont Older in arranging for the famous graft prosecutions—finding the prosecutor, hiring the investigator and helping to finance them. Alas, when the trials reached beyond the politicians to the rich and influential who paid the bribes, Society—at least some of it—turned against Phelan and Spreckels. But he managed to outlast the freeze.

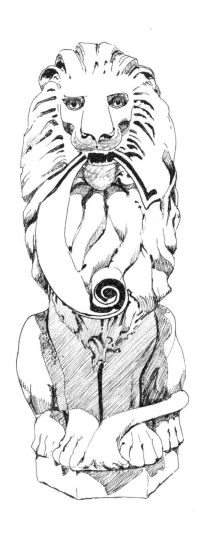

No. 63

2190 Washington

Lion at Attention

This marble lion and his twin have sat proudly at 2190 Washington since 1904, even though the apartment house whose presence they currently announce from virtual street level was only completed fifty-seven years later. In their earlier role they crowned eight-foot-tall pedestals and guarded a carriageway and curving double staircase, appurtenances these of the Irwin mansion ruined by fire in 1956. Only the walls and the lions survived.

These admirable pets were designed by one Professor Petrelli of Florence and executed in Carrara marble no less. Well, for William G. Irwin, who commissioned them, money was no object; when he died in 1914 his fortune was estimated at over ten million in the dollars of the day. Most of this pile came from Hawaiian sugar: he controlled the Hilo Sugar Company and half a dozen sugar plantations, and the "Spreckels" of sugar fame was for a time merely the "company" in William G. Irwin and Co.

And Irwin once bought the entire island of Lanai for a dollar!

This shrewd operator helped Anglicize Hawaii. As a boy with a British Navy father en route from Australia to Gold Rush California he'd been washed up on an Oahu beach during an operatic storm. Father and son stayed in the Islands and young Irwin became a bank clerk, and then, not so many years later, a bank president. He served in the cabinet of King Kalakaua, built a mansion in Honolulu and donated a fifteen-acre park.

Irwin and his wife didn't move to San Francisco until 1899. For their mansion here they commissioned the Reid Brothers, architects of some of California's best buildings, for instance the Hotel del Coronado near San Diego (1888), San Francisco's Fairmont Hotel (1906) and First Congregational Church near Union Square (1913).

The ill-fated 2190 Washington was a perfect cube, very Classical Revival. Constructed in steel and brownstone, it had four major floors, Ionic columns two stories tall and three layers of stone balustrades. The interior featured Tiffany stained glass, French marble fireplaces and Gobelin tapestries, and the drawing room was Louis XV. In the great Gothic dining room carved furniture matched dark paneled walls, while below a 60-by-24-foot ballroom shone in gold and cream—carriages drove right up to its terraced entrance.

Here the Irwins lived and entertained, beginning in 1901. The lions did not come off the boat until three years later, but surely great saddles of beef, fresh strawberries, good Bordeaux, brandy and cigars were not about to wait for these late arrivals.

The biggest event chez Irwin was the 1911 wedding of daughter Helene to Templeton Crocker of the Southern Pacific Railroad clan. The young couple proceeded to build their own mansion in Hillsborough, the great ship Uplands which later became Crystal Springs School for Girls. Then after Papa Irwin's wife died in 1924 the house in town was sold to the San Francisco County Medical Society for their headquarters and library. Helene Irwin Crocker removed the choicest family pieces and the other furnishings were sold at auction in 1926.

On the eve of the United States' entry into World War II the Irwin Memorial Blood Bank was launched at 2190, especially through the offices of Dr. John Upton, who was working toward supplying plasma for Britain, and Dr. DeWitt Burnham, who was organizing a centralized blood bank for local hospitals. When they banded together and the medical society agreed to shelter their facility in the old

Irwin mansion the world's first community blood bank went into operation.

The ballroom became the donation room, the adjacent kitchen and laundry were turned into labs and plasma was stored in the old wine cellar. Ex son-in-law Templeton Crocker gave blood at the opening in June '41 and the Irwin family donated money to the British War Relief Association for Upton's plasma processing operation. As time went on the Irwin Foundation continued giving major donations to the bank, which was named for William G. Irwin, the lion king himself.

A decade after the war the blood bank and the medical society moved to a new building on Masonic Avenue, leaving the Irwin mansion vacant. The builder Louis Epp bought it thinking to replace such an arguably impractical behemoth with an apartment building. Ironically, he found the price of demolition too high and it was only after the frightful fire of '56 that he went ahead with his plan for a curve-faced modern high-rise.

Thankfully Epp remembered the lions...

No. 64

2360 Washington

Pacific Heights Bavarian

*N*ot just a box with decorations, this countryish house at 2360 Washington: it has a steeply pitched roof complete with an asymmetrical set of dormer windows, a second floor making crisp shadows over the first, a nice side balcony, and there used to be a window box too. A cozy Swiss or Bavarian chalet if you will, designed by the popular Edgar Mathews in 1898 to grace a lot on the old Tuckerville block.

Although the owner's father had come from Bavaria and may have paid for the house, it was likely the reputation of Mathews as an imaginative architect rather than the more or less Bavarian style on offer that earned him the commission from William Lewis Gerstle, who lived here for three and a half decades.

Gerstle was born in San Francisco in 1868, his family involved in a great variety of San Francisco business ventures. He grew up living next to his aunt's family, the Louis Sloss clan; his father, Lewis Gerstle, and his aunt's Sloss husband were partners with Gustave Niebaum in the Alaska Commercial Company, which was fabulously successful for twenty years gathering sealskins in the Pribilof Islands under an exclusive contract.

Walrus heads from the company's demolished building still adorn the modern bank that replaced it at 370 California Street.

William Lewis Gerstle and his wife, Sara Hecht Gerstle, lived here on Washington Street next door to his brother's and her sister's house, in other words that of Mark and Hilda Hecht Gerstle. The Hechts were in shoe manufacturing. Meanwhile William's sisters married Lilienthals (as in the Haas-Lilienthal house) and a Fleishhacker in banking and electricity, and his first cousins included Haases, other Lilienthals, Isaac Walter of the decorating firm and a Koshland. The usual genealogical ragout.

William's more distant cousins make up half the membership of Temple Emanu-El and listing them would take more space than most publishers would allow.

All these families are descendants of Jewish immigrants from southern Germany who made fortunes as merchants in the wake of the Gold Rush and frequently focused on philanthropy. They established social, but not marital, equality with their non-Jewish peers in a refreshingly unpolarized upper-middle-class community and intermarried to an incredible degree.

Besides making a tidy fortune with Alaska Commercial, William Lewis Gerstle was president of the San Francisco Art Association, whose school is now the Art Institute. He himself painted seriously, and like his sister Bella Gerstle Fleishhacker he could boast of having had a one-man show at the Legion of Honor museum.

No. 65

2249–51 Webster

Mirror Image on Webster

In November 1879 the contractor/developer Henry Hinkel bought a corner lot at Webster and Washington measuring 78 by 69 feet for $3,650. Under today's regulations he would only have been able to build two, maybe three houses, but he managed to squeeze five into this space, each only 15 feet wide.

Not surprisingly they have walls in common, and since they were served up for many years as rentals, you could call them vertical flats.

The mirror image 2249 and 2251 Webster are two of the five; like the copy-cat pair just to the south, 2245 and 2247, they share a single rise of double entry stairs. The house at the corner, 2253, has its own narrower front steps. These houses' party walls make them almost if not quite unique in San Francisco. New York and Baltimore, of course, are famous for their common-wall row houses. And think London, too, where the term is "terrace house."

The construction date of 2249-51 and their siblings indicates houses in the Italianate style. And yes, the half-octagon bay windows, the acanthus-leaf brackets at door hoods, the arched window tops on the second floor and the rounded top corners of the first-floor fenestration, all these details are straight from the Italianate rule book.

The false mansard roof above the cornice was Henry Hinkel's nod to Second Empire style, a late subset of Italianate.

Henry was the oldest of five brothers of German parentage who all worked in the Bay Area as contractors and developers at one time or another. All his houses were Italianate—in part because he died in 1882 before much stylistic change was prevalent—but they didn't all have mansard roofs. Usually somewhat wider than 15 feet, they tended to have virtually identical floor plans: double parlor, each "half" separated by sliding doors, then a dining room with a diagonal corner fireplace and a side wall set in from the main house line to provide light, then at the rear a kitchen and small garden.

In the *California Architect and Building News* of February 1880 Hinkel announced he was putting up the five narrow houses on Webster Street. The following month he sold the whole package to a widow named Elizabeth May for $15,000 (and one might add that one of these $3,000 houses sold in the year 1999 for $1.5 million). She lived with her son George on the north fringe of Nob Hill and didn't need any of the Webster quintuplets for living quarters so she rented them out for fifteen years before they passed into the hands of the Raisch family. The Raisches kept all five "flats" until 1945.

Because renters are hard to trace I can offer only a sampling of the people who actually lived in these houses.

At 2249 the tenants in 1880 were Alfred Whitaker, head librarian for the Mercantile Library, which is now part of the Mechanics Institute, along with his wife, daughter, infant twins, mother-in-law and, probably stuck in the basement, a Chinese servant. Rather a tight fit at fifteen feet! Then in 1900 came a sixty-three-year-old widow, Kate Blevin, with her adult son and daughter, followed around 1910 by a French clerk, Charles Jardine, with his wife and their son and his sixteen-year-old bride.

At 2251 the tenants in 1880 were Alfred Barney, a deputy U.S. shipping commissioner, his wife, infant daughter and an "Irish maid"—not Isolde. From 1886 to 1901 attorney Simon Rosenbaum hung his hat at 2251, with two grown children and a maid on deck. And then from 1910 to 1914 the occupants were John Barnes and his wife, who had a bar—not a coffee-house!—on Fillmore Street nearby.

By 1901 the owners of the architectural quints were Gottfried and Anna Raisch, he being a street contractor. In 1909 they deeded the package to their youngest son, William, the family drifter. In 1916 William and his wife, Mae, handed it over to brother Fred, a plumber, and in 1929 Fred gave it back to Mae but not William.

As time went on the Raisches put off much needed maintenance, and when two African American couples bought the property in 1945 the building inspectors came down on them hard. This was one of the ways prejudice restricted civil rights in those days. But the couples persevered, made repairs, split the property into five individual lots and sold them all off in 1949.

About this time a delightful African American woman name of Mrs. Miller bought one of the larger houses on this block of Webster. With her carpenter husband she maintained it as one of the most attractive properties in the neighborhood for more than forty years. Mr. Miller loved to sit in his car listening to ball games and that is where he died, peacefully, in his eighties. There was a grand funeral in Third Baptist Church over by Alamo Square.

...And speaking of the Hinkel clan, Henry's brother Charles was responsible for a tract of eight houses around the corner on Washington Street, 2405 through 2461, built in 1888–89. A tract? you might well ask, because only the first, third and sixth of this Stick Eastlake octet look essentially like their original selves. Assorted Mediterraneanizing (Meddling?), Modernization, just plain Terrorization, have turned the others into hybrids, attractive enough in most cases but still, their face-lifts—nose jobs if you will—have toyed with architectural truth in quite alarming ways. The vaguely "Gothic" face of the Japanese church, the second house in the series, is perhaps the most appealing corruption.

The fate of this Hinkel-ville one must chalk up to the fears of being thought old-fashioned that swept over a still-Victorian San Francisco in the middle years of the twentieth century. Appreciation of historic authenticity is much stronger today than it was fifty, sixty, seventy years ago, and for this we must all of course sing Amen.

No. 66

2318 Fillmore

Here's Looking at You

*D*id you know that the popular Mayflower grocery kitty-
corner from Calvary Presbyterian Church at Fillmore and Jackson
used to be called the Foxhall Market, and
that the Foxhall in an earlier time (from
1897) was established in the large building a block and a half south—that's 2318
Fillmore—which retains to this day grand
pairings of oval windows staring impas-
sively as if through giant lorgnettes at the
passing parade?

Amusing, perhaps, that the building
now houses an eye research institute.

There were, back around 1900, at least
four "stallholders" operating under the
merchandising hat of the Foxhall, two
butchers, a greengrocer and a milk dealer.
Also there was a drayage company operating out of the basement. Later 2318 became a van and storage company, then
an auto repair garage before assuming its
present more office- and lab-oriented
identity, with a bit of exterior remodeling
to make an appropriate entrance.

Originally the building was a stable,
and it was, as it remains to this day, the
most substantial structure in the immediate area of the Upper Fillmore, with
some competition from another ex-
garage across the street, the Pets Un-
limited facility which recently expanded

somewhat beyond its earlier not inconsid-
erable dimensions.

The Gertrude Bowers Brick Stable
Building, that being 2318's official historic moniker, is significant as one of the
few surviving "industrial" buildings put up
by the distinguished architectural firm of
Percy and Hamilton, not to mention its
having brick bearing walls in an area where
frame construction predominates.

And then there's the fact that here was
a creative investment in the economic life
of the neighborhood instigated by a woman at a time when a lady's place was in the
home pouring tea.

The firm of George W. Percy (1847–
1900) and Frederick F. Hamilton (1851–
1899) ranks high among northern California's best late-nineteenth-century
architects. Alas, they both died relatively
young, but not before designing the Art
Museum and Roble Hall, then the fresh-
man women's dorm, at Stanford University, the Alameda City Hall, the Bourne
(later Christian Brothers) Wine Cellar at
St. Helena and the First Unitarian Church
in San Francisco.

Except possibly for the Sperry Flour
Mill at Stockton, and 2318 Fillmore of
course, most of their industrial buildings
are gone.

Most of their public and semi-public

work was Romanesque, reflecting their training in Boston during H. H. Richardson's reign there. 2318, however, seems with its stucco front, tiled cornice, rope moldings and mildly Churrigueresque surrounds to have been one of the early responses to Willis Polk's trumpet call for architects to build on California's Spanish heritage.

This response may in fact have been an introduction to the professional association which Percy established with Polk after Hamilton's death, and which, in a brief time, netted the Kohl Building downtown on Montgomery Street and the Wilson Building on Market.

Gertrude Bowers was the millionaire widow of George M. Bowers, a "capitalist" who probably made his fortune in mining and who in 1885 had Percy and Hamilton design him a residence (no longer extant) at 2610 Jackson, just next to our Old House No. 58, that Coxhead masterpiece of architectural whimsy. Widowed in '93, Mrs. Bowers ordered up the stable as one of her earliest investments of the fortune just bestowed on her.

A smart woman, she probably opted for a brick structure for its fire-resistant qualities in relation to hay storage. But it's not likely she was directly involved in a far-out decision to suspend the second floor from a truss system above. Meanwhile one thing is sure: Mrs. Bowers made hay, economically speaking, while the sun shone.

No. 67

2400 and 2402 Steiner

School of Maybeck by the Park

*N*o, the crisply shingled 2400 Steiner is not a Maybeck. Or a Willis Polk, as I was once told on a house tour. But its design certainly was influenced by Maybeck, and its architect, John White, was in fact Maybeck's brother-in-law and sometime partner.

2400 represents very well that style known as the Bay Area Tradition, a style in which, as Professor Longstreth puts it, "elaborate Classical elements [are] set off against relatively plain, vernacular-inspired masses." The vernacular vocabulary here, straight out of medieval Europe, includes plain walls, steep roofs, multi-pane windows, roof dormers, noticeable chimneys, common materials in general.

As for Longstreth's "elaborate Classical elements," look for them at the entrance. Huge consoles with acanthus leaves hold up the second-floor balcony just above, there's a proper pediment over the front door, and the door itself features pillowy panels and a light surrounding garland.

Note that the house is only forty-seven feet deep on the Washington Street side. Immediately to the east stands a shingled building frequently mistaken for a continuation of 2400 Steiner, but this is a completely separate piece of real estate. Fooling us seems to have been the intent when a different architect built this different building for a different client three years after 2400 went up in 1900.

White's clients at 2400 were Edward G. and Alice McCutchen Schmiedell. Her family founded the well-known law firm of McCutchen et al. and his pioneer father was a successful stockbroker and real estate investor, so money flowed on both sides. The Schmiedells were art patrons and environmentalists besides being Social Register types and he was first cousin to the Monterey painter Charles Rollo Peters and brother-in-law to the architect George Howard, about whom more in a moment.

As a student in Paris Schmiedell may have studied art. But business took precedence when he came home to become a highly successful manufacturer's agent: from 1897 he was half of the firm Maillard and Schmiedell in partnership with an ancestor of longtime San Francisco congressman William Maillard.

2400 Steiner was merely the Schmiedells' property in town; their lifelong residence was No. 1 Upper Road in Ross, the posh Marin County suburb where Alice Schmiedell helped found the Marin Art and Garden Club. The San Francisco house was rented out, first to attorney and Yehudi Menuhin–benefactor Sidney Ehrman, who later settled into 2970 Broadway, Old House No. 30. The house in Ross was also designed by John White, in 1896.

White had grown up in Kansas City where he worked as a draftsman for Henry Van Brunt, the noted post–Civil War architect and theorist, from 1886 to 1891. In 1889 Bernard Maybeck moved to Kansas City, met John White, and the following year married White's sister Annie and moved to the Berkeley he'd be so associated with. John White followed a year later.

White's first commission came in '94, Maybeck's in '95. Then while Maybeck was in Europe managing the UC Berkeley Master Plan competition he entrusted his local office to White. In 1900, the year 2400 Steiner was designed, White went to work for George Howard.

After the 1906 fire four still-young architects, Maybeck, Howard, White and his younger brother Mark were joined in a single office, then two years later that partnership was amicably broken up and the firm of Howard and White (that's John White) continued into the late twenties, specializing in Peninsula mansions for Howard's family connections.

One suspects John White met George Howard through the latter's connection by marriage to Edward Schmiedell. And perhaps Schmiedell met White through acquaintance with Maybeck in Paris. At all events, the Schmiedells became valuable patrons: White or the firm of Howard and White designed Ross' landmark

firehouse and Lagunitas Club and possibly its town hall, also houses for Edward's partner Maillard, his cousin Peters, and maybe the Schmiedells themselves at Tahoe and Carmel.

...And now to 2402 Steiner, that's another Schmiedell house. In 1900 Edward signed contracts for *two* houses on Alta Plaza Park, a $12,500 "residence" at 2400 and a $7,000 "frame building" at 2402. These terms suggest the Schmiedells intended to use the "residence" as just that, while leasing the "frame building." Actually, as time went on each served briefly as a town pied-à-terre, but that Marin address in Ross was always basic *home*, until their deaths in 1959 and 1964.

Where 2400 and 2402 Steiner still stand, two earlier houses had been put up by The Real Estate Associates, a premier tract developer, in 1878. These residences faced Washington Street and resembled the remaining 2572 Washington. Now, in 1878 Alta Plaza Park wasn't much to look at, just sand and rocks and junk, so no wonder the TREA houses averted their gaze from such an eyesore.

By the turn of the century, however, the park was up and running as a community asset and the Schmiedells' idea was to build a pair of houses in the latest style and point them at the nice landscaping across Steiner Street. Well, one should say two styles, for 2400 was shingled and 2402 half-timbered.

And that makes sense because while shingle expert John White, much associated with Berkeley and Marin, designed 2400, half-timber specialist George Howard, White's boss at the time and a Hillsborough mansion architect, did 2402. Evidently there was no problem with a subordinate in the Howard office going against the "house style." If, in fact, there really was one!

Today we miss 2402's half-timbering under the universally applied white paint. Originally the house must have been especially striking with the counterpoint of dark wood, white plaster and deep red clinker brick. Those winged gargoyles jutting like errant Pegasuses between floors would have matched the wood.

In spite of their differences, 2400 and 2402 do share the design philosophy of the Arts and Crafts movement with its advocacy of simple living and that interesting thing called "created rusticity."

Of the several noted architects practicing this philosophy, Maybeck and Ernest Coxhead among them, George Howard was the wealthiest. His stepfather, one of them at any rate, owned the 6,500-acre Rancho San Mateo. Educated in Switzerland and Paris, Howard was also inspired by his mother's head gardener, John McLaren, who went on to be the boss of San Francisco's giant Golden Gate Park. Howard's second known commission, executed when he was thirty years old, was the Burlingame train station, which is generally acknowledged as the first permanent building in Mission Revival style.

Howard was one of the founders and first councilmen of Hillsborough, the posh suburb built on his family's land. And he had money enough to sometimes waive a fee when designing houses for Hillsborough friends. The Howard and White partnership was harmonious, an interesting blend of contrasting personalities: the charming and attractive Howard with his rich family connections and the introspective White, friend and brother-in-law of Maybeck.

No. 68

2301 Scott

A Parliamentary Architect's Work

*N*ow, what does 2301 Scott Street have in common with the Pacific Union Club (ex-Flood mansion number two) on Nob Hill?

Not much actually, but the architect is the same—Augustus Laver. If you don't compare the august P.U. and 2301 too closely the latter has quite a lot going for it. The round tower at the corner commands the house's hillside location and Alta Plaza Park across the street, the Ionic colonnade which seems to carry the tower gracefully on its shoulders is well-proportioned, and the attendant balustrade lacks nothing in cheerful delicacy.

Then there's the roof which is certainly "picturesque"—as a review of the house when it was new in 1898 exclaimed—thanks to its steep incline and wide overhanging eaves.

Also of note are the deeply shadowed entry porch, the projecting balcony behind the balustrade and the undulating wall on the Washington Street side. An estimable Queen Anne, in short, and it was Laver's last building, one of three known to remain in San Francisco: besides 2301 Scott and the P.U. Club there's a residence on Golden Gate Avenue near Scott in the Alamo Square neighborhood.

2301 is a shade busy, and perhaps some of the over-busyness should be attributed to Laver's partner at the time, Patrick Mullany, who'd been a draftsman in the much-senior architect's office. On the other hand, Laver himself designed some pretty fancy stuff. As he conceived it, the Flood mansion was somewhat less dignified than it emerged after Willis Polk's post-1906 alterations including side wings. The pre-1906 City Hall from Laver's drawing board was certainly on the wild side ornamentation-wise.

Born in England in 1834 and trained there, Laver practiced architecture for several years in Canada, designing some of the parliament buildings in Ottawa. He also worked for a time on New York's State Capitol at Albany, which riders of Amtrak's Lakeshore Limited may spy as they wait for the train's Boston and New York sections to link up at a station across the way.

Then in 1870 he won the competition for San Francisco's old City Hall design. But after coming West he became embroiled in a stormy relationship with a very political building committee and ultimately gave up the project in disgust.

Meanwhile he peppered the letters pages of the local newspapers with his unflinching opinion that City Hall was being built all wrong, and the fact is he was proved absolutely right when it collapsed like the proverbial house of cards during the '06 quake.

The first owner of 2301 was Patrick Mullany's lawyer brother, Michael, like him an immigrant from Ireland. For half a dozen years both brothers had quarters in the big corner house along with a third sibling, Thomas, and Michael's wife, Ellen. Almost a variation, this, on the recurrent theme of "spinster" sisters sharing a Pacific Heights mansion. But the Mullany clan didn't stay nearly as long as some of those tenacious single females of Pacific and other avenues.

According to the 1900 census there were no servants in residence at 2301. An example of Irish frugality?

Interlude

Walk a block west from Augustus Laver's swan song, turn left, and there on the west side of the street is the charming and rather improbable 2229 Divisadero, two Italianate Victorians actually—they date originally from 1877—but the more southerly of the houses, a kind of sidecar to its mate, only has one story and its front door, slighter than that of its neighbor, is framed by a pair of narrow windows suggesting serious rethinking of the house's fenestration somewhere along the historical way.

The explanation I can give is largely thanks to Sara Holmes Boutelle's copious biography of Julia Morgan. When, about

1929, the illness of the diminutive architect's mother made it impractical to keep up the family home in Oakland she bought the houses on Divisadero, then numbered 2209 and 2211, remodeled the more uphill one into an apartment for herself, doubtless upstairs, plus two rental units, and meanwhile lopped off the second floor and attic of its neighbor just to the south and connected the pair, the principal reason for the decapitation of 2209 being to provide good south light for the upper floor of 2211. Rarely has a head been lost so elegantly!

And today there remains a slight air of mystery about the complex, because one flight of front steps, and one house number, lead to two somewhat different but equally impressive "front" doors; neither is remotely a "tradesman's" entry.

Continuing out Washington Street it's hard not to notice and be charmed by Engine Company No. 23, that's to say the former firehouse at 3022 with its ecclesiastical hose-drying tower. This gem was designed by Henriksen and Mahoney, the same firm responsible for an almost identical firehouse at 1152 Oak Street a little south of Alamo Square. The initial construction cost was $4,880. Engine Co. 23 went into service in 1894, a time when weekly inspections were held to determine how quickly the horses could be harnessed to the steam engines—more than twelve seconds was considered a poor show. It was decommissioned in 1963 when it was sold for $50,000, a fairly princely sum at that time, and became an interior designer's studio-residence and literary party venue.

—*Arthur Bloomfield*

No. 69

2107 Lyon

The Gem behind the Wall

And now what is very probably the greatest work of art in this series, the Church of the New Jerusalem, the Swedenborgian Church at the corner of Washington and Lyon. As if one could say it has a location, this church behind a retaining wall and grove of trees. It retreats so from the distractions of the city, physically and spiritually, that it seems in this lyrical process to almost melt, as it were, back into nature.

And all this aura of pastoral self-effacement behind a picturesque but almost crouching entrance is consistent with the personality of the church's first clergyman, Joseph Worcester, a very special guru who inspired a number of cutting-edge architects to collaborate harmoniously on a project blending numerous arts.

You enter the slightly stunted archway on Lyon Street, turn left into a roughly stuccoed passageway, expecting perhaps to see an operatic monk or two, then come onto a gentle lawn enclosed by trees and bushes, with an antique mission cross and some stepping stones. You have to turn about-face to find the church itself, and then you must cross to the lawn's far corner and duck under another archway.

The place exudes peace, and with mind at rest you enter the church to discover nature is indoors as well as out, propelling your meditation. There's a brick fireplace nearby, and benches next to it where you enter at the rear of the hall. A short, unthreatening aisle leads between rows of starkly simple handmade maple chairs with rush seats. And on the left wall: glorious paintings of the seasons! The feeling is more meeting-house than church.

The wall opposite is a series of metal windows admitting light, often strong, from the garden. Madrone trees with the bark on are the raw material for pillars and braces strapped together to hold up the two-sloped ceiling—the trees were specially chosen from a farm in the Santa Cruz mountains and personally brought to the church by the farm's owner. And notice two bits of stained glass, one a dove of peace, just enough to hint at traditional church architecture.

No, the Swedenborgian is not traditional. But neither is it revolutionary, in the way, say, of Nervi's St. Mary's Cathedral on Cathedral Hill. The architecture is unique, but it employs familiar imagery from California missions and Italian country churches. Don't laugh at the analogy—the blend here of local and perhaps Mediterranean inspiration recalls today's California Cuisine.

The Swedenborgian came to be in 1894 through a combination of talents, no one of whom ever took credit for the whole.

Rev. Joseph Worcester commissioned it, Renaissance man Bruce Porter sketched a prototype Italian hill church and made the stained glass, A. Page Brown, the architect of San Francisco's Ferry Building, took responsibility for working drawings and supervision of construction, Bernard Maybeck of Palace of Fine Arts fame (he was in Brown's office at the time) made a presentation drawing of the project, and A. C. Schweinfurth, probably also in Brown's office and an inspired architect who espoused the use of primitive materials in artistic buildings, very likely had a hand in the design as well.

The legendary nineteenth-century landscapist William Keith contributed his marvelous *Seasons* as an offering from a humble member of the congregation. And the name of Willis Polk should be added to the all-star cast of designers because as a neighbor and disciple of Worcester's he doubtless put in his thoughts on the fascinating matter at hand.

Each of these men produced by himself wonderful art in other contexts. But which of them is chiefly responsible for this place? The question has defied the attempts of numerous architectural historians to pin down The Name. Well, I think we will never have just one name. I think all these competitive egos were able to subdue themselves for this one project, and the reason for their cooperation was the inspiration of Joseph Worcester.

This gentle, unassuming clergyman whose sermons were abstract and almost inaudible and who attracted a highly intellectual congregation and inspired people to great works of charity was an amazing person. Son of a Swedenborgian minister in New England, he espoused a religion in which nature shows the path to God. Utterly selfless, he struck at least one of his students as the closest man to Jesus Christ on earth.

Worcester had considered architecture as a profession and he remained an amateur architect—he kept an excellent library filled with scrapbooks on design. When Brown, Polk, Coxhead and other budding architectural giants came to San Francisco Worcester stood back and pushed them forward. The mentor extraordinaire, he conducted a virtual salon where the young men discussed the philosophy, the mission of their work.

They idolized him, and only such a man could have inspired such a great work of art as the Church of the New Jerusalem.

On or near

Clay Street

east to west

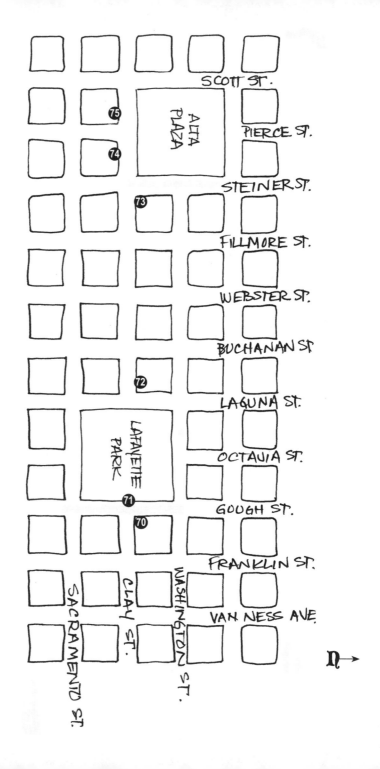

No. 70

2000 Gough

Architecture According to Smith

*A*ficionados of photographs from the earthquake and fire of 1906 will recognize 2000 Gough, one of the three oldest buildings opposite Lafayette Park. An oft-reproduced shot of the devastation just to the east shows the house and its neighbor 2004—which a son of 1952 presidential candidate Adlai Stevenson once called home—standing in the foreground very much intact and symbolic of San Francisco's intention to carry on.

Looking now pretty much as it did then, 2000 Gough, which dates from 1885, is a distinctive house, even if its architect was a Smith that I once confused with another Smith when writing about one of his Pacific Heights houses. Pseudostructural "sticks" and other verticals divide the surface into a symphony of rectangles (this, of course, is a Stick style house) and there are nice Queen Anne bits as well: the round bay windows, fish-scale shingles and a complex roof, all well harmonized.

Credit for the appearance belongs not only to a Smith (initials W. F.) but to a man named Jones who contracted for the house. Nearly impossible names to research, as you know if you ever tried to find that particular Smith or Jones—in San Francisco add Lee, Wong and Ng—in the phone book. But this time I was lucky.

William F. Smith, active as an architect in San Francisco for more than three decades, has managed to remain quite unnoticed by most architectural historians. But he conducted a healthy practice, mostly residential and much of it in Pacific Heights. His clients included no less than Adolph Sutro before he became mayor. His oeuvre was mostly in mid-range houses: no mansions, that is, but there were hardly any cottages either.

Among his works are our Old House No. 37 at 2505 Pacific along with its tract-mates just to the west; the original of the strenuously remodeled Old House No. 26, which achieved its new form via the drawing board of Frank Van Trees, at 2536 Broadway; and also Old House No. 96 at 1900 Pierce, which I confess to attributing wrongly to an A. W. Smith who would have been about twenty-one when it was built. Another building from W. F. was the brick and stone garage, formerly a stable, which sat dutifully across California Street from Grand Central Market until it was demolished some years ago for a parking lot, not bringing many tears in its behalf.

Once I had the correct identity of the architect of 2000 Gough *and* 1900 Pierce, I saw only too clearly their points in common, not only the rounded bay windows but the elongated eave brackets and the shadowy entrances from porches incised in each case into the main mass of the house.

The Joneses involved with 2000 Gough were three: a wholesale grocer named Michael P. Jones who bought the lot, signed for the water and contracted for the house; his son and junior partner, Webster Jones, and Webster's bride, Beulah Hobbs Jones, to whom Papa Jones gave the house as a wedding present, nothing less. Young Webster, that well-housed fellow, was just three years out of Harvard.

The lengthy newspaper article about Webster and Beulah's marriage, on June 1, 1885, concluded: "The happy couple...will return to the city toward the close of the month to reside quietly until the completion of their future residence on Gough and Clay Streets, the gift of the groom's father. Cards will not be sent out until the dwelling is ready for occupancy."

The "happy couple" did reside in the house, according to *Our Society Blue Books,* until they separated about 1898. They divorced in November 1899, trying to be hush-hush by going to court down in Santa Barbara. Divorce just wasn't done in those days. Four months later the *Daily Call* reported rumor of Beulah's engagement to Count Vladimir Artsimovitch, Russian consul general in San Francisco. The story accompanied a photo of a handsome and headstrong-looking "Mrs. Webster Jones." In April the Count's convenient transfer to Berlin—should we picture a dashing fellow out of Tolstoy?—and the couple's now official engagement were announced.

And one supposes Webster slunk off to his club.

So the house was sold, to Ludwig Schwabacher, manager of Crown Paper Company, a predecessor of Crown Zellerbach. It was inherited by his son James, who lived at 2000 before moving to 2520 Pacific—that's our Old House No. 39.

No. 71

1925 Gough

Apartments in the Park

925 Gough Street is the apartment building inside Lafayette Park. How it got there is quite a story, and it begins a century and a half ago when San Francisco was essentially empty west of about Stockton Street downtown.

Once upon a time, I mean until 1855, San Francisco had no parks west of Union Square. But early residents and speculators laid out claims all over the place. In 1855 the city fathers passed the Van Ness Ordinance, named after the mayor at that time, to legalize land claims, including those of the City itself.

This law provided for the laying out of streets from Larkin west to Divisadero, and the reservation of land here and there for public use. A surveying commission comprised of Messrs. Hayes and Gough—whose names presently grace one of San Francisco's busiest gourmet-ghetto intersections—chose the streets we have now, plus twenty-eight school lots, twenty-five firehouse lots, a hospital space, and nine parks, including Lafayette and Alta Plaza, in what we know as Pacific Heights.

But the parks remained undeveloped until the 1890s. There were years and years of lawsuits by persons who said they'd established claims to the parklands before 1855. Some of the claimants had political pull, and most of them persisted with multiple suits.

One of the noisier ones was attorney Samuel W. Holladay (not to be confused with Hallidie the cable car inventor) who lived at the northeast corner of Clay and Octavia in what is now the middle of Lafayette Park. The site of his house, just above the slope where sunbathers gather on good days, is still a rectangular lawn surrounded by trees—as if Holladay had willed some special remembrance.

In any event, in 1867 the Fourth District Court accepted his argument that the land had never been dedicated as a park and it awarded him both sides of Clay Street, from Octavia east to Gough, half a block deep. Holladay's possession of this space was still legally recognized as late as 1913, with the park around him already up and running. But somehow the City managed to reduce his land to just what's occupied by 1925 Gough, the St. Regis Apartments as it was originally known, which went up in 1914.

The property was developed by sixty-four-year-old Alexander William Wilson, a Swedish immigrant who'd built a fortune in San Francisco apartments and hotels. He claimed to have constructed the very first apartment building in the city. In the earthquake and fire of '06 he lost all his units, a whole lot of 'em, but he soon rebuilt, starting with the Grand Hotel at Turk and Taylor, near the present-day Original Joe's in the Tenderloin. He also developed and owned a hotel at Eddy and Mason, a better corner then than it is today, and apartments at 840 Powell on Nob Hill and 2135 Sacramento and 1810 Jackson in Pacific Heights.

His architect of choice was our old friend C. A. Meussdorffer, apartment specialist to the upper crust. Meussdorffer was said to be a tyrant with his employees, insisting on correct construction standards, and no wonder the socialites liked him.

The St. Regis must have been A. W. Wilson's crowning glory: it's a very satisfying building, with just enough lovely curves to make it interesting. Incidentally, all four sides are finished, which is most unusual. There are two apartments to each floor, but each runs a copious three thousand square feet. A corporation owns the building, has always done so, and the stockholders—which have included two Bank of California presidents and oldtime Hearst newspaper executive Edmond Coblentz, editor of the *New York American* in the 1930s—are the apartment owners. This makes for longtime residents: Wilson's widow, for instance, was still living at 1925 Gough in 1953!

...And all those Gough Street commuters who pass the gently undulating 1925, which looks as if it belonged in Cannes, the sixteenth arrondissement of Paris or one of the better blocks on Manhattan's Upper West Side, probably never stop to think: how curious, that building is *in the park.*

No. 72

2214 Clay

The House That Climbed the Hill

Have you ever seen a house move?—besides in an earthquake, that is. Well, it gets jacked up off its foundation, placed on wheels or skids and ignominiously hauled to the new site where the process is reversed. Lots of buildings have been moved—for redevelopment, freeway construction, some other new project. But it's astonishing how many were moved more than a hundred years ago, how good the technology was even in those far-off times.

2214 Clay, until around 1905, was not on upper Clay near Lafayette Park but down on Polk Street on part of the lot where the Alhambra cinema, now a whopping gym, stands today. Moving this sizeable house had to be quite a project. I can easily imagine it being jacked up by human muscle and hauled by mules up gentle slopes on Pacific, but how did they get it up the steep Clay Street hill between Buchanan and Laguna and level it at such an angle to the slope? Jacks? More and more I respect our ancestors' skills and inventiveness.

It was one Annie Wallace who had the house carted up the hill from Polk Gulch. She lived in it both before and after, a total of some forty years. It had been built for her in 1885 by an indulgent father—familiar scenario, this!—an entrepreneur named George Bradley who started out in the wholesale liquor business, eased into real estate and proceeded to live off his healthy income.

The year before he had the house built he gave the nineteen-year-old Annie a wedding that was the Social Event of the Week. The *San Francisco Call* described the gowns and jewels of twenty-eight ladies, commencing with:

> *The bride wore a magnificent white satin court train. The petticoat was beautifully arranged with rich point lace one yard deep, and marabout feathers; the train was also edged with the same feathers; the corsage was in points, cut square at the neck, finished with point lace; a bunch of feathers were worn at the corsage; elbow sleeves, and long mousquetaire gloves were worn; the coiffure was draped in two flat coils...*

Etc., etc., etc. yackety-yackety-yackety...

The article took over a full newspaper column to chronicle the flowers, gifts and socialite guests. But the writer, clearly not a foodie, skipped over fine points of the supper which the guests "discussed for a full hour."

The marriage that followed, like some others noticed in "Old Houses" of Pacific Heights, was, alas, less successful. The couple were separated for the last dozen years of Ryland Wallace's life, which ended in 1911. Though he was a lawyer he never made much of a career, unlike his father, who was chief justice of the State Supreme Court.

The early years of the marriage must

have seemed brighter; that's when George Bradley had this house built for his daughter—in an area, the west flank of Lafayette Park, where the neighbors included Union Iron Works president Henry Scott, noted ophthalmologist Adolph Barkan and the rancher Henry Miller (no, not the novelist) who controlled fifteen million acres of land in the Central Valley.

The architects Bradley chose were Samuel and Joseph Cather Newsom of Carson House (in Eureka) fame. In San Francisco they're responsible for 1737 Webster (our Old House No. 105), 2402 Bush, the store with a hole through the second story at Oak and Divisadero and many other buildings.

The Newsoms attained fame by exaggerating the latest fads, but this house, which cleverly balances the prim and the rather racy, seems relatively quiet. It is, though, more than up to date. With its complex façade and roof and the variety of wall surface materials (from wavy to hexagonal shingles and horizontally grooved boards) it looks a good ten years later than its actual date of origin.

And with that jutting "summer house" bay at the left just a little bit, perhaps, like a house out of a Chekhov play.

Interlude

It must be one of the earliest still-active cinemas in San Francisco: the Clay Theater down the hill at 2261 Fillmore with its simple but garlanded façade, a handsome female mask at its center. Put up in 1913 by the father-son team Rousseau and Rousseau and known during the 1920s as the Regent, it was originally a nickelodeon and has been an "art house," showing foreign and independent films, as long as anyone can remember.

As a schoolchild in the forties I saw silly Austrian musical comedies there with the tenor Leo ("When does the next swan leave?") Slezak, whimsical Hitchcock thrillers from his prewar days, and crackly French classics like *The Baker's Wife* and *Fanny*. The Clay may have been a homely palazzetto, but Jean Gabin, Robert Donat and Leslie Howard were the draws. A decade later, past adolescence and madly in love with a pink-ankled piano student at Stanford, I was weeping over Micheline Presle and Gerard Philippe in *Devil in the Flesh* one murky Sunday afternoon on Fillmore.

In the fifties one could lick one's emotional wounds at a convivial pastrami emporium across the street—site of the present Via Veneto—which went by the name Bon Vivant. This was a ray of light on a nuts-and-bolts high street where the prospect of today's forty or so eating places would have put frowns of disbelief on the faces of people in the 'hood.

...And, as we continue out Clay, here's a song from the Stanford Medical School spring show of 1944, a confection hatched just up the hill where California Pacific hospital is now:

Clay Street, Clay Street, the Do or Die Street,
I Was Your Slave Completely...

I suspect the vocalist is referring to cramming for exams, not the charms of the rue!

—Arthur Bloomfield

No. 73

2302 Steiner

An Unidentical Twin

302 Steiner has sometimes been considered a near twin of 2100 Scott at Sacramento three blocks away. Now it's conceivable both designs—the time is 1897—came from the same pattern book, but they differ in important details. Here's what's similar: both houses have elaborate entrances on the long rather than the customary short side of the lot, and each is a totally symmetrical two stories with basement and attic, narrow clapboard siding, Ionic corner pilasters and elongated hip roof with dormer windows.

Lots of very lovely detail at 2302, most noticeably perhaps the festive wreath-and-garland frieze below the roof and over the front door. The house seems to have gone to a fun and elegant party! Notice as well how the balustrades on the second-floor balconies curve down from matched posts in graceful U's, a typical Colonial Revival device. Other interesting curves include the three arches at the entrance and the arch that makes a Palladian ensemble of the three windows over the stately pillared entrance.

And there are two porthole windows peering out at Alta Plaza Park across the street.

The architects here—pastry chefs of the drawing board, you might say—were the little known John J. Laferme and Otto Collischonn. They were not, by the way, involved in the fraternal 2100 Scott. San Francisco directories list Laferme only from 1896 through '98, and Collischonn 1897–98, 1904–05, 1908–10 and 1914. This is the only building I know of on which they collaborated—and a felicitous collaboration it seems to have been.

Whether the architects or their clients decided so, it was an obvious decision to put the entrance facing a park that had recently been transformed from a rocky wilderness to a proper pastoral space. The Victorian sitting kitty-corner from 2302 has its entrance away from Alta Plaza and that of course is a reflection of the state of the unfinished park in the 1880s.

The owner who may have suggested facing 2302 toward Alta Plaza was a somewhat mysterious widow named Clara Kluge—her surname, by the way, meaning "wise one." She appeared in city directories for only three years and I've not been able to find the name of her late husband. Previously she had lived at 1903 Divisadero near Pine—that was in 1894—and at 2319 Van Ness (very fashionable) two years later. She must have been well off, as the building contracts for 2302 Steiner amounted to nearly $8,000, about double the average price for a house this size. At all events, she moved in when the house was finished, stayed somewhat more than a year, then vanished. The party, I guess, was over.

The next owners were Annie and Joseph Bier—Joseph was at 2302 all the way from 1899 to his death in 1947, with his brother Hypolite, who also had quarters in the house, beating him in residential longevity by a year. Incidentally, Joseph's wife, Annie, and Hypolite's wife, Minnie, were sisters. The right side of the upper floor, including a "red room," was Joseph and Annie's suite, while the left side belonged to Hypolite and Minnie. Downstairs they shared the double parlor to the right of the entrance hall and the dining room, kitchen and breakfast room on the left. Compromise gulch!

Joseph and Annie had a son, Allan, who grew up in the house and was a noted concert pianist in the 1910s and 1920s. Allan's daughter reports that he collected ancient jade, and her reclusive grandfather precious stones, antiques and oriental rugs. Joseph was a diamond importer and money broker who seems to have virtually retired after the catastrophic events of '06 and dabbled in real estate; Hypolite was in wholesale cigars.

No. 74

2673 Clay

On Writer's Block

The group of Victorian houses facing Alta Plaza Park in
the 2600 block of Clay Street
have been known for forty years at least
as "the Clay Street block," a special seal
of approval in light of the fact the houses
have been constantly well maintained, a
veritable fashion show in the best taste
demonstrating how Victorians can be
beautifully preserved.

The Clay Street block looked good at a
time, mid-twentieth century, when there
was still great ambivalence about whether
to treasure, remuddle or demolish such
gems. Prominent San Franciscans took to
the block before it was considered "proper Pacific Heights": the physician Cabot
Brown, for instance, who was on deck as
early as the 1940s.

In later decades (all at 2661) there was
bookseller Scott Martin from a posh old
family, attorney Charles Breyer whose
brother is a Supreme Court justice, and,
most notably, the elegant novelist Alice
Adams who chronicles the highs and lows
of trendy, pouting denizens of variously
broken homes who, if I'm not mistaken,
sometimes even lived in the neighborhood,
with their suntans, vodka and angst.

The house at 2673 was built in 1876
along with the other seven in the row, all
boasting nice south gardens and, at that

time, views of the absolutely unperfected
park across the way. It is, oddly enough,
the only one not enlarged this way or that
over the years. And it was a rental for
three-quarters of a century, until that
dapper gentleman George Brady, a lawyer
known for his trademark straw hat, bought
it in 1952.

The last tenants pre-Brady were the
family of lawyer Scott Knight Smith whose
parents, the Reginald Knight Smiths,
lived across Alta Plaza in the Coxhead-
designed house (Old House No. 58) at the
socially unimpeachable corner of Jackson
and Pierce.

Especially interesting is the fact George
and Hope Brady commissioned their
neighbor Ursula Knowles' father, the great
Houghton Sawyer, to design the garden of
2673. Sawyer, the architect of the Verdier
mansion on Russian Hill, 1001 California on Nob Hill, and 2518 Buchanan and
2100 Vallejo (Old House No. 9) in Pacific
Heights, was in retirement at the time and
must have found the little challenge a nice
diversion.

Now for some program notes on the
tract builder, TREA, that put up the Clay
Street block and more than a thousand
other houses in San Francisco during the
1870s. TREA stands for The Real Estate
Associates. The organization bought the

land opposite Alta Plaza in 1870 as part of a three-block parcel extending from Clay to Sacramento going north-south and Webster to Pierce east-west.

At that time those blocks were just heaps of sand—heaps of sand worth $80,000.

TREA's first venture into house construction was on the middle block of the three and examples of that 1870–71 project can still be found at 2503 Clay, 2229 Fillmore and 2530-2564 Sacramento. Those first TREA houses had almost all the design elements that persisted, with occasional exceptions, through their whole oeuvre: Italianate style, multi-faceted bay windows, false fronts with heavy bracketed cornices, high interior ceilings and a strong vertical emphasis on the façade.

Other groups of TREA houses may be found at 2115-2125 Bush and 1701-09 Gough in Lower Pacific Heights and in the 1500s of Golden Gate Avenue near Alamo Square (all built in 1875), on more than half the block bounded by Mission, Valencia, 20th and 21st Street (1876) and at 18-30 Hill Street, also in the Mission (1878), plus 2311-2321 Webster back in Pacific Heights (also 1878).

The company's president and manager was William Hollis, an experienced real estate developer who, however, based profitability on rising land prices rather than a just appraisal of actual costs of construction and financing. When a local depression slowed the market in the late 1870s his very productive empire fell into bankruptcy.

But many of Hollis' houses survive him still, providing gracious living in a city claiming many a "painted lady."

No. 75

2721 Clay

Not Cookie-Cutter Uniform

By 1900 Alta Plaza Park was a pastoral asset to the neighborhood, and one Caroline Wingerter, widow of a real estate speculator, engaged the architect Maxwell G. Bugbee to design a "tract" of four houses, 2713 through 2735 Clay, just across from the greenery. But Bugbee, whose architecture has been described as "romantic" and "eclectic," was not about to make these houses cookie-cutter uniform.

Our titular 2721 Clay is a delightful stew of elements. Find in the pyramid roof and delicate balusters of the balcony Colonial Revival, in the decorative plaster around the entry recess Italian Renaissance, in the semicircular bay window Queen Anne. Look closely at the dormer and you'll see a round-headed Palladian window lacking the shorter windows usually placed, like faithful dogs at their master's feet, to each side.

And notice how at the second-floor window's classic Ionic capitals are juxtaposed with wide paneling instead of the more conventional narrow fluted shafts. And how the dentil molding below the roof is too big by classical standards but pulls the whole façade together. Well, all this adds up to a turn-of-the-century American architect seeking like many of his colleagues to come up with an American style borrowing selectively from many past styles and integrating them into new wholes.

Mrs. Wingerter's late husband, Charles, had come to California from Bavaria in 1849, doubtless with gold in his eyes. At all events, he must have done fairly well because in 1873 he bought a sizeable chunk of real estate, the eastern half of the square block on which the Bugbee tract would go up a quarter-century later. The Wingerters' own home originally stood alone, crowded into the southwest corner of the property at the present location of the left half of an apartment building at 2744 Sacramento Street.

Interlude

If you continue two blocks west on Clay there's a childhood favorite of mine at 2961, a baby Norman château tucked next to a set of flats which has about it a certain air of enchantment. Well, 'twasn't always a turreted Gallic cutie. Originally built as a Victorian in 1877, perhaps as the near twin to its neighbor at 2965, it was virtually demolished in 1929 and reconfigured for the magnificent sum of $500.

—*Arthur Bloomfield*

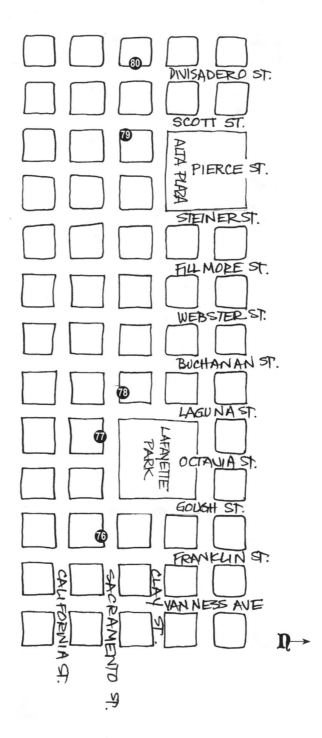

DIVISADERO ST.

SCOTT ST.

ALTA PLAZA

PIERCE ST.

STEINER ST.

FILLMORE ST.

WEBSTER ST.

BUCHANAN ST.

LAGUNA ST.

LAFAYETTE PARK

OCTAVIA ST.

GOUGH ST.

FRANKLIN ST.

VAN NESS AVE

CALIFORNIA ST.

SACRAMENTO ST.

CLAY ST.

N →

On or near

Sacramento Street

east to west

No. 76

1911 Sacramento

Brownstone West

The celebrated 2600 block of Clay Street has long had competition from the five elegant and not entirely uniform houses at 1911-21 Sacramento Street, just one block and change above the hurly-burly of Van Ness Avenue, street of churches, exhaust fumes and homeless people. The lovely set reminds us that Italianate Victorians didn't always come with five-sided or half-octagonal bay windows: four of the Sacramento block are flat-chested.

1911 is the most unusual of the lot, thanks especially to the fancy window surrounds only duplicated so far as I know on one other San Francisco house. Why 1911 and not its siblings on Sacramento is fancied up in this way, reminiscent of florid New York brownstones of the 1850s, is a mystery.

This Sacramento quintet were developed by a real estate broker with the pun-ready name George Dam. He it was who bought 192 front feet of raw land in February 1868 and sold the houses from September of that year through April 1871. The March 1871 announcement for the sale of 1911 noted that a house was on offer as well as a double lot.

The customer who seized on this opportunity was one Howard Havens who worked for a private bank—and that gives me a chance to write a little about early banking in San Francisco. The bank Havens worked for was called Donohoe, Kelly and Company, and it was private because California's first constitution permitted no chartering or incorporation of banks and no creation of any paper substitute for hard cash.

The founders remembered only too well the troubles caused by banks that failed and could not redeem that paper following the panic of 1837. They wanted money dealers to be personally responsible for their transactions.

The state's earliest banking houses consisted of individuals or partnerships who bought and sold gold dust, loaned funds at high interest, held deposits of gold dust and money for their customers and dealt in paper drawn on banks and businesses in other states.

The first commercial bank in the modern sense was the Bank of California, founded in 1864. Its incorporators gambled that public opinion had changed enough to let them get away with their venture. The principal founder was William C. Ralston, that operatic California booster, business incubator and creator of the Palace Hotel who died, by accident or suicide, in 1875 when the Bank of California had to close because he'd overextended it. His extravagant life should have been set to music by Tchaikovsky.

Ralston had organized the Bank of California on the sly because his cautious partners, Joseph A. Donohoe and Eugene Kelly, objected to some of the loans he was making. Their firm, Donohoe, Ralston and Company, had been handling more bullion than anybody else.

So when Ralston opened his new bank Donohoe and Kelly re-established their own private banking organization which flourished for a half-century, highly respected in financial circles. Howard Havens was their book-keeper for a time, then was made a partner in 1876. The firm incorporated fifteen years later with Havens now vice president.

The Havens family lived at 1911 until about 1890 when ownership passed to Palmyra Nickelsberg, wife and later widow of Siegfried Nickelsberg, president of a wholesale shoe firm. Palmyra was in residence on Sacramento Street for more than half a century, long enough to see the cable cars running outside her front door made, alas, redundant.

Should we imagine her ordering shellfish from Swan's down on Polk Street, and stopping in now and then for a sweet at Blum's a few steps away?

No. 77

2151 Sacramento

The House Sir Arthur Conan
Doyle Didn't Sleep In

*D*on't believe everything you read in brass!

The plaque outside the attractively garlanded and balustraded 2151 Sacramento proclaims that "this house, built in 1881, was once occupied by Sir Arthur Conan Doyle."

But 'taint so. The creator of Sherlock Holmes lived in Britain all his life and came to the United States only on lecture tours, and besides, the house was not built until 1921. But the person for whom it was designed might have been a character out of Doyle, or H. G. Wells. His name was Dr. Albert Abrams and he was a notorious physician/charlatan, a relatively harmless Jekyll and Hyde, you might say.

He'd begun as a conventional and highly respected doctor. Born in San Francisco in 1863, he earned his medical degree at the prestigious University of Heidelberg in Germany. Then back home he opened a downtown office specializing in diseases of the chest and saw patients at Mt. Zion and the French Hospital out on Geary.

He experimented with x-rays, he published, he was known as a brilliant diagnostician. And sometime in the 1890s he joined the faculty of Cooper Medical College at Sacramento and Webster as professor of pathology. Cooper, by the way, had been founded in 1882 by Dr.

Levy C. Lane and went on to become Stanford Medical School.

After living for a while on the somewhat commercial 2400 block of Fillmore, Abrams established a more luxurious home-and-office at the southwest corner of California and Van Ness, along a pre-1906 mansion row. Then after being burned out in '06 he moved to the Fairmont Hotel when it was ready for guests.

By 1908 the plot thickens.

Abrams was no longer associated with the medical school, I don't know why. The school was experiencing many changes at the time, Dr. Lane had died, and because state law didn't permit leaving one's whole estate to charity he'd left part of his to Cooper's president, the Dr. Ellinwood of Old House No. 43 up on Pacific, who inappropriately treated the bequest as his personal property rather than for medical school use. Other faculty took Ellinwood to court and lost, but they got a new president and eventually allied themselves with Stanford.

Somewhere in all this mess Dr. Abrams dropped out—dropped out in the modern sense, almost. It may have been bitterness over the business at Sacramento and Webster that caused him to cross the border into charlatanism. Or perhaps he suffered a mid-life crisis of large proportions.

In any event, about 1909 he published a book on "spondylotherapy," this mouthful describing a more or less chiropractic system. The book was very popular and went through several editions. And then came his involvement with "splanchnic neurasthenia," which sounds like something out of "Zippy the Pinhead." Interviewed about S.N. in 1915, Abrams impressed a reporter with his domineering presence, his rapid speech, his aura of knowing everything about you. Aaargh!

Next, in 1918, Abrams startled the world—yes, the publicity reached wide—with a couple of machines he'd invented to take advantage of the characteristic electrical vibrations he claimed every disease gave out. The "dynamizer" was for diagnosis through vibrations, and the "oscilloclast" for healing. These comic-strip apparati were sealed boxes with lots of wires—and, one presumes, they emitted no rabbits.

Abrams would also heal you with vibrations produced by special drugs or salves in exotic colors!

The heyday of all this healing-and-such was 1918 to 1924, with three thousand disciples throughout the U.S. and Europe adopting ERA, "Electronic Reactions of Abrams." Customers paid $250 down and $50 a month to lease each machine. But the *Scientific American* wasn't buying ERA and spent a year investigating it. The verdict: Worthless. But by that time Dr. Abrams had died, and without his key to the machinery, so to speak, ERA collapsed.

But while all those payments for rented machines were roaring in he bought the lot at 2151 Sacramento and had a young architect named Mel Schwartz design a lovely clinic with dwelling unit, costing a not insubstantial $45,000. A late Beaux Arts gem, the building rewards careful examination of its lavish decoration. The interior must have been amazing, displaying as it did the good doctor's tapestries, huge brass Buddha, Chinese ebony dragon chairs, the works.

Dr. Abrams only lived to enjoy all this for a couple of years, but he left his siblings $2 million. I leave it to you to decide if this was hard-earned cash.

Postscript

Conan Doyle *did* set foot in 2151 Sacramento once, probably on June 5, 1923. He came to town to give four lectures on spiritualism and stayed at the Clift Hotel. Perhaps he had tea with Dr. Abrams, whose inventions quite impressed the romantic Doyle.

No. 78

2212 Sacramento

Eternal Georgian

High above the sidewalk, 2212 Sacramento's serene Georgian façade overlooks the busy modern street—an electric bus every five minutes on weekdays!—as if the rich men's neighborhood of its youth had never changed. Proud it should be of its lovely half-round porch, the fine ensemble at the second floor of Palladian window and curvaceous balustrade, the satisfying proportions all about.

Architect of this visual treat was A. Page Brown, author of the Ferry Building and arguably the man who led San Francisco's architectural fraternity into the neoclassical. No relation to City Hall architect Arthur Brown Jr., Page Brown trained under McKim, Mead and White, those architects of beauty in New York, and had his own office there until the widow of railroad magnate Charles Crocker brought him to San Francisco in 1889.

Just thirty, Brown had only seven years to live, but his driving ambition and captivating social ways won him a very large practice. And he employed Willis Polk, Bernard Maybeck, Charles Rousseau, William Knowles and Frank Van Trees!

An architectural drawing and description of 2212 appeared in the *Chronicle* August 22, 1895, mostly matching what was built and exists today: "walls twelve inches thick...Italian Renaissance order... spacious vestibule in native marble... double-landed staircases...large marble fireplaces...hard woods of different varieties..."

The article trumpeted on about two bedroom-suites upstairs and one major room in each corner of the main floor, call-bell labels identifying said rooms as, clockwise from the right front, the Library which was in burled redwood, the French Room (a drawing room), the Music Room with musical motifs, and the oak-paneled Dining Room.

Construction set back the original owner, a businessman/investor named Richard Edward Queen, a princely $35,000. Queen, who gave memorable parties at 2212, appeared on the San Francisco scene about 1883 when, still under thirty, he was president of the California Fig Syrup Company, sellers of a sweet laxative. He later managed Golden Gate Advertising and died in 1924 while on a world tour. A faithful son of the Catholic Church, he willed it the house, keeping a life interest for his relatives.

In the 1940s and 1950s, 2212 Sacramento did a turn as Hawley Manor Guest House. Such boarding houses peppered the neighborhood then, in the wake of the Depression and concurrent with wartime housing shortages. Evidently some of the "guests" weren't very finicky in the house-keeping department: new owners coming in in the mid-fifties repaired eighty-three damaged windows and replicated stolen hardware, not to mention contending with a crane falling through the roof during high-rise construction next door. Real preservationists!

Interlude

And further out Sacramento at 2395 don't fail to notice the Health Sciences Library, originally the Lane Medical Library of Stanford University School of Medicine, a noble stone pile designed by Albert Pissis and put up in 1912 at a cost of $150,000. My father, after retiring as professor of medicine across the street, had a desk in the library and wrote thereat his monumental *Bibliography of Communicable Diseases*. Pissis' credits include the old Hibernia Bank building at Market, Jones and McAllister downtown. The library's interior features a four-story oval spiral staircase and murals by the highly regarded Arthur Mathews, one of them depicting Hygeia, the Greek goddess of health, along with other muses.

Then at 2695 there's an enchanting house with a landscaped loggia running along the Pierce Street side. Built in 1894, it was for a number of years the Peters-Wright dance studio. With many a cigarette break, I suppose, out on the loggia.

—Arthur Bloomfield

No. 79

2100 Scott

The House That Isn't 2302 Steiner

The United States Coast Survey map of 1869 shows a lot of open space—fenced-in open space—in the vicinity of Sacramento and Scott Streets. The two nearest houses to this intersection were on California just west of Scott and on the south side of Sacramento a little west of Steiner, two latter-day blocks away.

The fences were evidence of land claims, perhaps also to contain livestock with wanderlust. Both Scott and Sacramento existed as dirt streets between the fences, but California, now a major boulevard, was scarcely a road beyond Scott. The topography was rather like pieces of Sonoma County, rolling hills in Contra Costa, orchards in Santa Clara County, other country spaces that became subdivisions later on.

Then about 1871 horse-car lines reached this western part of Pacific Heights. There was one along Bush to Fillmore, then out California, and another along Pacific to Fillmore. When plans for these lines were made known the real estate rush was on. Forty houses sprouted on the block bounded by Jackson, Webster, Washington and Buchanan, a dozen more on the block framed by Clay, Steiner, Sacramento and Fillmore.

More development near the now-developed Alta Plaza Park was stimulated by a cable car line built along Sacramento Street in 1892 by the Ferries and Cliff House Railroad. This is an ancestor of the current No. 1 bus line which, before it was electrified in the 1980s, was scarcely a match for its phased-out cable car predecessors. The diesel buses couldn't always make it up Nob Hill with full loads, so rush-hour passengers were sometimes requested to get out and walk!

But back to the 1890s. It was in '97 that the beautiful 2100 Scott went up at the corner of Sacramento, a lovely house characteristic of its time in its blend of Queen Anne and the more serene Classical Revival, but by no stretch of the imagination could you call it just another nineties residence. Even if it feels like a sister to 2302 Steiner.

2100 Scott claims Queen Anne aspects in the triangle-topped dormer windows on its north and south (Sacramento Street) sides, and in the frieze bands hung with cornucopias under the eaves and boasting anthemions above the entry. The perfect symmetry of the façade, even to matching dormer windows on the side roofs, is characteristic of Classical Revival. But the bell-shaped gable end above the dormer window over the entrance is Mission Revival. The sum total? A felicitous hunk, you might say, of architectural "cabinetwork."

Note meanwhile that 2100 lacks the bay windows which were common to San Francisco Queen Annes and Colonial Revival houses alike. And did you spot the subtle convexity of the Ionic columns at the entrance? This "entasis" was a device invented by the Greeks to create the illusion of increased height.

The architect named in the contract report for 2100 is one C. A. Robertson. No one by that exact name was listed in city directories of the time, but there was a Clinton F. Robertson who practiced architecture independently from 1896 through 1900. Earlier he'd been a draftsman in the office of A. C. Lutgens, who would design the city of Sonoma's City Hall. The 1901 directory listed this Robertson as a draftsman again—with George W. Percy, one of the Bay Area's best nineteenth-century architects. Maybe this was Robertson's route to security.

At all events, this probably-the-right-Robertson designed thirteen other known houses, costing from $925 to $4,333.

Although 2302 Steiner is as we've observed a bosom design buddy of 2100 Scott, that house was the work—a year earlier—of Laferme and Collischonn, architects scarcely better known than the obscure Mr. Robertson.

The first owners of 2100 were Frank and Sarah Marvin, he from upstate New York, she from Philadelphia. Marvin's father, William Waldo, had sailed to California in 1850, tried some gold mining, run a hotel in Georgetown up in the Gold Country and later owned a music store in Sacramento. Young Frank went to school in Sacramento and moved to San Francisco in 1875, marrying the following year. He was long in the wholesale shoe business, but after the catastrophe of '06 was secretary of Taylor and Spottswood, which sold supplies for blacksmiths and horseshoers.

Then, around 1914, Frank Marvin was back in shoes for two-legged customers. And his house, so neatly placed on the corner of Sacramento and Scott, was, you might say, a good fit.

No. 80

2131 Divisadero

An Imaginary Castle

*I*n one of Alice Adams' dryly ironic novels set in San Francisco a character drives from, North Beach I think it was, out Sacramento, then Clay on the way to the Avenues west of Pacific and Presidio Heights. Maybe this character's jaw dropped a little at the sight of the picturebook 2131 Divisadero, between Sacramento and Clay.

The design of this house is most unusual, I'm not sure there's another quite like it in the city. The witch-hat tower spells 1890s, but the round-headed windows with their eyebrow pediments look straight out of the 1870s. The rectangular-plan bay window at the right shows off a shape from the 1880s, as does the gable end with hexagonal shingles and a sunburst motif.

But all this fits together, as if 2131 were some imagined castle.

The only relevant building contract I've found is dated June 1883, for two thousand dollars' worth of "additions." No architect is mentioned, just the contractor-builder John P. Shepard or Shepherd. At that time this amount of money could have paid for a simple house, possibly even one with two stories, but not this elaborate a building. So I think the people involved were "adding" all right— to something fairly substantial, a sizeable "cottage" say, that was there before '83.

That "something" in the previous sentence is elusive indeed. We know from a Coast Survey map dated 1869 that the lot where 2131 now stands was vacant at that time. Fair enough, but there's no report of water service until August '83. The use of the word "additions" in the contract, plus the round-headed windows, passé by 1880, hint at an earlier structure including, I suspect, the center section of the current house, the hipped roof and basement logically being part of this original package as they almost certainly extended into the area at the left now covered by the turret.

The rectangular bay window at the right was up-to-the-minute for 1883, so it must have been added at that time.

And the turret as well, however 1890s it looks. Well, the steamer captain and real estate investor, James O. Van Bergen by name, who owned 2131 Divisadero in 1883 had just contracted for a pair of houses on Bush Street, 2100 and 2102, that were designed by Samuel and Joseph Cather Newsom, whose designs were frequently several years ahead of "their time." The Newsoms very likely suggested the turret for 2131.

Very sensibly Van Bergen was careful on Divisadero Street to continue the window style of the "original" (see especially the center of the house) in the "additions"—

including, I think, both bays—honoring in the process a non-trendy obsolescence in order to create an appealing and necessary unity.

This is a lesson not learned by some current-day architects who impose on houses stylistically combative partial fenestrations that may in a particular and conspicuous segment of the façade look rather handsome but condemn such houses to split design personalities until such time as the remuddling is corrected.

Van Bergen's name is associated with several other unusual buildings, those twins on Bush as well as 2560 Washington and possibly 2401 Jackson as well. The Washington Street house, a double Italianate, was his home from 1880 through 1885.

The first known resident of 2131 Divisadero didn't move in until 1889. He was Max Ordenstein, a Bavarian who came to this country around 1870 and in due course owned a company that manufactured cigars and sold them wholesale. Ordenstein became a naturalized citizen but he never registered to vote. After the '06 catastrophe he conducted his cigar business—the selling, doubtless, but not the manufacturing—from his residence. He died around 1925 and his widow remained on Divisadero well into the 1940s—a long run.

One suspects the Ordensteins didn't pay much attention to the origin of the name of their street, known as Devisadero until 1909. Well, there are different theories, and the one I like best has it that part of the street followed the original trail "dividing" the turf, actual and metaphorical, of the Presidio and the Mission. Between these Spanish institutions, church and state so to speak, there was quite a bit of friction.

Sounds kind of modern, doesn't it?

On or near

California Street

east to west

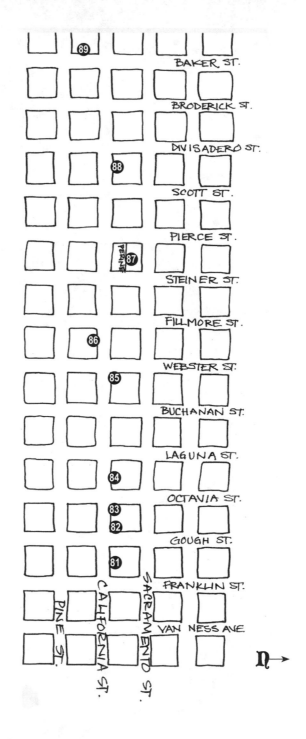

No. 81

1834 California

Elegant Amalgam

For thirty years I frequently passed this lovely Victorian/Queen Anne, a sensitive amalgam of 1875 and 1895, and always the green window shades would be arranged in perfect symmetry, at about half-mast. The house was immaculate, yes, but seemed to be inhabited by ghosts (wealthy ones, obviously, and obsessive-compulsive ones too) who required no groceries to be delivered, received no callers walking up the front steps in view of the California Street traffic, opened no parlor window to a warm spring breeze.

A house, in short, lost in time. And was it inhabited by a "little old lady of means?"

Why of course. Her name was Persis Coleman and she lived at 1834 for at least eighty-five years, maybe more. Doubtless she must have known that the center and the right side of the house as it currently stands constituted the original building from '75 with its half-octagonal bay window and Corinthian columns at the door, and that twenty years later the tower was added, as well as some width on the left and the side bay windows. Probably the roof was raised for the third floor at that time as well.

The original building mustn't have cost much more than the 1895 alterations—"cabinet work" these alterations were called in an architectural magazine of the day—which came in at $3,750. One O. F. Griffin bought the large lot, probably vacant, for $18,000 in January 1875 and seven months later sold it, presumably with the house thereon, for $23,000. That's $5000 for construction costs and profit.

O. F. Griffin is unidentified but could have been the wife of a developer named John Griffin, or one of several carpenter-builders named Griffin active at the time. The purchaser in '75 was Isaac Wormser, a wealthy merchant from Germany. Two years later he and his wife, Louisa, were joined for a couple of years by daughter Emilie and son-in-law Samuel Sussman, a nephew of the Alaska Commercial Company's Louis Sloss. Around this time there were also three live-in servants, German, Irish and Chinese, the last-named probably the chef de cuisine.

Before his marriage Samuel Sussman had already become a partner of the wholesale grocer Myer Ehrman. Then his brothers-in-law Samuel and Gustav Wormser joined the firm which in due course became Sussman, Wormser and Company before evolving into what is known today as S&W Fine Foods, a name brand if ever there was one in canned goods.

The noted architects Percy and Hamilton, authors of the First Unitarian Church a half-mile away, were responsible for the 1895 remodel instigated by new owner John Crisp Coleman, an elderly Englishman who'd been a Gold Country senator as well as the owner, with his brother Edward, of the Idaho Mine in Grass Valley before retiring to San Francisco.

The 1900 census showed the seventy-six-year-old J. C. Coleman as residing at 1834 with his wife Persis of thirty years and five of their seven children, plus two servants. No wonder they wanted a twenty-room house.

No. 82

1801 Gough

Lobbyist at Work

Early twentieth-century apartment buildings in Pacific Heights that don't quite suggest ultra-luxury addresses tend still to look rather elegant on the outside. Their lobbies are frequently even ritzier, sometimes looking as if they were bucking for a role in Julia Morgan's Hearst Castle.

The point was that the proportions and decorations of these buildings' exteriors should imply a fair degree of luxe inside, even if most of the units were studio-size rather than three-thousand-square-foot palazzi. Yes, the designers planned such confusion on purpose: they believed that a person living frugally in a small apartment at a "good" address would want to give the impression of living fairly high on the hog.

It was also true, of course, that extremely wealthy inhabitants of very toney apartment spaces in many cases preferred to live in a building that didn't shout its luxuriousness from the rooftop, and the fashionable architects of the 1920s knew that too.

Here at the not exactly ultra-luxe 1801 Gough, where a typical longtime resident was Ferdinand Claudio who played at the second or third stand of the San Francisco Opera Orchestra's violins for half a century at least, the exterior is scored to look like stone and it's decorated with shields and flower patterns. The top of the building features an ornamental parapet and two cornices with deep moldings, and as for the entry, it boasts an arch two stories tall with a paneled surround and three concentric sets of spiral columns.

The lobby is also two stories high, and complete with marble floor, balcony arcade, deeply coffered polychrome ceiling and the pastry-like Spanishy decoration so typical of the time, 1927, that 1801 Gough went up.

The designer here was a specialist in apartment buildings, Herman C. Baumann, a fellow who considered an elegant lobby as vital as three square meals a day. Oakland-born, he was active for nearly fifty years beginning in 1914, with son John following in his steps and grandson Bruce continuing in the business, as a developer.

Herman Baumann produced reliable, budget-fitting designs with that handsome lobby trademark, but he was never fashionable or innovative. Among the five hundred or so(!) buildings he designed in the Roaring Twenties some of the most ambitious are the white Deco charmer 1101 Green, high on Russian Hill—the iconic English food writer Elizabeth David used to hang out there on local visits—as well as the old Gaylord Hotel (very Spanishy!)

on Jones above Geary, and the rather New Yorky Bellevue-Staten Apartments on Lake Merritt in Oakland.

Like quite a few of Baumann's other buildings, 1801 Gough was commissioned by the Marian Realty Company, a real estate and development business conducted by the Rousseau family, themselves prolific architects. What Baumann could do better than they themselves I don't know, but they certainly used his services and let him take design credit time and time again. The Rousseaus must have figured they could make more money marketing than designing.

Interlude

And just up California Street on the left there's the strange case of 1969, an English Tudor Gothic house whose grand portal ends surrealistically with its second half—seemingly for a companion house that was torn down or never built—missing. The fact is, the other house was never built. The extant 1969 California was put up in 1915 by Willis Polk for Constance Tobin, one of the heiresses of the de Young clan, owners of the *Chronicle*. A mirror image was planned for her sister Helen Cameron, but George and Helen Cameron decided to settle on the Peninsula.

A few yards further and dating from approximately the same time, 2001 California should not be missed, a finely detailed palazzo of an apartment house, the work of the prolific but scarcely remembered Edward Eyestone Young who also designed 2000 California, a marginally less exciting apartment building across the way, with a low-rise Spanishy affair next to it which was his personal studio.

—*Arthur Bloomfield*

No. 83

1990 California

A Quiet Millionaire's Remodel

This is another house that had two births, so to speak. Not to speak of being haunted, probably.

It went up in its original form in 1881, commissioned by Dominga de Goñi Atherton, a five foot, two-hundred-pound Chilean aristocrat, quite a tyrant apparently, who was the widow of the well-heeled merchant Faxon Dean Atherton who owned a huge ranch down the Peninsula on the present site of, yes, the town of Atherton. She was also the conservative mother-in-law of the decidedly unconservative novelist Gertrude Atherton, the bored-stiff wife of Faxon's ineffectual son George who, according to the chronicler of "haunted" houses Antoinette May, "barely had the initiative to tie his own shoelaces."

Then in 1891 a millionaire Sacramento banker named Edgar Mills bought the house, called in a disciple of the New York architects McKim, Mead and White and radically changed the look of it. It's difficult today to identify anything on the crazy-quilt exterior that belonged to the original house, except perhaps the bulk of the main block behind the tower.

Dominga Atherton spent twelve thousand 1881 dollars to buy the land at California and Octavia, and another $22,000 to build the house. According to the building contract she engaged no architect, just the builder/contractor brothers Charles P. and George H. Moore. The original structure was probably a box shape, Italianate with a couple of bay windows and no tower—Dominga was not, it seems, imaginative enough to commission such a new-fangled accoutrement—and for that kind of money it must have been large, and very elaborate inside.

Now advance ten years and Edgar Mills makes his entrance. Trained as a civil engineer, he'd arrived in California in 1849 and conducted the first surveys of the Feather and Sacramento rivers. Much of the 1850s he spent in mining towns buying gold dust for the Sacramento bank of his older brother D. O. Mills. In due course Edgar became president of the bank and some small railroad companies as well, but for a millionaire he led a quiet life.

About 1879 he moved to the Bay Area, acquiring and remodeling a twenty-one-room mansion at 40 Noel Drive in Menlo Park—that's next to Atherton, by the way—but keeping quarters at the Pacific Union Club in San Francisco when he needed to be in town. Then, aged sixty-three, he bought 1990 California from Dominga Atherton and set about having it remodeled.

To bring Casa Dominga up to date, Edgar Mills took his cue from older brother D. O., who'd hired out-of-town architects Burnham and Root to build his eponymous Mills Building which still stands tall in San Francisco's Financial District. Edgar's choice was A. Page Brown who'd worked with McKim etc. in New York and had been brought to San Francisco by Mrs. Charles Crocker of the Nob Hill Crockers. The darling of local Society, Brown produced for his clients the latest in architectural fashion from the East Coast.

Only one contract has come to light regarding Brown's alterations for 1990: it calls for three thousand dollars' worth of plumbing. Surely, though, there must have been other agreements to account for the complex redo of the house under Brown's direction.

Brown's stamp can be seen in the multiple roof shapes resembling those on Eastern Shingle Style residences built by McKim, Mead and White in New Jersey and at that supreme exurb Newport, Rhode Island. The shapes also recall the long-gone roof of Brown's second San Francisco project, the Crocker Old People's Home at Pine and Pierce, in its original configuration. To suit Edgar Mills' urban setting Brown eschewed shingles and used smoother wood cladding punctuated by horizontal bands boasting remarkable carvings of foliage, deeply three-dimensional.

From the street, 1990 with its binocular front door, idiosyncratic dormers and rather mischievous vitality looks much as it did in Edgar Mills' day, even if it was converted into apartments in the 1930s. And now it's San Francisco Landmark No. 70! Well, it survived the years 1923 to 1974, when Carrie Rousseau was on board with her fifty cats.

No. 84

2026 California

The House with Jellyfish Panels

2026 California was built in 1878 but it isn't pure 1870s by any means. Shortly after Simon and Emma Meyer bought the house about 1904 they made a number of changes, curving the side windows of the bay, jettisoning a mansard roof with its corner urns, and letting mirror-image jellyfish panels intrude between the rounded window tops and a squared-off cornice. A photograph from 1891 also tells us that the front stairs originally marched straight down to the street (there was of course no garage) and they sported curving handrails.

What the Meyers, who lived here for more than fifty years, retained and what they scrapped makes for a fascinating study in taste. Exhibit A: the sides of the bay were rebuilt to create curves but they kept the tall narrow window proportions, the cornices between floors and, especially notable, the Italianate colonnettes between the windows.

Meanwhile the entry side of the façade seems not to have been changed at all: the photo from 1891 shows exactly the same portico we see today, with wide, exaggerated Corinthian capitals on those sturdy columns. The balcony and the elaborate surround to the single window above are likewise nineteenth century. And the photo shows plainly the same keystone to the portico arch that still suggests an Egyptian head.

The Meyers made a number of interior changes, Frenchifying the living room, for instance, with paneling and new hardware. They rebuilt the fireplace, perhaps because of '06 quake damage, and they reconfigured the main staircase from a straight run along the west wall of the house to a "dog-leg" with landing; in so doing they had to move the door into the front parlor. The new banister in Queen Anne style was crowned with a square newel post and at the new stair landing they inserted a beautiful Tiffany-like stained glass window, signed in 1911 by Ingerson and Glaser, local "art glass designers and craftsmen."

Quite a bill must have been run up for all this remodeling. Well, Simon T. Meyer inherited, and ran, the private bank which his great-uncle Daniel had founded in Civil War days before California permitted the incorporation of banking institutions.

Before the Meyers bought 2026 its owner was Christine, the wife of Paul Breon, a wholesale provision merchant. Mrs. Breon received callers on the first and third Thursdays of the month—when, that is, she wasn't in residence at her place in Coronado down by San Diego. Mrs. Breon was a generous lady: after selling

2026 she gave the people of San Francisco the great entrance gates to Golden Gate Park at Nineteenth Avenue and Lincoln Way, and she also donated a room at the de Young Museum and willed most of her $2 million estate for medical research.

The original owner on California Street was one Joseph Haber, a German-born jeweler. He bought the lot in 1878 from Samuel Lewis, a tobacco importer and small-time speculator who'd acquired the whole vacant block fronting California, Sacramento, Laguna and Octavia Streets the year before. The price of this land? About $70,000.

The 1880 census shows the thirty-five-year-old Haber living at 2026 with his considerably younger wife, Fannie, two little sons and a live-in servant girl, Hannah Healey, who was still a teenager. Haber must have been fairly prosperous, for this was not a small house.

Which brings us to an interesting point: this Italianate fits a lot thirty-four feet wide exactly the same way my Italianate fits a twenty-four-foot frontage. The trick? Identical proportions. The houses look the same—until you walk into 2026 and realize the ceiling is two feet higher than you're used to.

No. 85

2266 California

Vintage Temple Near Rue Boutique

The great architect Albert Pissis (pronounced PEE-sees) usually produced Classical Revival buildings like the Emporium department store, the Hibernia Bank and Flood Building downtown and the Lane Medical Library at Sacramento and Webster. Temple Sherith Israel at California and Webster, a block east of Fillmore and its cutting-edge boutiques, is something else: here we're met by the steamroller of a weighty round-arched Romanesque tinged with the Oriental. Architectural fusion cuisine, anyone?

None of Pissis' other buildings lays such an emphasis on the heavily horizontal, on such thickly layered clusters of columns and concentric arches. Also unusual for this classicist are the dense sandstone carvings of foliage at the tops of columns, the dark and deeply recessed entry porch and the great rose window. Architect and clients must have wanted the building to announce itself as a religious structure but not quite a Christian one.

Sherith Israel was one of two Jewish congregations that emerged from tent meeting holiday celebrations at the height of the Gold Rush. The rivalry with Temple Emanu-El has continued to this day. Sherith Israel has always been the more conservative and less prestigious of the two, while the lion's share of membership has, interestingly enough, swung back and forth between the competitors more than once.

The name means "loyal remnant of Israel," which the Jews in Gold Rush California must have felt themselves to be. But Congregation Sherith Israel has not trumpeted itself about the community at large or produced any books about its own history; it has gone about its work quietly, among its own people.

The Congregation's first building was dedicated in 1854 on Stockton Street north of Broadway in the neighborhood where Chinatown and North Beach now overlap. China Beach? Then, from 1870 to 1905, they met at Post and Taylor on the site now occupied by the Bohemian Club. The present building was dedicated September 23, 1905 before a throng estimated at 2500 worshippers, and that, of course, was seven months before the great earthquake and fire of '06.

Well, it would have taken a Samson to pull down Sherith Israel; all Nature could do was produce a thousand dollars' worth of damage.

And soon the City was borrowing the building, at a handsome rental fee, for a temporary courthouse. Here, under the blue dome with hundreds of sparkling electric lights, by windows parading psalms in interlace patterns, and under ancient religious symbols painted by Attilio Moretti, the political boss Abe Ruef and other shady characters stood trial for corruption in the City's great graft clean-up.

Ironically, Ruef's parents were members. Their rabbi, Jacob Nieto, tried without success to arrange some sort of plea bargain between Ruef and the crusading district attorney, Francis Heney, but neither was willing to compromise and in the end Ruef was the one grafter who went to jail.

By the time a new DA dropped the graft cases a new Hall of Justice was functioning on Kearny Street across from Portsmouth Square (where the Chinatown Holiday Inn may currently be found) and Temple Sherith Israel had returned to the purposes for which it was built. It has remained true to them ever since.

Postscript

It has recently come to light that Pissis' brother Emile (1854–1934), a prolific painter who rarely exhibited his work, designed several of Sherith Israel's impressive stained glass windows.

No. 86

2373 California

An Uptown Villa

"A very popular style of dwelling. For architectural beauty and interior arrangement this plan cannot be surpassed." So proclaimed The Real Estate Associates' advertisements for a trio of villas on the south side of California Street running toward Fillmore from the alley halfway between Webster and Fillmore—which used to be called, logically enough, Middle Street and is now Orben.

Although "very popular" in marketing lingo, these so-called villas which attempted to ape eastern country residences—2373 does the job nicely, I think—were in fact relatively rare items in San Francisco's housing stock. The Associates, known as TREA—and they were the city's biggest housing developer in the 1870s—built just forty or fifty of them, mostly in the Mission but also in the Western Addition, which includes the present-day so-called Baja Pacific Heights.

Their longevity record is not good. Other than 2373, the one house remaining of the California Street tract, the only TREA villas still visible are at 271 and 279 San Jose Avenue north of Twenty-fifth Street.

Villas were bigger than the usual box-shaped Italianate of 1870s San Francisco. They were built on wider lots with an L-shaped plan, no false front above the roofline and separate geometrical blocks for entrance and one-story bay. Their interiors were very probably more elaborate than the usual TREA house, witness the price difference, two thousand dollars or more, with only a small portion of that for the larger lot.

Villas generally related especially well to the outdoors with three extra façade windows, and it was not unusual to find a rear bay window replacing the more standard flat arrangement. Among non-villa Italianates the wonderful TREA houses on the south side of Bush Street east of Fillmore are the only ones I know that have similar rear bays.

TREA president William Hollis bought the 108-foot frontage on California Street that includes 2373 in July 1875; his cost was $5,000. Then he built his trio of houses and sold them in the second half of '76 for an average of $6,500.

In the case of 2373 the buyer probably had a great deal to say about the interior: he was the distinguished architect Albert A. Bennett and bought the house a little less than three months after the first ad for the California Street villas appeared. Bennett was New York-schooled, came to California at the height of the Gold Rush and designed the first Sacramento County

Courthouse in 1850. He was also responsible for a hotel, hospital, waterworks and Masonic hall in that city.

Later Bennett worked on the State Capitol and he built UC Berkeley's first mining building in 1879. He must have liked his California Street villa, because he lived in it for at least a decade.

...And if you're driving down the Central Valley note that his quite beautiful Merced County Courthouse (1874) survives!

Postscript

The replacement apartment building just east of 2373 California is certainly no villa, but drop in your tracks at the sight of the lobby ceiling, an essay in sculpted cake frosting that's nothing less than extraordinary.

No. 87

62–64 Perine

Not Quite Gasoline Alley

*J*ust behind that nice gas station at Steiner and California Streets that pipes classical music through its self- and full-serve corridors you'll find Perine Place, one of the city's many sheltered alleys containing generally tiny houses along with an above-average tranquility rating.

In Pacific Heights there aren't so many: just Wilmot, Austin, Orben (formerly Middle), the posh Raycliff Terrace and the quaint Cottage Row, plus Bromley which only has garages and qualifies therefore as a genuine "gasoline alley." Alleys are particularly plentiful on Telegraph Hill and in Chinatown where sometimes two or more crowd into a single square block and where some of the "main" thoroughfares aren't all that wide either.

In North Beach, just behind the police station, I'm always amused by the junction of alleys known respectively as Emory and Card, each seeming to need a Board.

Historically alleys developed to increase profits for real estate speculators. San Francisco's original lots were large squares, 137.5 feet to a side, six lots to a block: that was more space than most urban buildings required, so developers were quick to subdivide. The new lot sizes they arrived at depended of course on the economic level of the targeted clientele. Not surprisingly very few of the original 137.5-ers are left: perhaps the most conspicuous in Pacific Heights is the one containing that proud house and garden at 1901 Scott, our Old House No. 99, behind the Cobb School playground.

If a developer owned a whole block he might cut an alley through it either to create more lots with marketable street frontages or to provide service access. Perine Place, running from Steiner to Pierce parallel to California Street, was probably one of the latter, turning very gradually into a residential street. The houses appear to date from about 1880 to 1920 or so.

The house at 62-64, like its neighbors less than thirty-nine feet deep, was constructed in 1909 as one of four buildings, ten flats in all, under a single contract. The lot involved was fifty-two feet wide, running from Perine to Sacramento, the next normal-sized street to the north. A pair of two-story two-flat buildings was erected on Perine—the other is 58-60—along with a pair on Sacramento, each containing three stories and three flats.

Nine months after the building contract was filed, with construction complete, the lot was split in two, north to south, so that each of the new owner couples owned one building on each street. Then, thirty-five years later, the Perine buildings declared independence so to speak and were no longer jointly held with Sacramento Street frontages.

There was an architect for the four buildings, Arthur J. Laib who practiced full time only from 1907 to 1916, then turned salesman. He specialized in residential work, often flats or small apartments. I've long been especially fond of the graciously Colonial Revival 1360-68 McAllister in the Alamo Square neighborhood, set high behind a retaining wall, forming an L around a southwest garden.

On Perine the style is also Colonial Revival but in a very modest vein. You see it in the nice proportions of the windows, the consoles or brackets under the window hoods (now apparently removed) and especially in the high moldings, dentil above egg and dart.

The original owners of the paired Perine and Sacramento properties, including 62-64, were the brothers Abe and Meyer Abrahams and their wives, Belle and Lillie. The brothers did business together as A. and M. Abrahams at their not-very-fancy clothing store on the Embarcadero opposite the south end of the Ferry Building, long before this area was spiffed up with the likes of restaurants such as Boulevard and One Market.

Around 1914, 62 Perine was rented by Emilio and May Lorenzini. Emilio had a fruit and vegetable business on the corner of Washington and Fillmore where

a succession of restaurants have located (following in about 1980 the legendary Joe's Smoke Shop, a well-tobaccinated den for old salts from neighboring boarding houses, relics these of the days before Pacific Heights was almost *totally* gentrified). At the time, presumably, when Emilio sold to Joe's he moved downtown to own and manage the San Mateo Produce Company in the old produce district where the towers of Embarcadero Center now soar.

Emilio was, I suspect, the uncle of the Lorenzini brothers—including Max, a stalwart member of the San Francisco Opera Chorus—who operated a popular carriage-trade grocery at the southwest corner of Fillmore and Sacramento, where yuppies may now be found sipping their lattes.

Interlude

Jog back to California Street and try not to be fascinated by the much-shuttered 2652, a house that seems to have leapt full-grown from the Italian Riviera. Its date is 1922 and its author the magnificently named Edward Eyestone Young who lived in Presidio Terrace and practiced architecture 'neath a Wagnerian panorama in his wrought iron-balconied studio at 2002 California. He also designed the exquisite Francesca Club downtown at Sutter and Mason and the comme-il-faut apartment house at Green and Baker, in a particularly cozy part of Cow Hollow, which is now the Russian Consulate.

Around the corner from 2652 California enjoy the fun 1938-40 Scott with its delightful fan-patterned corbels, complex massing of roof and pseudobalcony, etc., etc. Interesting people lived in this Stick/Queen Anne mix: Russian born Mary Prag, for instance, who retired from schoolteaching aged eighty-two only to serve on the Board of Education and fight for teachers' pensions and women's rights—this was around 1927. Mary's daughter Florence married U.S. congressman Julius Kahn after whom the playground at the foot of Presidio Heights—marvelous tennis courts!—was named. After he died in '24 she ran for his seat and served in Congress for a dozen years. She was the first Jewish congresswoman, and also FDR's first Republican dinner guest!

No. 88

2766 California

Witch-Hat Eclectic

Pigeonholes are often flimsy affairs when assorted critics, commentators or architectural historians set to work, trying to categorize their prey. Think of the word "eclectic," about which Walter Kidney has written a whole book, *The Architecture of Choice: Eclecticism in America, 1880–1930.* My architecture dictionary offers: "Eclecticism: The selection of elements from diverse styles for architectural decorative designs."

And this brings us to 2766 California Street: what are its diverse elements?

Let's start at the top with the witch-hat towers which, along with the rest of the roof, constitute the multiple shapes and volumes placing 2766 at least partly in the Queen Anne pigeonhole. The rounded bay windows push it in a little further. But then there's the quadrifoil, or four-leaved, central window, the little Cyclops in the stew, that's surely Mission Revival. Meanwhile the geometrically patterned stained glass—a "how many squares?" puzzle—is pure Stick. The symmetry of the house is Beaux Arts, the Ionic colonnaded porch Colonial Revival, the stained glass around the door mildly Renaissance Revival, and the siding good old channel rustic, the standard covering for San Francisco houses from the early Italianates of the 1860s.

So how many pigeonholes will we need?

The idea of eclecticism in American building was to create a distinctively American architecture by borrowing—selectively—from specific historic periods and melding it all into a dignified but comfortable whole that fit contemporary lifestyles. I'm not sure the melding altogether worked here at 2766 (although the house does come into better focus as one becomes accustomed to its fussy face), but it's fun to dissect all that diversity.

It was put here, this model of eclecticism, in 1900 by three Irishmen: John Elliott, the owner, and Shea and Shea (Frank T. and W. D.), the architects. Frank, who is supposed to have studied at the Ecole des Beaux-Arts in Paris, was the better known of the pair; they practiced together from 1890 to 1906, then again in the late 1920s.

Shea and Shea designed the dome and other parts of San Francisco's City Hall that collapsed so disastrously in '06—and it must have been on that uncomfortable note that the partnership went under. But most of their work held up. Among their credits are a string of Catholic churches: St. Paul's, Holy Cross, Corpus Christi, early parts of St. Brigid's (Old House No. 17) and also St. Rose in Santa Rosa and St. Thomas Aquinas in Palo Alto. Other Catholic commissions included St. Mary's Hospital and the entrance to Holy Cross Cemetery.

Doubtless Shea and Shea came to the attention of their client through the Olympic Club, which they designed in 1899. John Elliott had joined the club in 1884, a scant four years after arriving from Ireland, and only five years after that he was a director of the organization. He put together its boat club and was the Olympic's track and field captain (a noncompetitor) in 1890 and 1894.

And he was, in fact, Mr. Amateur Athletics of the Pacific Coast, refereeing at least fourteen Big Games between Stanford and UC Berkeley, serving four years as president of the Pacific Association of the Amateur Athletics Union and, with two other local AAU officials, cleaning up the amateur boxing scene, disqualifying quite a number of errant contestants in one evening's sweep.

Elliott made his living as secretary-treasurer of a large grocery firm, West, Elliott and Gordon, that had stores on Third, Fourth, Sixth, Polk and Hayes Streets and Columbus Avenue. But his heart belonged to the AAU. And obviously to his young bride, Maude Gray—he built 2766 for her to come home to.

Elliott died in 1926 aged about eighty-two and respected to the last as "honest, square John Elliott," and Maude lived on at 2766, *her* house, until she died about 1950, the California Street cable car line still operating outside the door. The little red and yellow cars were frequently operated, Arthur remembers, by pink-cheeked Irishmen. The cars were noisy, making a grating—pleasantly grating—sound as they gripped their rope set in motion, one likes to think, by pleasant old Norns pensioned off from a Wagnerian opera.

Interlude

Walking along the increasingly gentrified outer California Street portion of Pacific Heights with its multi-ethnic "gourmet ghetto," one of many in the city, passing the new Drew School building at Broderick, gasping perhaps at 2915 California with its crazy balconette atop an overweight scallop shell, then turning left at Baker, one reaches...

No. 89

1705 Baker

A Cottage with Three-Star Trim

*1*705 Baker has a mirror twin, 1707, and in the years since construction in 1885 neither seems to have lost, or added, one stick of exterior trim, in spite of having had a number of different owners. Such integrity is hard to find.

And the trim, characteristic or idiosyncratic, is truly three-star.

Now, the rectangular bay window, of course, indicates Stick style. Standard Stick details include the corner boards, elongated brackets, lowered column capitals, gouged-out vertical decorations and the paneling on porch columns. Meanwhile a little triangle above the center of the bay window hints at the huge roof triangles to come on Queen Anne houses, but it's a very minor gesture.

Then there are several trim ideas that seem unique to 1705 and its twin: the suspension bridge motif in the center of the bay window's frieze, the highly textured oval plaques interrupting the porch columns, and the round window tops, exceedingly rare in Stick houses.

The single story of these houses is not particularly rare for the time or this neighborhood, outer Baja Pacific Heights as the saying goes. It was quite far out indeed in 1885, though one could commute downtown on the California Street cable cars which had run out to Presidio Avenue since '79.

Not far from Laurel Hill Cemetery (where Laurel Village shopping center is now) and Holy Cross Cemetery (now the Anza Vista neighborhood), the Baker Street twins didn't boast an especially fashionable address when they were built and perhaps it is only with the recent need for good housing for "young urban professionals" that lower Baker and other cottage-dotted streets in the area have taken on, with their painted little ladies, a touch of class.

Unusual for its day was the fact that the quite modest 1705 was individually designed by an architect as the residence for a specific client. Most of the city's small houses were erected as speculations by contractor-developers, or else by loving hands at home. Few people on modest budgets could go to the expense of hiring an architect. And modest is the word here: total construction costs for 1705 and its sibling were estimated at only $3,000.

The architect in question was Henry Geilfuss, best known perhaps for the towered Westerfeld House on Alamo Square, that great party venue the Brune-Reutlinger house on Grove Street, and St. Mark's Lutheran on O'Farrell. The prolific Geilfuss was active from at least 1879 into the 1910s. Born and raised in Germany, he arrived here in 1876 as a young man and developed in due course a good practice with many Germans among his clientele.

Including on Baker Street someone named Schutze.

The first name here is a puzzle. An "E. Schutze" signed the building contract with Geilfuss and builder William Pluns, but no E. Schutze appeared in city directories of the period—maybe E. was somebody's wife (nineteenth-century directories notoriously left out women). Then, two months after the contract notice appeared, one "James Schutze" signed to have the water turned on, but he's not listed in directories either. The Schutze who was listed was Frederick, and he it was (perhaps with a middle name of James?) who lived at 1705 from 1886 to 1892.

The directory-certified Schutze was a wholesale millinery salesman who became enough of an expert on ladies' hats that, about the time he sold 1705, he and one Vincent Butler founded a wholesale millinery business of their own which survived up until the '06 catastrophe. The next owner was an insurance salesman named James Simpson who had a wife named Annie, a daughter named Annie, and employed a Norwegian servant named Annie. I wonder how they knew which one was being called.

On or near

Pine Street

east to west

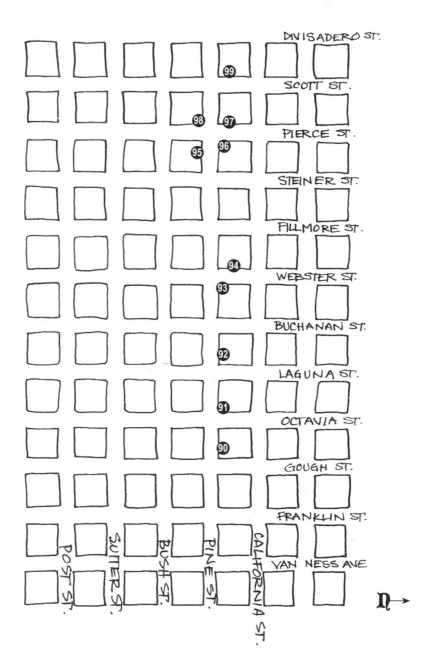

No. 90

1848 Pine

The First Koshland House

Early in June 1875 one Simon Koshland bought 1848 Pine and its big side garden, which as a matter of fact is still there, for $5,500. He needed a big house—there were of course bigger houses around but this one would do—because he had eight (or were there ten?) children. They ranged in age from about three to twenty.

Simon Koshland was already a prosperous merchant, but he remained at this good but not quite posh address until his death in 1896. It was only after his widow Rosine's death about 1911 that the family sold the house.

This was a close-knit patriarchal family: sons went into the family business, children lived at home until they married, grandchildren came back. And Simon's habits of attention to his temple and unostentatious charities have been emulated down the generations as the Koshlands became an extremely important San Francisco family.

Son Marcus built the most famous Koshland house, that stately pile at Washington and Maple in Presidio Heights which imitates the Petit Trianon. Concerts by the Blinder brothers' string quartet, sometimes with a guest pianist of the calibre of the ethereal William Kapell, were a regular feature there in the 1940s and 1950s—each of the programs was played once at the Koshlands' and once downtown.

Marcus' son Daniel Koshland was a president of Levi Strauss, a faithful philanthropist and a gentle, urbane figure walking up the aisle at the Wednesday night concerts of the San Francisco Symphony. Meanwhile in New York Daniel's cousin William (Billy) Koshland became a celebrated executive at the publishing firm of Alfred A. Knopf. He was a key player in the launching of Julia Child into cookbook glory.

Other descendants continue to make waves in San Francisco's business and philanthropic communities, many of the Koshlands having intermarried with their friends and relations from other pioneer Jewish merchant clans.

Simon Koshland himself was born in 1825 in Ichenhausen, Bavaria and before the age of twenty he was in the U.S., probably alone. He became a citizen in Philadelphia where he met and married Rosine Frauenthal. Then it was a case of Go West.

Directories show Simon in Sacramento in 1853, a wholesale clothing merchant working with his brothers Nathan and Max. Then he seems to have followed the trajectory of Nathan, who came to San Francisco in 1858 because it was the center for shipments to Canada. By the time

Simon bought 1848 Pine, Koshland Brothers was a significant firm of commission merchants and dealers in wools, hides and furs.

Four years after that Simon and Nathan split up, Simon founding S. Koshland and Company with Joseph, his oldest son, who became the New York representative. Simon and Joseph seem to have bought wool from producers all over the West and marketed it in the East, especially Boston, which was the shipping point for New England mills.

By 1908 Simon's sons Abraham, Jesse and Joseph all lived in Boston and Marcus was the only partner left in San Francisco. Well, Marcus' three-star "Petit Trianon" with its stunning double staircase remains in rarefied Presidio Heights to be stared at by walking tourists, but it's the relative modesty of 1848 Pine, with endless traffic passing below its Italianate door (and a slightly enlarged front), that symbolizes best the solid foundation of a great old San Francisco family.

No. 91

1801 Octavia

A German Priest Spoke Japanese Here

*I*n 1913 a Japanese resident of California wrote to the Bishop of Tokyo for permission to make his confession by mail. And that started the ball rolling. Thanks to this communication Father Albert Breton founded a Catholic mission and community center for San Francisco's Japanese population. It was originally in the next block to the south, where the Montessori school, formerly Morning Star School, is located.

At first the mission was just a Sunday school and parlor chapel in an old mansion, one of the early pastors-in-charge being Pius L. Moore, who was president of the University of San Francisco from 1919 to 1925. Then, under the forceful influence of William W. Stoecke of the Divine Word fathers—he served the Japanese Americans here from 1925 to 1951—this mission came up in the world.

Slowly and carefully Father Stoecke proceeded. In 1929 the old mansion at 1715 Octavia was torn down to make way for the "Morning Star" schoolhouse with the Asian-style tile roof. Then he and his flock began to raise money for a proper church. Ten years on it was dedicated, the new St. Francis Xavier at 1801 Octavia, named after the sixteenth-century missionary to Japan.

The site had been the home of architect John Cebrian's family, who may have donated it or willed it to the church. The location, corner of Octavia and Pine, placed the Cebrians right on the edge of the Japanese American community which, before World War II, was concentrated in the area from about Pine to Geary and Gough to Fillmore.

Nobody in 1939 had the least notion of a "Baja Pacific Heights"—people from Pacific Avenue went to Bush Street to buy their goldfish from a Japanese aquarium.

And this was before sushi too!

Father Stoecke was a perfect example of the Catholic Church's international organization. Born about 1879 in Germany, he was educated in Holland before spending a dozen years as a missionary in Japan. By the time that tour of duty came to an end he was well versed in the Japanese language and customs: giving a sermon in his parishioners' tongue was not a problem.

But the fact is the Catholics were not by any means the first Christians to establish missions for San Francisco's Japanese immigrants. A Gospel Society was aimed at this group in 1877, by 1910 the Methodists and the Presbyterians had founded Japanese missions, and there was also a Japanese YMCA. The Episcopalians and Congregationalists soon followed.

Japanese immigration, overwhelmingly

of male laborers, had begun in the late 1860s. The 1890 census counted 590 Japanese in San Francisco, by the turn of the century there were 1781, then 4,518 by 1910, this steep ascent motivating the launching of the assorted Christian missions.

The American government excluded additional Japanese laborers in 1908 but allowed wives and children to enter until 1924. So the census figure in 1930 was 6,250.

The designer of St. Francis Xavier—now St. Benedict Church for the Deaf—adopted a number of Japanese motifs. The plain stucco walls are typical of Japanese shrines, and like a shrine the building is surrounded by landscaping. The tile roof with turned-up corners strikes another Japanese note and the entry portico borrows from the ideas of a torii gate and the multiple brackets of a Chinese temple roof.

By the time St. Francis Xavier opened, on Christmas Eve in 1939, the congregation numbered a healthy two hundred. But their days were numbered. On December 7, 1941 the Japanese attack on Pearl Harbor unleashed prejudice that had been simmering for years in a city considerably less diverse than it is today. California's Japanese Americans were herded into concentration camps far away from their homes, the deportations beginning to empty the neighborhood in March 1942 and continuing throughout the war.

Father Stoecke went with his parishioners to a camp at Topaz, Utah!

The church probably stored some of the congregation's possessions and in the absence of Stoecke, Father William Zimmerman while abandoning the Japanese language for services did bring in people of half a dozen different nationalities. Then Father Stoecke returned after the war and picked up where he left off, offering shelter to other returnees in the house next door.

Gradually a number of the original congregation came back to the fold. But it was difficult for them geographically. After the war the Japanese Americans dispersed themselves over the Bay Area and while a charming "Japantown" retail area eventually sprang up in the neighborhood—with, of course, dozens of places to eat sushi, sashimi and tempura, and some worthy real estate bulldozed in the process—the old residents vowed they'd never segregate themselves again.

And now, around that Japanese retail core, is the diverse and rather "upper Bohemian" neighborhood of Victorians known as "Baja Pacific Heights," wherein sits St. Benedict Parish for the Deaf at St. Francis Xavier, a church with quite a story.

No. 92

2016 Pine

The Second Story Came First

This is a Victorian club sandwich of a house, sporting all three of the styles popular in San Francisco during Queen Victoria's reign. The first floor with its rectangular-plan bay windows, column capitals and anti-Classical balusters is Stick-Eastlake, the second floor with its round-headed windows falls under the heading "early Italianate," then the crown of the house with Palladian window and garlands on the frieze just below is Queen Anne.

The cooking up of this sandwich seems to have resulted from three major remodels at least, including the basement and right-side addition dating from the mid-twentieth century. Note meanwhile that the present staircase up to the porch doesn't match the nineteenth-century fabric, and the original stairs through the sidewalk retaining wall don't line up with an entrance.

Here's the story as well as I can make it out...

In May 1869 one William Horton paid $1,000 for a vacant lot now occupied by 2016 Pine, then in July of the same year sold it for $5,000. The huge price difference means a house must have been built on said lot. Now advance to August 1873, one Dr. Edwin H. Parker having sold the property to bookkeeper James F. Hough, and *Magee's Real Estate Circular* reports, "There is a one-story frame house on the lot, No. 2016; rent $27.50," this presumably for a month.

So the building in question must have been what is now the second story, early Italianate in style, with a different top. The house was square in plan and, with the centered door, twice the size of most houses being built at that time.

The next information we have is that Hough sold the property to a merchant named Joseph Moody in 1875 for $6,000. Then in 1880 a widow named Rebecca Gordon with three children paid $7,000 for the house and was the first owner to live in it. Also resident was Nicholas Gordon, presumably Rebecca's brother, a stockbroker's clerk, and it was very likely the Gordons who had the house jacked up and the present main floor added, providing more room for a probable population of at least five, plus a live-in servant or two to do the laundry and pastry.

This remodel would have been in the 1880s to judge by the Stick-Eastlake details mentioned above.

Our tale continues as the widow Rebecca marries widower and fellow Ohioan Charles Boone—he was a barber downtown—about 1894. Mr. Boone has four minor children of his own, that ups the population at 2016 considerably, and lo, a Queen Anne attic and rear addition sprout, with a sidewalk retaining wall thrown in too. We're growing like the proverbial Topsy.

Now, records show Rebecca Gordon as the owner of 2016 from 1880 to 1901, but the 1893 contract for a big remodel (with, of course, her marriage in sight) was signed by Mary Ellen Pleasant, a prominent African American businesswoman and fearless crusader who'd sued to desegregate public transportation in San Francisco. One suspects Rebecca was her protégé, partner or client.

At all events, by 1906 this house that grew and grew belonged to another widow, Katherine H. Withrow, whose husband, a Virginian with the euphonious not to mention alliterative name of Woodward Withrow, had been a construction engineer on the San Francisco sea wall.

Two daughters joined Katherine at 2016 Pine, Marie who was a music teacher and Evelyn Almond Withrow who was a painter of some note, doing portraits, still lifes and depictions of Indians in the Southwest and southern California.

After Woodward's death in 1881 Mrs. Withrow had taken her daughters to Europe, where Evelyn studied for four years with J. Frank Currier in Munich. Edan Hughes' *Artists in California* reports that the three women "lived for seven years in London where their attractive studio in Kensington became a rendezvous for the artistic and literary elite of that era. They gave teas and were the talk of London for their salons…" Do you suppose Henry James stirred sugar into his tea at their address?

And the article goes on to say that the trio maintained the same sort of studio-salon in San Francisco when they returned "to the old family home at 2016 Pine Street."

Some years on, toward the end of her time in San Francisco, Evelyn—or Eva as she was generally known—was the first president of the Society of Women Artists. Katherine had given the house to her daughters in 1911 but continued to live with them for another decade. When the daughters moved to San Diego in 1926 it was rented out.

After Eva's death two years later Marie sold the property to the Property Control Board of the American Nichiren Mission, a Buddhist organization led for many years by the Reverend Ishida. They had the side addition constructed, perhaps as temporary housing for Japanese Americans returning from the World War II concentration camps.

To make room for the addition the mission had the house moved to the left on a new basement—and that explains why the sidewalk stairs don't line up with any doorway!

No. 93

1900 Webster

The White House

The house at 1900 Webster with its immaculately preserved wrought iron fence stands out because it's white and on a corner. Now, if you stop for the Webster Street light coming out Pine on a regular basis, the chances are very good you've wondered about the filled-in window shapes: were there really windows there at one time, or is what one sees simply the intended decoration of an otherwise blank wall?

Well, a careful look and a thought to the inside arrangements tell us it's the latter. The moldings in the "window" spaces match the house and its proportions too well to be anything but original. The inner side of the wall they adorn at the first-floor level must be the front parlor's south wall, and remember that the Victorians did seem to like dark parlors: anything to keep the furniture from fading prematurely!

The architect of this white house was Bernhardt Henriksen, born in San Francisco in 1851 and trained by the city's first French architect, Prosper Huerne. Henriksen's work is virtually unknown: three Eastlake cottages in Alameda, a pair on Guerrero Street in San Francisco and, in partnership with one Mahoney, a couple of firehouses (see Interlude after Old House No. 68) and a round-bay affair at Fillmore and Grove.

In 1886 Henriksen was secretary of the city's brand new chapter of the American Institute of Architects. However undistinguished his output, he did produce a good design at Pine and Webster, worth every penny of the $280 he received for it. The building contractor signed for $8,300, a sum indicating luxury well above average for its era. Luxury rather than up-to-dateness was evidently what the client ordered: by '84, when it was built, the house's Italianate design would have been thought conservative, even old-fashioned.

The original owner of 1900 Webster was Pierre or Peter Berges, until 1882 part owner of Miner's Restaurant, an enterprise prosperous enough that its stock and furnishings were assessed in 1875 at $2,000. By the time Berges moved in on Webster he was a wholesale wine and liquor merchant.

French-born (this might signal a tie to Henriksen's mentor Huerne), Berges came to the U.S. in 1869. The 1900 census records that he had a French wife, three sons and a daughter. All of the family, including the two sons who were grown, were living in the white house at that time, along with a French—but of course—servant. Ah, coq au vin on Webster, that sounds like a nice idea.

Amazingly, descendants were still living in the house a century, and many coq au vins, after it was built, passersby occasionally seeing an elderly Asian servant—attired in feng shui white jacket to match his pristine surroundings—sweeping 1900's front steps.

No. 94

1935 Webster

"Civilian Exclusion" Happened Here

In 1934 this 1879 Victorian was bought from the long-resident Ellert family by Shotaro Tsuruoka, the teenage son of Tokutaro and Dai Tsuruoka. The house was in Shotaro's name because California's Alien Land Law of 1913 prohibited ownership of land by "aliens ineligible for citizenship."

Shotaro was a U.S. citizen, having been born here, but his immigrant parents were denied citizenship by laws in effect all the way up to 1952—when, as far as certain basic rights were concerned, this country was still a lily-white home of the brave. Tokutaro probably came over before 1908, which is when immigration was closed to Japanese men. Wives and families were admitted until 1924.

Father Tsuruoka was listed in a 1933 directory as a salesman on Post Street, then in 1940 without occupation; in '41 Dai was listed alone, working as a florist. Doubtless she had a hand in creating the house's Japanese garden in back.

But the Tsuruokas had scant time to enjoy it. On December 7, 1941 the Japanese attack on Pearl Harbor threw the U.S. into World War II and immediately the FBI arrested some two thousand Japanese nationals. On February 19, 1942 President Roosevelt authorized the mass expulsion of Japanese Americans and in March the head of the Western Defense Command followed suit by announcing the removal of all persons of Japanese ancestry, alien or citizen, to camps in remote areas of California and other western states.

Over the next four months, 108 separate "Civilian Exclusion Orders" were issued, each for a particular area. Residents were ordered out of their homes, to be transported with only what they could carry. For citizen or alien, baby or grandfather, there was no hearing, no trial, no appeal—viewed with hindsight, this was, to put it politely, government hysteria in high gear.

Civilian Exclusion Order No. 20, issued Friday April 24, 1942, zeroed in on the San Francisco area bounded by California and Sutter Streets and Presidio and Van Ness Avenues. Family representatives had according to this edict to report for instructions on April 25 or 26. And evacuation, they heard, would take place on Friday, May 1. No pets allowed, everything carried would have to be packaged. And oh yes, one week to wrap up one's life. Think of what it must have been like trying to get a night's sleep.

When May Day (date of irony?) arrived, the travelers to the windy sands of Utah and eastern California were labeled, as if they were packages themselves, and herded into transition quarters in horse stalls at Tanforan race track down the Peninsula. And in this manner ended the Tsuruokas' sojourn at pretty 1935 Webster—where Levi Ellert, mayor of San Francisco in 1892, had lived happily. "Memories of a Deportee," alas...

Many years earlier a different problem had made life difficult for a previous resident, the widow of David Colton who was a junior partner of the infamous Big Four "robber barons" of the Southern Pacific Railroad. Ellen Colton was being pressured to return her late husband's SP-related holdings and at first she gave in, but she felt defrauded and in due course sued.

1935 Webster has had only six owners in more than a century. The fourth stripped off the trim and covered the house with stucco. But the sixth stripped off that abysmal covering and luckily found "shadows" of the original trim to guide in restoration. Good show!

No. 95

2475 Pine (not extant)

St. Rose Academy, Alas

*A*ll good buildings, it seems, have the potential to become parking lots.

This is what happened to St. Rose Academy on the south side of Pine Street just east of Pierce, a lovely pile designed by Albert Pissis who, as a colleague of his put it in the local architects' magazine in 1909, is "responsible for more graceful, dignified and well-planned structures on the streets of San Francisco than any single practitioner in the Bay City."

This article went on to toast a mere forty-four Pissis buildings, including the Emporium, the Flood Building across from it on Market Street, the old White House department store (now housing Banana Republic) at Grant and Sutter, the Mechanics' Institute on Post, and of course the Hibernia Bank from 1889, San Francisco's first Beaux Arts Classical building.

Mentioned too, naturally, was St. Rose Academy, a building which always reminded Arthur of an opera house on some great street like Berlin's Unter den Linden. Dedicated in March 1906, it weathered the great earthquake of the following month with only $10,000 in damage to plaster and such—and how much did it cost to demolish it eighty-five years later?

Born in Mexico in 1852 and a San Franciscan from the age of four, Albert Pissis—remember to pronounce it PEE-sees!—was trained at the Ecole des Beaux-Arts in Paris and was San Francisco's earliest confirmed product of that prestigious institution, which influenced so much American architecture of the early twentieth century, including the "Bay City's" Civic Center. He poured his training into St. Rose and his other buildings as well, all models of taste and finesse, and let's take a closer look...

St. Rose had three stories and an attic with dormer windows, the middle story which was the tallest and most ornate following the Italian tradition of "piano nobile." A grand external double staircase led up to this floor's roofed porch where four fluted columns defined the spaces for three semicircular arches on the main wall.

Italian Renaissance styling also influenced the rusticated coating of the lower floor and the individual fenestration of each floor. Symmetrical as can be, in the proper Beaux Arts manner, the windows—while different in size, shape and ornament from level to level—were arranged in repeating threes: three on each floor of the projecting pavilion at each end of the façade, three for the centered entry porch and three to each side of it.

Well, no beautiful voices like those of Tiana Lemnitz or Friedrich Schorr rang out from this operatic façade, but St. Rose Academy was harmonious indeed. Enough, for now, of the past tense: the Victorians facing the "St. Rose" parking lot look more lovely than ever.

No. 96

1900 Pierce

Sinuous Design on Pierce

A year after this Queen Anne/Craftsman house at Pierce and Pine was built—we're talking 1887—it was photographed for a newspaper series titled "Artistic Homes of California." Except for minor details the picture might have been taken today: it shows the same sinuous brackets at the entry and in bay windows, the same unusual fern relief in gables galore, the same elaborate roof with wavy dormer, and so on.

The house lost a tall brick chimney along the way (probably in '06), a rear porch, square upper sash panes on the parlor's bay windows facing Pine Street, stained glass in an adjacent window and a few entry details. But what would you expect in a century and more? Meanwhile it's managed to acquire a flagpole, fire escapes, basement window bars and the wrought iron fence on Pine.

Aesthetics here, security there: a house walks somewhat in step with changing times.

Now with that photograph from 1887 came a quaint description of the interior, a sort of architectural laundry list: "The main hall is nearly square, finished in redwood, with wax polish. The hall fireplace cuts off the further right-hand corner. The chimney-piece, supported on Corinthian columns, is very effective. The staircase rises from the left. The dado is panelled, with a circle in each square. The side walls are terra-cotta, and the ceiling is marked off by deep mouldings. The staircase makes one turn and then is walled in."

Not a text, this, to win the Booker Prize but it and the picture from 1887 reveal changes at the entryway. Originally there were double front doors with little squares of leaded glass, and on either side of the marble steps the porch had a long bench sheltered not only by the gabled door hood but also a pair of L-plan balustrades.

This inglenook effect, and the curious brackets, adventures-in-roofing and unpainted redwood interior relate 1900 Pierce to turn-of-the-century Craftsman houses by Julia Morgan, Bernard Maybeck and lesser architects. Basically a Queen Anne, but designed on the cutting edge of style for 1886, it draws these new elements to its bosom with flair and a good feeling for continuity. 1900 is complex but not too busy for its own good.

"Artistic Homes of California" attributed the house's design ideas to the owner and only their execution to his architect, but this may well have been a case of sloppy reporting. In any event, the architect was named as A. W. Smith, an "interesting practitioner" who had an office in the East Bay and was very busy in residential work from about 1895 to 1925.

Smith built many Craftsman houses, often with curious design twists of his own. Quite a few Oakland and Berkeley houses said to be by Morgan or Maybeck have proved, upon solid research, to be the work of none other than this A. W. Smith who could, it seems, have used a good public relations man.

Postscript

And as Anne admits in connection with Old House No. 70, further research indicates that the correct Smith here was not A. W. but W. F. This is the sort of mistake she almost never made; the only mortal who may have a better track record in this regard is the archivist Gary Goss.

No. 97

1919 Pierce

Perfect Italianate

*T*he house at 1919 Pierce Street is *the* typical San Francisco Italianate house: a tall thin wooden box with a fancy front, the tux shirt so to speak on the chest of the ordinary man.

The following you must have read before...

A half-octagonal bay window rises through two floors into a top cornice that rests on ten brackets plus two on the sides hiding a sloping roof; window tops have "segment" arches or rounded corners; a pervasive verticality is offset by the main cornice as well as two subsidiary ones on the bay, a big projecting front door hood and a smaller hood/cornice/entablature over one second-floor window; moldings, panels and attached columns fill the spaces between these projections, leaving scarcely any main siding of horizontally grooved wood; and as if foreseeing a late twentieth-century need, the house has been placed far enough above and behind the sidewalk to allow for a later basement garage.

The paragraph above describes almost any Italianate house built in San Francisco in the 1870s, except a few didn't have the bay window. Of course in the 1860s there'd have been more variety, and in the 1880s builders began to vary the mold, mainly with a rectangular bay and slightly different trim.

What's special about 1919 Pierce, the Cunningham-Dodd house, is the perfection of its type—except for the garage and lost stair rail. Then too, it's one of five still-matching houses that graciously thumb their collective nose at serious alteration. It is a tract house, but that's nothing to be ashamed of; tracts were typical of the era and the older they become, the more charming they look to us today. We drink in Victorians in bulk as shoppers buy strawberries by the ton at Costco.

This particular tract was built by Henry T. Hinkel in 1881. Yes, it was a little old-fashioned, but he did add the pretend-Mansard roof above the main cornice to create a fashionable Second Empire look.

Henry Hinkel, whose name turns up repeatedly in the annals of San Francisco Victoriana, was one of five house-building brothers, each in business independently. Faithful aficionados will recall Charles Hinkel's no longer "pure" set of houses on Washington Street between Webster and Fillmore, and you step to the head of the class if you know that John Hinkel donated Hinkel Park to the city of Berkeley.

Their father was a carpenter named Charles (aka Karl) Hinkel who'd emigrated from Germany to Galena, Illinois where he married the daughter of a Welsh miner. The couple came to California about 1851 and descendants are here still.

Sudden thought: what sort of houses would the Hinkel boys have been designing if father and sons (born, presumably, of a non-Welsh mother) had remained in Germany?

At all events, Henry was the oldest child, born in 1846. By 1869 he was out on his own as a carpenter, and five years later began listing himself as a contractor. By the time he built the Pierce Street tract he had a lot of experience. Alas he died in '82, only thirty-six, with about a hundred houses to his credit, some now demolished but enough remaining to make a fitting homage to this good craftsman indeed, a carpenter's carpenter if you will.

All five of the Pierce Street houses are handsome enough for a chapter of their own in a study of San Francisco's Victorians, but 1919 had at least one especially interesting owner-occupant.

About 1886 it was bought from the first owner, a widow or divorced woman named Alice Cunningham, by a mining and hydraulic engineer named Willis Gorman Dodd. By 1890 Dodd had become manager of Pacific Iron Works on First Street north of Mission and for this company he invented the "Sigmoidal Water Wheel," which rather sounds like something out of a comic strip (remember Alley Oop?) but perhaps the engineers among you know what the obviously accomplished Mr. Dodd came up with at his workspace.

About 1892 Pacific Iron Works was acquired by Union Iron Works, the West's first iron foundry, begun in 1851 by Peter Donahue who's remembered in the Mechanics Monument at Bush and Market Streets. In the 1890s Union was the West's premier shipbuilding company, with a huge plant that's still visible east of Potrero Hill a century later.

With the Union takeover Dodd continued to manage his old foundry, but as the First Street branch of Union Iron Works. Evidently his management was good because early in the next century (before Bethlehem Shipbuilding took over) the Pierce Street Dodd became Union's president—still, one presumes, taking the handy California Street cable car downtown.

No. 98

2501 Pine

Old Folks Were at Home Here

Note: Anne wrote about 2501 Pine a decade before the Dominican Sisters—who could not apparently afford a seismic retrofit of St. Rose Academy—restored and comprehensively remodeled this languishing property into an attractive complex including affordable housing units, child-care center, community meeting hall, chapel, gardens and convent. In the process 2501 regained at least one story of its original height.

Behold here the remains of a wonderful building. Now two stories high and an L-shaped plan on the lot, it was once four stories high and an E-plan with a tower at each corner and an astonishing roof.

The third story began like the surviving second, shingled and with a window above each window below. Wall met window with softly curving sides but sharp tops and bottoms while the shingles between floors were arranged to make one large band of alternating circles and diamonds that relieved the 230 feet of wall without making it fussy. You can still see the lower half of each circle and diamond.

What's tantalizingly missing is the complex two-story roof. It was shingled, and flared at the edges. It sloped up from the top line of the third-floor windows on all four sides of the building to make what's called a hip roof. For adequate third-floor ceiling height a dormer rose above each pair of windows and each dormer had its own hip roof with a pointed cap.

The curved sections of wall sprouted into turrets with upturned funnel roofs, one at the Pierce-Pine corner and three along Pine. The walls of the two end turrets rose higher than the others, and little fourth-floor windows peeped out from under their roofs. More such miniature windows sprouted halfway up the main roof, each with its own dormer, hip roof, flared edge and pointy top.

This roof was a whole symphony of shapes, its composer A. Page Brown, then a twenty-nine-year-old graduate of McKim, Mead and White, the great New York office of eclectic architects whose work includes the Villard Houses, the Boston Public Library and assorted mansions at Newport. At home among the cream of society, Brown opened his first office in New York under the patronage of the Chicago multimillionaire Mrs. Cyrus McCormick.

Her friend Mrs. Charles Crocker of Nob Hill, widow of one of the Southern Pacific Railroad's founders, heard her extol the talent of the young Brown and quickly from the hill came a commission for Brown to design a family tomb and also 2501 Pine for a favorite Crocker charity, San Francisco's Old People's Home—the design of which comes, reports Professor Longstreth, from McKim, Mead and White's hospital for railroad employees in Brainerd, Minnesota.

Brown arrived in San Francisco in July 1889 and within days the two projects were under construction. Mrs. Crocker introduced the young architect around town and he had an immense success almost overnight. As for the Home, a group of prominent women had started it in 1874, their noble purpose "the founding of a Home for the needy, sick and destitute of all nations."

At first the facility was in North Beach, on Francisco Street. For a number of years it was managed by a clergyman, doubtless an Episcopalian, given the Crockers' religious orientation: Grace Cathedral, of course, is on Crocker land. At 2501 the residents lived upstairs in the huge E-plan building while on the main floor there were parlors, dining rooms (note the plural), a kitchen and library.

In 1942 the Dominican Sisters took over the building which, for reasons not entirely clear, had fallen into disrepair; conceivably the dismantling of the third floor was a necessary precaution, the fourth level having been seriously damaged by fire. So now...behold the remains of a wonderful building.

Postscript

Anne was writing in 1989. Well, the present Rose Court is neither exactly the remains nor, of course, the original of this building whose story suggests a cake that collapsed and was put back together again by a different baker. Perhaps it's most accurate to describe the relaunched 2501 as the latest variation on an ongoing architectural theme. Meanwhile the Sisters with their affordable units are carrying on in the spirit of those Nob Hill ladies who wanted to do something for the needy: that is a mission with which even preservationists cannot disagree.

No. 99

1901 Scott

A "Vara" Nice House

Observe at the corner of Pine and Scott a low brick fence, a hedge and a row of cypresses. Nothing can be seen behind them except more trees and hints of a rather large white house, an excellent Italianate specimen, it develops.

No, we are not out in the country, somewhere in idyllic Sonoma County or down by old Pescadero; this is San Francisco. And house, garden and driveway, surrounded by the L-shape of Cobb School playground, comprise a real estate entity that, while now exceedingly rare, was once a standard sort of thing, a fifty-vara lot.

The term comes from a Spanish measure, the vara, which is 2.75 feet long. Mexican San Francisco was surveyed—from Market Street out past 1901 Scott to Presidio Avenue—into lots fifty varas on each side, that's 137.5 x 137.5 feet. Many a nineteenth-century resident built his house—"castle" perhaps?—on a fifty-vara lot, gardening the considerable rest of his property. You see these big lots in old pictures, and here at 1901 Scott the picture, in danger one feels of going out of focus, comes alive.

The house here has lovely round-headed windows, a Corinthian-columned porch and a many-bracketed cornice around all sides. The present appearance results not only from its original design but also from a couple of major alterations, and from wonderful preservation by the current owner (in 1988), grandson of the original owner.

Grocer and liquor dealer John Frederick Ortman, born in Hannover in 1829, bought the big lot at 1901 Scott in 1870 for $5,000. He and his family had been picnicking in the scrub-filled vicinity and took a shine to the location. Soon they were established in the house that still stands today, with at that time a well and windmill nearby, and chickens and a cow in the area where elementary school children now play.

A photo from about 1885 shows the house with a widow's walk on top of a four-slope roof and no attic window. The building at that time was shallower and the front bay only one story tall. The fence was wooden pickets and the Norfolk pine that now towers over the corner came, in 1885, not quite up to the second floor.

With 1889 came alterations. A second story was added to the front bay and the roof shape was changed to accommodate an attic, a Queen Anne–style arch and gable appearing in the process. The house was also extended to the rear and a wrought iron fence replaced the pickets.

By 1914 Ortman had died and his son-in-law Thomas Shumate, a Missouri-born physician and pharmacist, in collaboration with designer William Merchant and his brother-contractor Christopher, put in a brick fence, walks and steps, plus a fireplace or two inside and other new hardware.

There were also garages and stables added behind the house, launching pads so to speak for the busy Dr. Shumate, who had a thriving medical practice as well as a string of pharmacies, the latter with their paternal druggists in near-clerical white well remembered by present-day senior citizens of San Francisco. There was one Shumate's at the southeast corner of Sacramento and Presidio across from the Vogue Cinema, another at the southwest corner of Fillmore and Jackson, now a coffeehouse.

In fact, on the threshold of this coffeehouse one can still read: SHUMATE'S.

Dr. Shumate—whose son Albert was also a physician, and a wonderful historian of Californiana as well—was born in St. Louis in 1871. As a young man he came to California for his health and got a job clerking in a drugstore. Meanwhile he went to night school to get a pharmacist's license. Then the obvious next step was to buy his own pharmacy so he could make enough money to attend medical school, tending the store at night after class.

Earning a medical degree in 1894, the first Dr. Shumate was hired on as a police department surgeon for five years. And when he married, in 1899, his father-in-law installed him and his bride in a new house on California Street in part of what is now the Cobb schoolyard. Soon he was building up his chain of pharmacies which eventually numbered the magnificent sum of twenty-eight.

A corner in San Francisco those days was almost as likely to house a Shumate's as a bar or restaurant.

But Thomas Shumate was not content just being a physician and druggist with all those tile-floored "corner-houses"; he also ran an import-export firm and a real estate company—the latter, come to think of it, almost inevitable considering his cornering the market on drugstores if you will.

And then he was a police commissioner from 1912 to 1937.

He also owned Fillmore Street's east side from Washington almost to Jackson where the Bond Cleaners, Symphony secondhand shop and a fancy china emporium are now located. And he had six hundred acres of orchards west of Los Altos. In Sunnyvale he owned and ran the Troy Farm Stables, the largest breeder of saddle horses in the country.

Thomas Shumate's obit called him "wealthy, debonair, of distinguished appearance, a notable figure in the city's professional, political and social life."

And in almost every detail Thomas' son Albert matched the distinguished record, and look, of his dad.

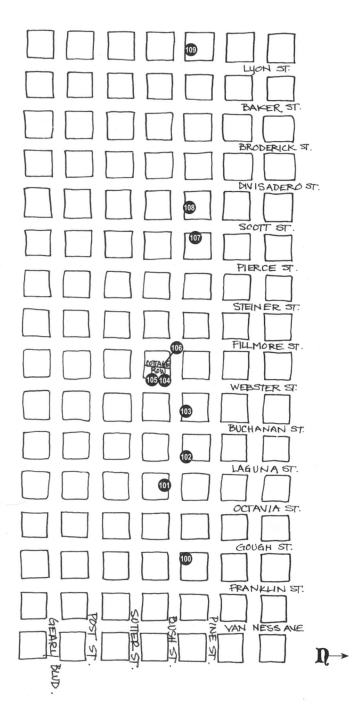

On or near

Bush Street

east to west

No. 100

1668 Bush

A Venerable Parish

*A*lmost a building out of one of Donizetti's Elizabethan operas, Trinity Episcopal has a touch of the medieval fortress in its 1892 roofline. The architectural details of this sometimes gloomy pile—pointed arches, wall buttresses, turrets—look ahead to 1920s Collegiate Gothic more than sideways to its Victorian Gothic contemporaries, St. Mark's Lutheran for instance down Gough Street toward Civic Center.

In essence the design trumpets Trinity's geometric forms and their being clothed in a rough-cut gray-green sandstone from Colusa up the Central Valley. And it speaks too of A. Page Brown's talent for creative, forward-looking architecture—although Brown himself was so busy networking in 1892 he relied heavily on his colleague A. C. Schweinfurth for design input and acted more in a supervisory capacity on this job.

For Trinity Episcopal Brown worked with typically upscale clients: the building committee consisted of William Burchell Hooper, a prominent hotelier; William Bourn, president of the city's water company and a Pacific Gas and Electric predecessor; and William H. Taylor, head of Risdon Iron Works. What a stalwart trio of ushers they must have made marching up the aisle, baskets in hand.

Well, only a parish of wealthy community leaders could have financed such a substantial and possibly operatic structure.

Now Trinity is the oldest Episcopal parish in the West, organized in the summer of 1849. Brown's (and Schweinfurth's) building, more than a century old, is its fourth church, and because it survived "1906" virtually intact it contains items brought from the immediately previous Trinity on the northwest corner of Union Square.

From the 1850s comes a plaque heralding the parish's first rector and his portrait painted by fabled California painter Charles Nahl. The brass chancel rail dates from 1888, the tail end of the Union Square period, and two small windows were made of stained glass pieces from that downtown church.

The current Trinity's interior is a cross plan, light, spacious and featuring pared-down decoration. The vaulting boasts a complicated geometry but few moldings while the crossing dome, sixty-three feet high, rests on plain ultramassive columns. Worth special notice are the Tiffany bronze angel who holds up the lesson, and the Tiffany angel window high in the left transept.

And where are Joan Sutherland and Beverly Sills, Sonia Ganassi and Edita Gruberova?

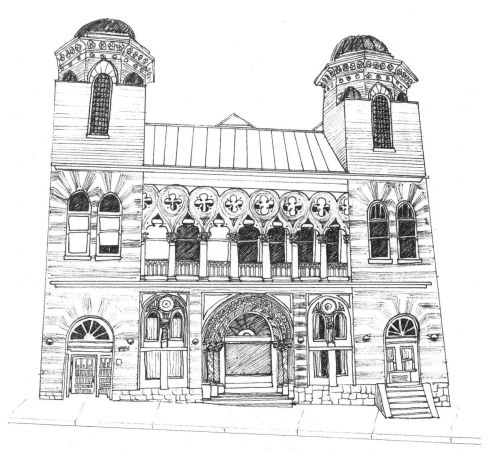

No. 101

1881 Bush

A House with Several Lives

A Moorish/Venetian head-turner on an urban raceway, 1881 Bush has had several lives, and sometimes no life at all. It's been a synagogue, a Japanese mission, a black Baptist church, and (prior to its new role as an assisted living facility) just a wreck waiting under Redevelopment Agency jurisdiction for its future to begin.

It was built in 1895 for Congregation Ohabai Shalome, which means "lovers of peace." Ohabai was San Francisco's third Jewish congregation, following Sherith Israel and Emanu-El, which were both founded in 1849. Its prime movers were a group of fifty-five worshippers, mostly from Bavaria, who split off from Emanu-El in 1864 because they didn't like certain reforms, especially a new prayer book (sounds familiar, doesn't it?).

Led by Rabbi A. S. Bettelheim, Ohabai remained conservative throughout its existence, attracting French, English and more German members through the years.

When the congregation was launched, a temple seating no less than six hundred and fifty souls was built on the site of the Native Sons building at 414 Mason Street downtown, a mere three blocks from a new temple Emanu-El. Then after a thirty-year run the group moved out to Bush Street and Dr. Julius Fryer, a new rabbi, dedicated 1881.

America's first Moorish synagogue was the 1865 Emanu-El. And 1881 Bush—Ohabai Shalome obviously knew a good thing when they saw it, even if the competition saw it first—may have been the last. The architect, Moses J. Lyon, clearly had a ball: the intricate loggia above the entry imitates either the Ca d'Oro or Ducal Palace in Venice.

Lyon practiced from about 1888 to 1930. He studied with the noted pioneer architect Henry C. Macy but he never made a name among his colleagues. He designed a number of residences, some apartments and a few business or industrial buildings. Most of his clients were fellow Jews, including the infamous political boss Abe Ruef for whom he built the gorgeous clinker brick garage at 731 Filbert in North Beach.

Lyon's Bush Street temple was the congregation's home for about forty years. It had a very active membership, men, women and young parishioners having their own clubs. Though less rigidly conservative than in earlier days, Ohabai Shalome became one of the focal points for the Zionist cause.

During the Depression the congregation, under Rabbi Mihail Fried, had to sell 1881 and relocated on Fourth Avenue near Anza. When Fried died in 1940 the once flourishing Ohabai seems to have curled up and died.

Next, under Teruro Kasuga, the former temple became the Soto Zen Mission which is now located in an absolutely
un-Moorish building around the corner
on Laguna. Then, following the building's Baptist period, and time as the San
Francisco Zen Center—with California
governor-to-be Jerry Brown among its
congregants—the Redevelopment Agency
acquired the property in 1973 as part of its
Western Addition Area Two project. For
several years the only occupant was a club
always open for a game of Go. But this was
not the way to go with such a building!

Spruced up now, this Jewish cousin to
a Grand Canal palazzo just about reaches the apotheosis of zing. Bring on the
gondolas!

No. 102

1801 Laguna

Cornering the Market

Corners, corners: one tends to think of them in terms of restaurants because, well, just about every other restaurant is at an intersection. But think residential, and how the corner house of a Victorian row always has a little more room than its neighbors, more expanse of wall, more windows, more ornament.

A corner Victorian was usually more expensive to start with because of the conspicuous location and good natural light—yes, nineteenth-century real estate prices confirm that corners were considered choice.

The corner house at 1801 Laguna Street anchors a large tract of generally similar houses, eleven on Laguna and two each on Bush and Pine. Built in 1889-90, they waver between Stick style and Queen Anne. The triangles above openings shout Queen Anne and so do the bays, which are different from the rectangles of Stick and the half-octagons of Italianates; meanwhile the topline cornice follows the Stick rectangular plan over the bays but leaves the actual corners hanging over air as in Queen Anne.

1801 Laguna and its brethren were built on speculation by William Hinkel, the fourth of carpenter Charles Hinkel's five builder sons. He probably copied the building plans from tradition and books, a standard approach at the time.

The first Hinkel born in California, William turned up in San Francisco's city directory—the 1869 edition—when he was just eighteen. He was, this directory tells us, employed as a sashmaker. And the directory of 1879 tells us he was a sawyer, and still living with his parents. By 1882 he was a millhand, no longer at home, and presumably married.

The next year, aged thirty-one, William started his own contracting business, a business that continued through 1901 after which he switched career gears and became a stockbroker!

At 1801 Laguna William's customer was one George E. Dow, a manufacturer whose life reads like a Horatio Alger story. A machinist by trade, Dow while in his twenties worked for a mechanical engineer who was the agent for "Cameron's steam pumps and Pickering's engine regulators, etc." By the age of thirty-two he and a partner had taken over the engineer's Beale Street location for a foundry and machine works, and four years later he'd patented and was manufacturing the Dow Steam Pump.

Dow's operation specialized in hydraulic machinery and heavy iron castings as well as pumps for marine, irrigation and reclamation uses. From about 1910 to 1940, under Dow's son, the company had massive facilities on the Alameda side of the Oakland estuary.

No. 103

2006 Bush

The Far Out House

The simple Greek Revival house at 2006 Bush is one of the oldest buildings in San Francisco, maybe the second oldest in Pacific Heights between Vallejo and Bush. It was built sometime between 1858, when the U.S. Coast Survey mapped the city with no structure at this location, and 1864, when the owner signed up for water service. So it's of Civil War vintage, more or less.

There are many signs of 2006's comparatively great age. The triangular gable-end for instance has no false front and the siding is wide clapboards that slant outwards rather than the horizontally grooved rustic used c. 1860–1895. The hall-less floor plan is early as well: to reach back rooms one must walk through front rooms. Furthermore, ceilings are not as high as in Italianates of the 1870s—sounds like a salt box back East.

Then the rare porch or veranda across the front resembles those in California photos and lithographs of the 1850s, and in every Western film.

The Coast Survey map of 1857 shows the area around 2006 Bush as undulating, barren sand hills, the nearest trees about three blocks north. Only one road came out this far, ten modern blocks west of downtown. Paved with planks, it ran roughly along Bush to cemeteries on the present site of Laurel Village and Lone Mountain. The thickly built part of town didn't extend much west of Powell where the St. Francis Hotel sits today.

To build a two-story family house this far out required a man of vision. And such was Charles Stanyan, the house's first known owner and occupant. His claim to fame was chairing the committee that organized the Outside Lands as they were called—that's everything west of Divisadero—into the regular gridiron street pattern, meanwhile setting aside space for Golden Gate Park, the present east boundary of which is, yes, Stanyan Street.

Charles Stanyan was a New Hampshireman, about twenty-six years old in 1858 when his name first appeared in a San Francisco city directory. Probably he'd come West earlier, to mine gold. At all events he gave his occupation in 1880 as "mining." It was while on the Board of Supervisors from 1865 to 1869 that the precocious Stanyan led the Outside Lands committee, serving with such other "street-names-to-be" as Messrs. Shrader, Clayton, Ashbury and Cole.

Think of it, if there'd been no Mr. Ashbury there wouldn't have been a Haight Ashbury to go down in history. Haight Cole just doesn't do it.

In *The Making of Golden Gate Park*, Raymond Clary notes that these five supervisors billed the city $10,000 each for their services, but had to make do with $2,100. Business as usual in City Hall.

The original use of the house at 2006 Bush is something of a puzzle. For three decades Stanyan listed his residence sometimes as 2006 Bush but more often near Polk and Sacramento, where his voter registration remained. Could the Bush Street house have been for tenants, or even vacations? It and its huge lot—with six houses added later—remained in the Stanyan family for well over a century. Its original balustrade-encircled garden looks out from page 117 of Roger Olmsted and T. H. Watkins' *Here Today,* a tree'd and grassy Time Machine space, cleansed of sand and filled with charm.

No. 104

1717–19 Webster

A Surviving Triplet

*T*his double house fascinated me for years with its bayless front, round-headed openings on the main floor and its elaborate trim. It was such a beautiful example of Italianate style but its age and story had never come to light.

Then, working on a historic district proposal for the Bush Street–Cottage Row area, I looked deeper. Turns out the house was one of a set of identical triplets, but the other two, next to it toward Sutter Street, were torn down and replaced between 1899 and 1913.

They were all rental housing. The original owner never lived in any of them but he held onto the full property for the eighteen years between their construction and his death. This absentee landlord was John H. Smyth, an Irish-born attorney who never wrote his own will.

Smyth lived around the corner on Bush between Webster and Buchanan in the late 1860s and early 1870s and it was on the last day of '69 that he bought one hundred square feet of bare land on Webster for $3,000—the seller was one Daniel McLeod. At that time there was hardly anything built in the neighborhood, except of course the Stanyan house at 2006 Bush. The first public transportation didn't arrive until 1873, a horse car along Bush.

But development was in the air. In 1870 The Real Estate Associates put up its first eleven houses at Fillmore and Sacramento—coffeehouse land today!—and a partnership built cottages on all sides of the block bounded by Washington, Jackson, Webster and Buchanan: that was Tuckertown.

In 1870 Smyth developed his Webster Street lot too. He had three identical duplexes built, stairstepping down the hill (by the way, Webster in this area was not a wide boulevard until relatively recently). The Sanborn fire insurance maps of 1893 and 1899 show them about fifty feet deep, a basement and two stories in height, and each one with a center front mini-porch and split from front to back into two dwelling units.

The fancy trim on these essentially simple boxes indicates that Smyth expected to attract a relatively high class of horse-car riders who'd be willing to pay above-average rents. Flat lintels would have been cheaper but the arches made the houses seem like expensive brick buildings whose structure required arched openings.

The delicate balcony, the exquisite window surrounds, the fancy topline brackets were all prestige items that added to costs. They were all the very latest style in 1870, and they look beautiful today.

After John Smyth died in 1888 the

court divided his property among his relatives. A brother-in-law, contractor John Francis Riley, was still living in 1717-19, half or all, in 1914 and doubtless his need for a home saved this building from the fate of its siblings. Some miracle has saved this remaining duplex from remodelers ever since.

No. 105

1737 Webster

Traffic Stopper

*T*his is the house that stopped traffic.

It happened one morning about 1972 as the Redevelopment Agency was moving the house from one part of its "Western Addition Area Two" to another. This was at a time when the agency bulldozed a tremendous number of Victorians to make way for new developments in and around the so-called Geary corridor, but moved a few: the about-to-be 1737 Webster, originally on the outer edge of present-day Opera Plaza, was one of the lucky ones.

As the previous night proceeded, a number of houses being moved had been waiting here and there on blocks. Power lines had been taken down, police enlisted, the works; everything had been arranged to make for a smooth nocturnal transit of the "vehicles." Except that no one remembered how old houses often have topline cornices that stick out to the sides as well as in front.

This house, a lovely and not un-frivolous painted lady—note the shingled flower petals—arrived at its destination on Webster Street and lo, it wouldn't fit. So there it sat, out in the street, all through the morning rush.

1737 was designed by Samuel and Joseph Newsom, architects of more or less outrageous houses all up and down the state, including the incredible Carson affair at Eureka which went up about the same time as this one. Architectural historian David Gebhard calls the Newsoms practitioners of "Low Art." They specialized in modern products built on time and within budget, with "Up to Date" their theme song, visual forms being changed almost with the rapidity of fashions in clothing, and their designs unblushingly borrowed from all the latest architectural publications.

They also created a few of their own publications to spread the word of their "modernity."

This particular architectural fantasy was commissioned by John J. Vollmer, a grocer who owned a large plot of land running down Turk Street from Franklin. At the corner stood his Italianate-style grocery store with a metal awning over the sidewalk and two stories of residence above. Next to it on Turk toward downtown was a double house with two bays, then the Newsom house and beyond it a cottage.

These buildings were constructed at different times, for Vollmer had been living and working at the corner since 1877; before that he and his brother Henry had had a big store near the waterfront. The 1880 census showed the forty-four-year-old

Vollmer living at Turk and Franklin with his wife, two children, one of his clerks and another couple, most of the adults hailing from Baden, Germany.

The John Vollmer family were solid citizens but not among the city's movers and shakers. Perhaps they hoped to attain that status by commissioning a house from the "with it" Newsoms, who advertised that prominent men owed their success to the architects who designed their striking houses!

If so, the Vollmers were disappointed; they moved back over the store after living in their zingy Newsom opus for about nine years. A case, I guess, of their being in over their aesthetic heads. Thereafter they rented it: their tenant in 1900 had two children and two servants, one Scottish and one German. It was that kind of house. The Vollmers never sold it, they simply passed it on by gift from one generation to another, until the Redevelopment Agency condemned it in 1967.

No. 106

3 Cottage Row

An Amewsing Little House

I recommend a stroll down Cottage Row. This narrow opening between 2113 and 2115 Bush ushers you into a vest-pocket enclave of redwood and plum trees and ivy, a brick footpath leading to six generally identical houses. No. 3 is in the center of this enchanted mews, invisible behind the houses lining Bush and Sutter Street to the south.

The houses are tiny, only twenty feet wide and twenty-three deep. Insides are even smaller, if you subtract for wall thickness, stairs, storage, etc. But each has a backyard, all of five feet deep.

Each house shares side walls with its neighbors, and so close are they that the right side of each one's eaves dies into the next-door roof. Only the left side of the eaves ends "properly," supported by a single bracket and with moldings carried around the corner. Miniaturization extends to narrow doorways and a window's trim melting into the eaves trim. Expertly managed proportions give the impression each house is bigger than its actual size.

Minor changes have occurred over the years, making the houses no longer strictly identical. No. 3 has lost the divisions in its windows and gained security grills. No. 4 to the left has acquired plywood panels below the windows and shingles on the basement. But the overall effect remains unimpaired, enhanced by the garden setting.

Cottage Row was built in 1882 for "Colonel" Charles L. Taylor, whose company owned them for the next thirty years. The houses, walkway and the masking house at 2113 Bush formed together a single piece of property, all developed by Taylor as rentals.

A Maine native, Taylor had sailed to San Francisco in 1850, carried on lumber and shipping businesses, then settled prosperously into marine insurance in the 1860s. At different times he was on the school board, the State Board of Harbor Commissioners and San Francisco's Board of Supervisors.

Who actually lived on Cottage Row is hard to trace in much detail. The first known inhabitant of No. 3 was Abigail Nash, the widow of Thomas Nash, the carpenter-builder who constructed it and its siblings. Nash may have received part of his pay in future lodgings because he lived in a Taylor house at 2103 Bush in 1882–83 and at No. 2 Cottage Row 1886–89.

After Thomas' death Abigail floated about Taylor Rental Land, continuing at No. 2, then moving to a unit at 2113 Bush, later resurfacing on the Row at No. 3 after disappearing for a while from city directories as women often did in those sexist days.

The 1910 census reported three residents at No. 3: a Finnish steam schooner sailor named John Laiho, his bride, Elinor, who also came from Finland, and their lodger, Mary Green, a dressmaker from Sweden. A tight fit for this trio, it seems.

By the 1930s so many Japanese Americans lived on pastoral Cottage Row it was nicknamed Japan Street. They grew vegetables in their tiny backyards and offered them for sale at an informal open market held Saturdays (shades of 2007!) along the row.

How delightful! And to be wrenched away from the Row to a wartime concentration camp must have been especially difficult for neighborhood people who were living hidden among the plum trees.

Interlude

Back on Bush Street, a little past Fillmore on the left, is the restored façade of an old auto repair shop with handsome central arch just behind which, not unwhimsically, a nest of simple-lined modern apartments has been erected. Decorated with lions' heads that were a faithful telephone company theme, this façade first saw the light in 1909 as the face of a telephone exchange where rows of female operators, just like in thirties movies, helped put through calls. The building's architects—the address is 2255—were Coxhead and Coxhead no less.

Then at the next corner proceeding west, Bush and Steiner, you can't miss the grand and rather English-looking St. Dominic's. Ah, another Joan Sutherland venue! This Gothic pile was begun in 1924, finished in '27 and its official architects were the Beezer Brothers of Seattle, specialists in the ecclesiastical. The Beezers sent down Arnold S. Constable as project manager and, I'm told by the amazing Gary Goss, he liked San Francisco so well he stayed on and set up shop as a church architect in the Bay Area.

From the sacred one returns to the secular with an even more impressive ex-auto repair shop at 2401 Bush, its triptych of arches on a gorgeously bare façade giving off aesthetic vibes that, truth to say, are not altogether unecclesiastical. The building's design roots seem to lie somewhere between Tuscany and Chicago and it is, I think, one of the most beautiful architectural creatures in town. James R. Miller was its author in 1916, the James Miller who worked for a while with Timothy Pflueger of Union Square and 450 Sutter fame.

—*Arthur Bloomfield*

No. 107

1806–08 Scott

Siamese Victorians

1806 and 1808 Scott Street are joined in the middle and have identical floor plans, only reversed. Their façades indicate that halls and staircases are located in the center of the pair, and that the parlors and bedrooms are on the outsides where windows let in light. This arrangement also creates a partial sound barrier.

Now, a similar arrangement exists with the pair of Italianate houses next door at 1810 and 1812. At these addresses the shapes are exactly the same but the trim is less elaborate. The increased complexity of our pictured pair includes corner boards and Corinthian porch columns with reverse fluting partway up the shafts—and they also boast little triangular pediments over the single windows and at the entries and centers of the bays on the first floor.

The similarities are no accident: all four houses were built for the same owner.

The plainer pair, 1810-12, came into existence in the spring of 1883, and the others apparently were erected somewhat later, anyway by the end of 1887. An indication of not exactly parallel construction is the fact that 1810 has a side bay window that's effectively blocked, in not very neighborly fashion, by 1808.

The written evidence also points to different construction dates. The water was turned on at 1810-12 on March 26, 1883. At 1806-08 water did not arrive until December 1, 1887, although it could have come earlier from the other pair.

I've found only one building contract, and a good question is whether it refers to two or four of these Scott Street addresses. In the local architecture magazine for March 1883 it's said to be for "two two-story frame houses" costing $5,000 to construct. "Two frames" could have meant 1810-12 and 1806-08, each pair freestanding, but $5,000 is a skimpy price for all four units. The differences in ornament and that date for water service, also the side bay window without an outlook, all point to quite different construction dates.

So, lacking evidence of early tenants, I must shakily conclude that this contract refers only to 1810-12.

Meanwhile we know for sure there was a single owner for all the properties, one Diedrich Lohsen. The architect, at least of 1810-12 Scott, was like Lohsen a German. His name was Henry Geilfuss, he was active in San Francisco from about 1877 to 1915 and he's perhaps best known for the house with the tower at Fulton and Scott on Alamo Square and St. Mark's Lutheran on O'Farrell (and also our Old House No. 89).

I tend to believe that Lohsen reused Geilfuss' plans from the "earlier" 1810-12 for 1806-08, updating the trim a bit. By 1887 the popular style was Stick with its rectangular bay windows and corner boards, but even Stick was beginning to be replaced by elements of Queen Anne. The Queen Anne style featured big triangular roof gables, and early combinations of Anne and Stick often used little triangular pediments such as we find on 1806-08.

Herr Lohsen and a partner ran a bar at Market Street and Hayes. He and his equally German wife, Anna, had four children, ages eleven to nineteen in 1900, who were all living in 1812 Scott at that time. Between bar profits and rents received from Scott Street units Lohsen had been able to move into real estate about 1890.

Mama and Papa Lohsen owned all four units until 1921, when they gave them to their children, who kept them until 1948; only then was ownership split between two parties.

No. 108

2520 Bush

Speedway Richardsonian

A nicely arched ecclesiastical echo here of that auto repair shop at 2401 Bush (see Interlude after Old House No. 106). And no sacrilege in writing that: both are lovely buildings.

Driving down the Bush Street speedway it's easy to miss the Philadelphian Seventh Day Adventist Church at 2520. What a fine example it is of Richardsonian Romanesque, the round arch and rough stone mode created by Boston architect Henry Hobson Richardson in the late nineteenth century.

The Philadelphian looks almost exactly like a newspaper photo taken upon its dedication as the West Side Christian Church on Sunday May 29, 1904. Almost a century later the gray sandstone and red brick betray no foreign painting, modernizing or remuddling, just a little repair, presumably after the 1989 earthquake. Well done, Philadelphians!

The façade here suggests what's within. The main entrance is centered and elevated for best effect, with more stairs inside leading up to the sanctuary, which is two stories high and lit by a stunning seven-part window.

In 1904 the *Examiner* described the interior space as an octagon finished in polished wood, with organ above the pulpit.

Large "girders" supported a dome and were striped with light bulbs. From the top of the dome, the report continued, hung a polished brass chandelier, cross-shaped, with sixty-four lights on its arms.

On the outside you should notice the special patterns of bricklaying; I count at least five. The intricate design was so completely carried out because a Mrs. Nancy Douglass, one of the congregation's founders, had willed her entire estate to the church. The building, which took a full year to construct, cost $45,000, a lot of money in those days—for a rough modern equivalent try doubling it and adding a zero.

The architect was Scotsman T. Paterson Ross who came to San Francisco with his family at the age of twelve in 1884. Only thirty-one when he designed West Side Christian, the much-in-demand Ross did most of his best known work after the '06 earthquake: some of his buildings were exotic, the Shriners' Temple/Alcazar Theater on Geary, for instance, and the two pagoda-topped buildings on the uphill corners of Grant and California.

Ross' client out on Bush was a church founded in 1892 by seven dedicated women who'd been worshipping in a smaller wooden building on the same site. Six of the founders' names are unknown and may be recovered if the cornerstone's time capsule is ever opened. The seventh, the generous Nancy Douglass, is something of a mystery because city directories, voter lists and other possible sources of that era tended to ignore the existence of women.

The men can be easily traced and we know that the earliest pastors were the Reverend William A. Gardner (1892–98), M. W. Williams (1899) and Walter M. White (1900–05).

Lay officers (two elders, thirteen deacons, four trustees and six deaconesses!) included two attorneys, two physicians, two clerks, two widows, a salesman, a pork packer, a lithograph foreman, a wagon-maker and an apartment owner/manager— which sounds pretty democratic. These parishioners helped conduct services, two on Sundays plus "Christian Endeavor," Sunday school, and Wednesday evening prayer meetings.

The congregation disappeared shortly after selling their gem of a building in 1960. Taking over were the fortunate Seventh Day Adventists whose home on Geary near Octavia was being removed by Redevelopment.

No. 109

2908–10 Bush

The Oldest House

The oldest house in Pacific Heights and Baja Pacific Heights is in the last block of Bush Street, set well back from traffic on an unusually wide, deep lot.

The porch or veranda across the front is a feature rare indeed in San Francisco now: it exists only on very old buildings like the Stanyan house at 2006 Bush (Old House No. 103), the Tanforan Cottages at 214 Dolores, the Phelps House at 1111 Oak near Divisadero, and Blackstone House on little Blackstone Court near Lombard and Franklin.

The house way out Bush belonged originally to Milo Hoadley, a pioneer surveyor and civil engineer who became city engineer in 1853. A controversial character, Hoadley recommended a set of official street grades that would have leveled Telegraph, Russian and Nob Hills! Fortunately these "Hoadley grades"—they would have turned San Francisco into a western Chicago, flat as the proverbial pancake—aroused huge opposition. Well, San Franciscans knew charm when they saw it, you betcha.

Hoadley still managed to lay out a lot of San Francisco as we know it without wreaking havoc and destroying the city's future meal ticket of tourism galore. He prepared the original maps for the Hayes Tract in Hayes Valley, the Beideman Tract from Bush to McAllister and Larkin to Laguna, and much of Bernal Heights. Scant flattening there.

Also, about 1870, Hoadley proposed a huge reservoir on the Peninsula to supply San Francisco with water from ocean-bound creeks and yes, that's Crystal Springs.

On his own behalf Hoadley laid out and recorded in 1862 "Hoadley's Extension" which subdivided into fifty-vara lots the land between Jackson and Post, Divisadero and Lyon, that's to say much of the most westerly Pacific and Baja Pacific Heights. His original land claim, established before 1855, may have included the present-day Laurel Village, Alta Plaza Park and Hamilton Playground near Mt. Zion Hospital. He was still litigating with the City over these parks when he died in 1887, victim of a fatal buggy accident up in Sonora in the Mother Lode.

Hoadley, you can see, had a San Francisco pioneer's typical mindset: make grandiose plans and speculate in lands and mines. He didn't end up as rich as some of his contemporaries and consequently has been forgotten, but he deserves better, even if he almost de-hilled the city's fabled northeast quadrant.

The house on Bush was Hoadley's

residence at least from 1858 and quite possibly earlier. His name appears in a city directory of 1850 but not in 1854 through 1857. I think it was left out because he'd moved beyond city limits—out, that is, into empty spaces next to the new Lone Mountain Cemetery dedicated in 1854.

A lithograph of the cemetery, drawn before 1867 when its name was changed to Laurel Hill, shows that its main roadway was a continuation of Bush Street, with smaller branches encircling every little hillock. The landscaping features trees, bushes and lawns which must have been a delightful sight in this barren western region where the fog still swirls on gloomy summer days.

(Arthur remembers being almost swept away by billowing sands while waiting for the old No. 1 streetcar at California and Locust when the cemetery was being dug up in the mid-1940s, pre-Laurel Village Shopping Center).

The main cemetery gate was originally on Bush about halfway between Presidio and Lyon, just beyond the intersection of "Cemetery Avenue" which ran at a steep diagonal about from the present Geary and Presidio (think Mervyn's and the Muni car barn) to a little east of Pacific and Lyon way up the Heights (where the city's spiffiest mansions may now be found with five- to ten-million-dollar price tags sometimes attached).

In the foreground of the lithograph stands Milo Hoadley's house, none other, and it's recognizably the same as what we see today except that the porch wraps around the east side and the roof's a little different. Behind the house are a wagon and a big water tank, while the yard is fenced and landscaped.

I think the Hoadleys must have enjoyed their view of the beautiful green cemetery which was, so to speak, "right in their front yard."

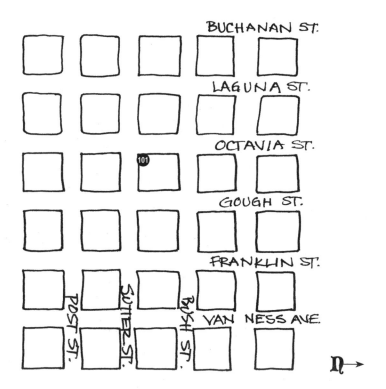

On
Sutter Street

No. 110

1590 Sutter

Young Ladies Were "Finished" Here

From boarding school to boarding house to a hotel, appropriately enough named the Queen Anne: that is the route of 1590 Sutter over a century and a bit.

Miss Mary Lake's School for Young Ladies, a fashionable and nonsectarian institution that grew out of Madame Zeitska's Young Ladies' Seminary in South Park (recently Dot-Com Land, that) held forth from 1890, with a faculty of eighteen. They taught their charges music, history, math, art, French, German, Latin, singing, elocution, and even pre–Isadora Duncan modern dancing. All the right stuff for young ladies of the time.

According to its brochure, "mental development" was the school's prime objective, the second "that molding of character which enables the pupil to express the kindly impulses of a fine nature with tact and serenity." In other words, don't argue with Hubby.

Students ranged in age from "infants," whose classroom seated sixty-five (!), on through high school, I believe. Some lived at home, others resided on the two top floors at 1590 where there was room for sixty-five or seventy boarders. Obviously no private rooms! Graduating classes averaged ten, giving a potential school population of one hundred and twenty or so in a dozen grades. So the student-faculty ratio wasn't bad, seven or eight to one.

Miss Lake herself was remembered as a beloved teacher of broad interests, keen wit and a warm, magnetic personality. Doris Day perhaps? She'd started as a teacher at Redding Public School, then joined Madame Zeitska's institute and risen to co-principal there. Later she taught at the still-operating Hamlin's.

But unfortunately her school at Sutter and Octavia lasted only seven years, 1890 to 1896. Maybe the end came because Miss Lake had health problems. Or maybe there were not enough students; or her budgeting was off; or the landlord raised the rent.

That would have been James G. Fair, one of the multi-millionaire kings of the silvery Comstock Lode. His own two daughters were being educated privately in the deportment and accomplishments suitable to their station as heirs to the Fairmont Hotel—one would marry a Vanderbilt, no less, and express, one supposes, kindly impulses thereto.

Although he seems not to have sent his children to Sutter Street to be educated, Fair was a fan of Miss Lake's and her educational mission and he had the school built especially for her, sparing no expense.

The $45,000 building was constructed in 1889 with marble plumbing fixtures, large closets, soundproofed double floors and solid partitions, oak paneling that survives and polished Scottish entry stairs that haven't come down to the present. There was a gym on the ground floor while the "main" floor was up a level with three classrooms plus triple parlor, cozy library and rooms for music and art.

These second-floor rooms are now hotel guest rooms as are the dormitory rooms above. The original central hallway remains with its waist-high oak paneling and squared spiral staircase beneath a large stained glass skylight. The present sitting room matches an 1889 description of the 20-by-30-foot dining room with "an open fireplace of ornamental brickwork from floor to ceiling and paneled wainscoting."

Yes, much of the original interior has survived, but important pieces are missing. A bell-shaped roof topped the corner bay window and one chimney is missing, others have lost their tops. Garages on Octavia fill the original side yard. The worst loss is on the Sutter Street side, the grand exterior staircase to a massively arched open vestibule before the main door. The arches have been filled in and a window with square instead of rounded corners substituted.

1590's architect was Henry Schulze, who practiced from 1887 through 1908, one year with Arthur Brown Jr. of City Hall fame. Schulze did Olympic Club interiors and the fine Richardsonian Romanesque church at Seventeenth and Franklin in Oakland. After the troubles of '06 he rebuilt the Wilson Building at 973 Market in San Francisco and his credits also include an interesting Mission Revival house for a Wells Fargo executive in Bakersfield. A solid, dependable architect.

After Miss Lake left, the Fair estate leased the building to the Cosmos Club, a gentlemen's social organization that counted among its members the capitalist James L. Flood, California governor George Pardee and Alaska Commerical head man Gustave Niebaum. Perhaps they met out Sutter Street because downtown was still a-building after the big quake.

At any rate, Virginia Fair Vanderbilt had inherited the property in 1904 and when she sold it in 1909 the club had to leave. The building was a boarding house for a while, then in 1926 the Episcopal Church bought it for the Girls' Friendly Society Lodge, a home for working young women two blocks from Trinity Church. Then from 1950 to 1975 it was a for-profit guest house called The Lodge.

In 1980 the Queen Anne Hotel Company bought what had become something of a stepchild, and while a total return to its original glory was not feasible they revved it up to its present Cinderella attractiveness. Good job!

And interestingly enough, the corner of Sutter and Octavia is where a daily set of walking tourists get off the bus from downtown and start their meander through the Victorian best of Pacific Heights...

Anne Bloomfield, for many years a member of San Francisco's Landmarks Preservation Advisory Board, was a highly respected consultant in architectural history and a keen preservationist. In her twenty-year career as a consultant she researched and prepared the nominations for six of the ten historic districts designated by the City of San Francisco and for eight National Register districts, as well as for numerous individual National Register listings and individual San Francisco landmarks. For a period of fourteen years she wrote the "Great Old Houses" column for the *New Fillmore*, a neighborhood monthly. A native of St. Paul, Minnesota, Anne Bloomfield grew up in Cincinnati and graduated with honors from Swarthmore College.

Arthur Bloomfield, the son of a medical professor, grew up in San Francisco's Presidio Heights, a sibling neighborhood to Pacific Heights, and spent five years in schools facing Alta Plaza Park, lunching with school chums in houses designed by Houghton Sawyer, William Wurster and Henry Howard (well, he didn't know that at the time!) before taking the Washington or California Street cable car to the movies downtown. A graduate of Stanford in music, he was for many years a music critic for the *San Francisco Examiner*, and also wrote restaurant criticism for the KQED *Focus* magazine. Mr. Bloomfield's books include *50 Years of the San Francisco Opera*, *Arthur Bloomfield's Restaurant Book*, *The Gastronomical Tourist*, and *Toscanini, Stokowski and Friends: A Guide to the Styles of the Great Historic Conductors*. He also wrote an extensive booklet for the CD collection *Sunday Evenings with Pierre Monteux*, which was nominated for a Gramophone Award.

Since its founding in 1974, Heyday Books has occupied a unique niche in the publishing world, specializing in books that foster an understanding of the history, literature, art, environment, social issues, and culture of California and the West. We are a 501(c)(3) nonprofit organization based in Berkeley, California, serving a wide range of people and audiences.

We are grateful for the generous funding we've received for our publications and programs during the past year from foundations and more than 300 individual donors. Major supporters include:

Anonymous; Anthony Andreas, Jr.; Audubon; Barnes & Noble bookstores; BayTree Fund; S.D. Bechtel, Jr. Foundation; Butler Koshland Fund; California Council for the Humanities; Candelaria Fund; Columbia Foundation; Colusa Indian Community Council; Federated Indians of Graton Rancheria; Wallace Alexander Gerbode Foundation; Richard & Rhoda Goldman Fund; Evelyn & Walter Haas, Jr. Fund; Walter & Elise Haas Fund; Hopland Band of Pomo Indians; James Irvine Foundation; George Frederick Jewett Foundation; LEF Foundation; Michael McCone; Middletown Rancheria Tribal Council; Gordon & Betty Moore Foundation; Morongo Band of Mission Indians; National Endowment for the Arts; National Park Service; Poets & Writers; Rim of the World Interpretive Association; River Rock Casino; Alan Rosenus; San Francisco Foundation; John-Austin Saviano/Moore Foundation; Sandy Cold Shapero; L. J. Skaggs and Mary C. Skaggs Foundation; Victorian Alliance; and the Harold & Alma White Memorial Fund.

For more information about Heyday Institute, our publications and programs, please visit our website at www.heydaybooks.com.